SPIRAL GUIDES

Travel With Someone You Trust

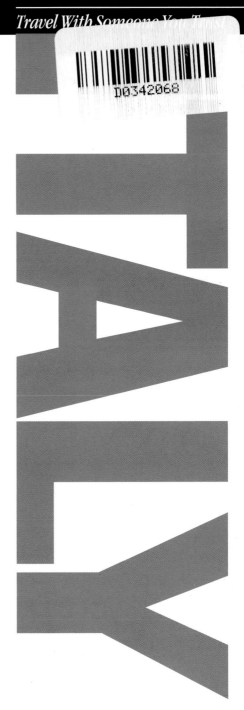

D0342068

Contents

The Magazine and Where to... sections by Sally Roy
Contributions from Teresa Fisher, Rebecca Ford, Tim Jepson

Original copy edited by Nia Williams
Verified by Frances Wolverton
Indexed by Marie Lorimer

Edited, designed and produced by AA Publishing
© Automobile Association Developments Limited 2005
Reprinted July 2005

Published in the United States by AAA Publishing,
1000 AAA Drive, Heathrow, Florida 32746-5063
Published in the United Kingdom by AA Publishing

ISBN-10: 1-59508-074-0
ISBN-13: 978-1-59508-074-5

Cover design and binding style by permission of AA Publishing

Color separation by Leo Reprographics
Printed and bound in China by Leo Paper Products

10 9 8 7 6 5 4 3 2

A02734
Map data © 1997-2003 Navigation Technologies BV.
All rights reserved

the magazine

Thousands of years of history have produced a diverse mix of saints and sinners in this country, all sharing a distinctly larger-than-life Italian character.

Julius Caesar

Julius Caesar was allegedly dragged from his mother's womb in the world's first Caesarean section

his love for the beautiful Beatrice. Dante was nine years old when he first saw her; she was only eight. Though Beatrice married

Plaque showing Christina of Lorraine (1565–1636), a member of the wealthy Medici family

Famous Italians ~

in 100 BC. Political manoeuvring and military success took him some way up the ladder, and in 49 BC he led his troops away from the battlefields of Gaul to challenge his rival Pompey for control of the Empire, crossing the River Rubicon without the legally required Senate approval. Pompey fled, the Senate's power collapsed and Caesar took his place as absolute ruler. Conspirators were gathering, however, and on the Ides (15th) of March 44 BC Julius Caesar was stabbed to death on the steps of Rome's Senate House.

Dante Alighieri

The Divine Comedy, Dante's epic poem, was inspired by

someone else and died young Dante never forgot her, using her as the narrator's guide in the *Commedia*, written around 1321. This vast work, a vision of a journey through hell and purgatory to eternal light, was written in Tuscan, the everyday speech of the people, rather than Latin. Dante worked as a diplomat in Florence, but after being sent into exile in 1321 never returned to his beloved home.

St Francis of Assisi

Francis was born in Assisi into a wealthy family in 1182 and during his youth enjoyed the good life of wine, women and song. But the revelry got out of hand, and he found himself in prison with time

Above (left to right): Leonardo da Vinci; Dante Alighieri; Marco Polo

to think. Here Francis heard the voice of God, and in 1209 he renounced his riches and left Assisi to preach a message of renunciation. His aim was to persuade everyone, rich and poor, to reject material goods, to love God in poverty, chastity and obedience, and to see God's hand in the beauty of the natural world. Francis gathered 12 followers and obtained papal permission to found a religious order, the Franciscans. In 1224 he received the stigmata, the five wounds of Christ; he died two years later and was canonised in 1228.

up the puppet Republic of Salò on Lake Garda, while Italy continued to fight – this time with the Allies. By April 1945 they were closing in and Mussolini and his mistress, Claretta Petacci, tried to flee to Switzerland. They were caught at Lake Como by partisans and shot on 28 April.

Giacomo Casanova

Casanova was born in Venice in 1725 and earned notoriety as Europe's leading sexual athlete. His exploits as a seducer – detailed in his memoirs – overshadowed a fascinating life story, which included introducing the

Above (left to right): Sophia Loren; Casanova; Benito Mussolini

The Good, the Bad

Mussolini

Benito Mussolini led the Fascist Party to public prominence in 1922, staging a 'March on Rome' from Milan. Within a couple of months he was prime minister, and assumed the title of Il Duce – the Leader – in 1925. In 1940 he took an ill-prepared and under-equipped Italy into war, a fatal move that ended with the armistice and his imprisonment in 1943. Hitler promptly freed him, setting

and the Ugly

lottery to France, being charged with sorcery, escaping from prison in the Doge's Palace and spying for the Inquisition. He was particularly fond of nuns; in the febrile atmosphere of 18th-century Venice convent parlours were the scene of major partying, and Casanova was definitely a big-league player.

> **"Casanova was a big league player"**

The Body Beautiful

Italian clothes designers work all over Italy, but the style capital, scene of the frenetic September whirl of glitz and glamour that is Italy's most important fashion week, is Milan. Whether you want the best of *haute couture* from the likes of Armani, Versace, Missoni and Prada, or affordable fashion that ranges from the classic to the quirky, the Italians make it. Given that Italians spend up to 50 per cent of their disposable income on clothes and fashion, and around 60 per cent of Italian women buy a new wardrobe twice a year, not to mention the huge overseas markets, it's hardly surprising that fashion is very big business indeed. Super-giant Benetton has over 7,000 stores in more than 120 countries and an astonishing global impact. But the real icons are the superstars: both Giorgio Armani and Gianni Versace have had 21st-century museum exhibitions dedicated to them in New York, while in Florence shoe designer Salvatore Ferragamo has an entire museum devoted to his work, effectively putting fashion on a par with mainstream modern art. Leather in all its guises plays an important role in Italy's fashion industry generally; it was Gucci, founded as a firm of Florentine saddlers, that introduced the concept of subtly logoed bags and shoes in the 1960s, with its unmistakable red-and-green trim and classy buckles.

Think Italian design and the image called to mind is of clothes, clothes, shoes and clothes. But fashion and design embrace much more than the rag trade in Italy, a country obsessed with high style and the *bella figura*, that barely definable concept that means, above all, looking good. It's all about seeing and being seen – great clothes, stunning architecture, fast cars. Add the age-old love affair with craftsmanship and luxury and it's easy to understand why the fashion and design industries are booming.

Bellissimo

Shopping is almost a national pastime for some

Bella macchina, bella casa

Italians love a stylish car, preferably by Ferrari, Lamborghini or Maserati, though, thanks to the genius of Enrico Piaggio, even the youngest generation of drivers can get about on stylish wheels. Piaggio invented and named the Vespa – *sembra una vespa* ('it looks like a wasp') – the beloved *motorino*, or scooter. It first buzzed on to the world stage to meet post-war affordable transport demands, and is

High-quality Italian leather goods

Ferrari – the pinnacle of Italian motor engineering

constantly updated in looks and image.

A casa, at home, you can experiment with Italian furniture. This ranges from beautiful reproduction Renaissance pieces to the cheerful primary colours and extraordinary designs of the Memphis Group, an avant-garde, international design team put together in 1981 by Milan-based Ettore Sottsass, expressly to revolutionise furniture design. More mainstream, but equally individual, are the classic pieces created by homeware giant Alessi: those wonderful stainless-steel containers for oranges you see in countless Italian bars are a superb example of his work.

If you're visiting, don't feel obliged to try and live up to the standards set by Italians: just sit back and enjoy it all. After all, the observer is an important part of the whole concept of *bella figura*; even if you feel lacking in innate style, you will be performing a vital service by providing an audience for the catwalk that is Italian life.

"It's all about seeing and being seen"

A TAVOLA!

From north to south and east to west, food is a major Italian preoccupation and one of the joys of life. You'll see the country's love of the table in the huge family groups enjoying Sunday lunch, in housewives shopping with care at the abundant markets, and in the mouth-watering displays in delicatessens.

Regional, fresh, seasonal

There's no such thing as Italian cooking: each region has its own distinctive cuisine, be it Roman, Tuscan, Milanese or Neapolitan. What appears on the table reflects the region, the dishes dictated by the time of year and local produce. Italian cooks are obsessed with freshness; in smaller places, food shopping is still often done twice a day and you'll notice the limited range of frozen and ready-prepared foods in supermarkets. Cooking is straightforward, its quality dictated by the superlative standard of the ingredients. Outside the biggest cities, most restaurants serve local food, so don't expect to eat Venetian dishes in Tuscany, let alone another country's cuisine. There are a few exceptions – you'll find *prosciutto* (dry-cured ham) and *parmigiano* (Parmesan cheese) all over Italy, and the pizza is available everywhere.

Vino, vino

The same story applies to wine; on the whole, you'll be offered the local varieties. In some areas, these are world-class wines with prices to match. In others they're plain country wines, grown on the same soil as the food on your plate. Whatever their background, Italian wine, *rosso* (red), *bianco* (white) and *spumante* (sparkling), will marry perfectly with what you're eating.

Top: Dining out in the shadow of the Rialto bridge in Venice

Above: Relax with a frothy cappuccino

The Northwest

There are great choices in the northwest, from the delicate Milanese *risotti* (rice simmered in saffron-flavoured stock) and intense white truffles of Piemonte, to the satisfying and classic *osso buco*, slow-cooked shin of veal, and Liguria's *pesto*, the famous basil, pine-nut and cheese sauce. Fish reigns supreme along the coast, where your evening dinner will have been landed that morning, while inland, you'll find polenta (maize meal) and rice, rather than pasta, providing the filling element.

lagoon and the Adriatic yielding an extraordinary range of molluscs and fish. Specialities worth sampling include *seppie* (cuttlefish), *sarde* (sardines) and *dorata* (bream), or a crisp selection of *fritti misti* (tiny fried fish and squid). Fill up on rice and polenta, or sample vegetable delicacies such as *carciofi* (artichokes) and *radicchio di Treviso*, a bittersweet autumn leaf vegetable. Further south, Bologna is the gastronomic capital of Italy, with high-quality *prosciutto* and *parmigiano* and lavish quantities of butter and

– a Taste of Italy

The big-name wines such as Barolo, Bardolino and Barbera are well worth their high prices, but a glass of well-chilled Asti, the region's major sparkling wine, won't break the bank and is a delicious aperitif.

Venice and the Northeast

In Venice the accent is on seafood, the waters of the

cream used in cooking. Up in the mountains there's a strong German influence – be prepared for *canerdeli* (dumplings), goulash, and *apfelstrudel*. Wines are excellent, from the Veneto's champagne-like Prosecco, hearty Lambrusco found around Bologna and smooth, dry whites such as Pinot Grigio and Chardonnay.

Pasticcerie – Melt in the Mouth and Sugar Sweet

Italian restaurants serve little in the way of desserts. To sample the best sugary specialities head for a *pasticceria*, where cakes, pastries and biscuits are made with pure, high-quality ingredients. They sell everything from creamy chocolate and fruit confections to single, traditional biscuits. You can choose at the counter and eat on the spot, or get the staff to make up a selection to take away.

The Bar

Bars are an integral part of Italian life, open from early morning till late, and serving everything from a breakfast *cornetto* (pastry) and cappuccino to lunchtime snacks, beer, wine and tea. You can pop in for a coffee or drink standing at the bar, or sit down – though that will cost you more – for table service and a sandwich lunch. Bars all have telephones, toilets and the daily papers.

Central Italy

High-quality ingredients are emphasised in the simplicity of central Italian cooking, where plain-grilled meats, game, superb bread and sheep's-milk cheese feature strongly. Tuscans, particularly, eat dried beans in many guises, such as soups or stews with oil and sage. *Crostini*, toasted bread with a variety of toppings, are another speciality, and make the perfect starter before tackling a juicy *bistecca alla fiorentina*, a prime-quality grilled steak, or *tagliata*, T-bone served with rocket and Parmesan cheese. In Umbria, too, simplicity is the keynote, with mountain food like smoked ham, *pecorino* cheese, salami and tiny lentils all on offer. Here you'll also be able to sample black truffles, best grated over homemade pasta. Central Italian red wines include the world-famous Chianti from Tuscany, the outstanding Brunello di Montalcino and Vino Nobile di Montepulciano. In Umbria look out for Orvieto, a light white wine, and the terrific reds from around Montefalco.

Rome and the South

Cooking in Rome is distinctive, though as Italy's capital it offers a greater choice of cuisine, with both international-style restaurants and those serving different regional food. Romans enjoy down-to-earth, strong flavours, so you'll find plenty of garlic in the offal dishes they love – *trippa* (tripe) and *lingua* (tongue) are great favourites. *Abacchio* (Roman lamb) well deserves its reputation, as does the delicious *saltimbocca alla romana*, thin veal slices wrapped in *prosciutto* and fried with sage. Rome's best-known local wines are Frascati from the Castelli Romani and Est! Est! Est! from Montefiascone – its

Below: Typical seafood salad from the coastal town of Portovenere

Bottom: Piazza San Domenico Maggiore, Naples

GASTRONOM

name comes from the words scribbled on a wine-cellar door by a papal envoy sent to find the best *enoteca* in town.

South from here lies Naples, home of the pizza and some of Italy's most imagintaive cooking. You'll find excellent olive oil, plenty of garlic, superb fresh vegetables and fresh milk cheeses like *mozzarella* and *ricotta*, along with seafood and fish. Meat doesn't play a major part, and in remote and poorer areas menus are limited – but the quality and freshness still shine through.

The best wine area is Puglia, where deep-flavoured reds are at their best in Primitivo di Manduria and Salice Salentino.

Sicily and Sardinia

Sicily's Greek, Arab, Norman and Spanish invaders all left their mark on its superb cuisine, while the climate contributes to the superlative fruit and vegetables. Expect fresh fish and seafood and imaginative *antipasti*, and sample street food in the shape of crisp

croquettes, fritters and *arancini* – deep-fried rice balls with a savoury centre.

Fish dishes star in Sardinia as well, along with excellent cheese, such as the salty *pecorino Sardo*, delicious with the paper-thin bread known as *carta di musica*. Both islands offer exceptional pastries and desserts – look out in Sicily for *cannoli*, fried pastries stuffed with ricotta, candied fruit and chocolate, and *cassata* ice-cream.

Sicily is also home to Marsala, a sweet fortified wine and Averna, a bitter *amaro* (digestive liqueur).

Top and above: Cured meats and locally made sausages

Left: Fresh seafood

THE GRAND TOUR
– the British Abroad

Twenty-first-century 20-something backpackers aren't the first to heed the siren call of Bell'Italia and her seductive pleasures. The British gentry were well aware that south of the Alps lay a land crammed with art and culture, where the sun shone, the wine flowed and girls were pretty. By the 1700s an Italian jaunt was a necessary part of every gentleman's education, and a procession of leisured young travellers headed south to enjoy the Grand Tour, a name coined by Richard Lessels in his 1670 book *Voyage to Italy*.

Rich young men – seldom young women – set off from England accompanied by their tutors and numerous letters of credit and introduction, for a trip that could easily last years. Rome was the honeypot, with Florence and Venice an additional option, and Naples joining the must-see list after the start of the excavations at Pompei in the 1740s. Apartments were rented, contacts made, and the months-long, sybaritic exploration of the cities of Italy began. For most, the attraction was the lure of ancient Rome, with the romantic ruins of the Forum, the Colosseum and the Pantheon topping the list. Hot on the heels of actual buildings were the great collections of classical statuary, and the leisurely inspection of the treasures of the Vatican and aristocratic private collections.

It all sounds too high-minded to be true, and the reality was very different from the cultured public picture. The Grand Tour's educational aspects also included serious tutelage in drinking, gambling and womanising, with profligate living and general debauchery the norm. Breakfast might be taken at the famous Caffé degli Inglesi in the Piazza di Spagna, where tales of all-night drinking were exchanged, before the *milordi*, as the young gentlemen were known, staggered off with their tutors, known as bear-leaders, for a morning's sightseeing. Afternoons were often spent at the Caffé Greco in Via Condotti, where the *milordi* rubbed shoulders

Panoramic view of St Peter's Square in Rome

with celebrities such as Casanova and Byron – 'mad, bad, and dangerous to know'. This was also a favourite time for shopping, and souvenirs generally meant the real thing: statues, furniture, mirrors, glass and paintings. With London portrait prices standing at around £150, Pompeo Batoni's £25 price tag was a snip, and many British country houses still house 18th-century Grand Tour souvenir portraits. Tourists were obsessed with shopping, prompting writer Horace Walpole to admit in 1740 that he was '...far gone in medals, lamps, idols and prints...I would buy the Colisem (sic) if I could...'

Twenty-five years later diarist James Boswell had other things on his mind: he caught crab lice and venereal disease after a series of nocturnal Italian adventures. Small wonder, then, that the journals and sketch books that were supposed to be completed as a record of the Tour often remain totally blank.

Roman delights exhausted, Venice, the great party city, beckoned. Carnival the ultimate anything-goes, weeks-long fiesta, was a favourite time to visit. With the entire population masked, and lace-bedecked and worldly nuns gaily entertaining in their convent parlours, it was the

natural choice for young men anxious to escape their tutors and let their hair down. Here too, Lord Byron was a familiar face, while far to the south, in Naples, voluptuous Emma Hamilton, Lord Nelson's mistress, had the visitors at her feet.

Pleasure was not the only reason for visits to Italy: it was also a favoured place in which to hide an unwanted and illegitimate pregnancy. Georgiana, Duchess of Devonshire and Lady Elizabeth Foster both gave birth here, and were by no means the only ones.

Years later, in 1820, after the Tour's heyday, poor John Keats, the English poet, arrived seeking warmth to alleviate his tuberculosis. He lodged in a room on the Spanish Steps, but Italian sunshine couldn't save him, and he died only three months after his arrival.

At the turn of the 18th and 19th centuries the Napoleonic Wars made European trips far more difficult and the arrival of the railways heralded the beginning of mass-market travel. But throughout Britain, in the great landscaped parks dotted with classical follies, in the Roman statuary, Italian portraits, marble tables, Venetian glass and furniture, is the tangible evidence of the way the Grand Tour shaped British taste for years after the last *milord* crossed the Alps and returned to the grey skies and damp climate of home.

One of several paintings of *The Molo* by Venetian-born artist Canaletto

Detail of a fresco at Pompei

Architecture lies at the heart of Italy's allure – the stately *palazzi*, the lofty churches, the elegant country villas, and the mellow stone and brick houses of the quiet towns and hilltop villages are the backdrop to the country's beauty. Italy has some of the world's greatest galleries and museums, but it's the buildings, many still performing their ancient original functions, that are the artistic essence of its cities and towns. Some cities' riches date neatly from a single epoch, others are a glorious mix, but all contribute to the pleasure of life in Italy.

ROMAN TO RENAISSANCE, BYZANTINE TO BAROQUE

Symphonies in Stone

Unlike paintings, which require a gallery or church visit, architecture is all around you, from the world-famous buildings of Rome, Florence and Venice, to the modest gems tucked away in provincial towns and villages.

There's a huge diversity of styles and materials; to make sense of it all, note that on the whole rounded means Romanesque, pointed means Gothic, harmonious balance signifies Renaissance and exuberant and complex decoration characterises baroque.

The present church of Santa Maria in Trastevere dates from the 12th century

The Architect's Role

An architect designs buildings; he also knows how to use materials, building techniques and practices. Through classical and medieval times his work was largely unsung; we're familiar with fabulous architectural works but we have no idea who designed them. All that changed with the Renaissance. Filippo Brunelleschi, designer of much of the Duomo in Florence, is reckoned to be the creator of the profession of architect. He was certainly the first to be recognised and acclaimed.

What's What in Architecture

Roman: 2nd century BC to 5th century AD

Italy has a wealth of ruins of monumental public buildings such as baths, amphitheatres and triumphal arches. Roman architecture borrowed its style from Greece, and made its own contribution with the invention of vaulting and the use of solid stonework, classical proportions and construction on a huge scale.

Byzantine and Early Christian: 5th to 7th century AD

Byzantine architects developed the dome, and gave Italy free-standing bell towers; examples are best seen in the northeast, particularly Venice. In Rome, church-builders based early formats on the ancient basilica, or public hall, with an altar at the eastern end.

Romanesque: 10th to 11th century

Look out for rounded arches, clean, simple lines and tall towers. Pisa, Lucca and Florence developed the style by introducing marble facing on the exterior and open arcaded galleries. In southern Italy you'll see a mix of Byzantine and Romanesque, featuring domes, mosaics and arches.

Gothic: 13th to 15th century

Light-filled interiors, pointed arches and soaring space are the hallmarks of Gothic, essentially a northern European style. It was adapted in Italy and here is marked by opulent façade decoration. The great Italian Gothic cathedrals are Milan, Siena, Orvieto and the main body of Florence's Duomo.

Siena's Duomo stands on the site originally occupied by a Roman temple to Minerva

Early Renaissance: 15th to early 16th century

Architects started looking back to the rules of classical architecture and using harmonious and rational proportions in churches, *palazzi*, public buildings and country houses.

High Renaissance: early 16th to early 17th century

More sophisticated spatial design was developed, with more decorative features and *trompe l'oeil* effects. These buildings are on a grand scale, with monumental courtyards and stairways and huge rooms.

Baroque: 17th to mid-18th century

Rome is the baroque city *par excellence*: over-the-top, self-confident, sumptuous and highly decorative, with the emphasis on town planning and the placing of buildings in their surroundings.

Neoclassicism: mid-18th to 19th century

As a reaction to the excesses of baroque, neoclassicism returned to the basic principles of classicism, with plain lines and ancient decorative elements.

Above: The domes of Santa Maria della Salute (Venice)

Left: Spiral cupola by Borromini at Sant'Ivo alla Sapienza, in Rome

Great Architects and Where to See their Buildings

Filippo Brunelleschi (1377–1446): Florence – the Duomo, San Lorenzo, Santo Spirito, the Cappella Pazzi.

Leon Battista Alberti (1404–72): Florence – façade of Santa Maria Novella, Palazzo Rucellai; Rimini – Tempio Malatestiano; Mantova – Sant'Andrea.

Donato Bramante (1444–1514): Rome – plan for St Peter's.

Michelangelo Buonarroti (1475–1564): Rome – Campidoglio, work on St Peter's, Santa Maria degli Angeli.

Andrea Palladio (1508–80): Vicenza – Basilica, Teatro Olimpico, numerous palaces.

Jacopo Sansovino (1486–1570): Venice – Zecca, Loggetta, Libreria Sansoviniana on Piazza San Marco.

Gianlorenzo Bernini (1598–1680): Rome – Piazza San Pietro (St Peter's Square).

Francesco Borromini (1599–1667): Rome – San Carlo alle Quattro Fontane, Sant'Agnese, interior of San Giovanni in Laterano.

Renzo Piano (born 1937): private work in Italy; Paris, France – Pompidou Centre; Osaka, Japan – Airport terminal.

LIGHT, COLOUR, FORM AND DEPTH

The world owes a huge debt to Italian artists. They invented new painting techniques, developed new materials and left a legacy of art that enriches not just their own country but also major collections all over the globe.

Left: Detail of a garden fresco in Pompei

Above: Early mosaic in the Mausoleo di Galla Placidia, Ravenna

The Originators

Even before the Romans, Greeks and Etruscans were painting and carving in Italy. Their work, and that of the Romans themselves, still survives in beautiful wall and tomb paintings and among the classical sculpture in Italy's museums. Romans made great use of mosaics, on walls and floors – a technique that was carried on after the fall of the Empire. From its eastern remnants came Byzantine mosaic art, with its stylised figures, rich ornamentation and glowing gold backgrounds. These became standard features of medieval pictures, which mainly concentrated on religious subjects and portraits of saints. The old fluidity and realism of classical painting and sculpture seemed to have gone forever.

The Renaissance – A New Birth

In the 14th and 15th centuries scholars began to explore classical art and ideas again. New money, earned from trade, paid for new art, and artists no longer had to churn out conservative, church-funded works. Conditions were right for an explosion of artistic creation in every field of the visual arts; the effects rippled out from Florence to Venice, Rome and smaller centres all over Italy. Artists studied the workings of bones and muscles, mastered perspective, and used realistic

Great Galleries

Above: Tondo of St Nicolas in Glory, in the church of San Nicolò dei Mendicoli, Venice

settings. Paving the way were Masaccio, who understood perspective, Donatello, whose sculpture breathed life into stone, and others such as Botticelli, Ghirlandaio, Filippino Lippi and the enigmatic Piero della Francesca. Later, the work of the towering figures of Michelangelo, Leonardo da Vinci and Raphael heralded the peak of this movement, now known as the High Renaissance.

Mannerism and Baroque

The confidence of the Renaissance waned around the 1520s as Italy's political situation grew increasingly perilous. In those uncertain times the strange, artificial style of Mannerism was adopted by Rosso Fiorentino, Pontormo and Parmigianino, who used intense colours and sinuous, distorted forms. The 16th-century Counter-Reformation – the anti-Protestant backlash – brought with it the showy baroque, seen at its best in Rome and the southern cites of Naples, Palermo and Lecce. Later, this was overtaken by neoclassicism, once again reviving the great classical ideal.

Above: The Fontana dei Fiumi, Piazza Navona, Rome

Left: Botticelli's *The Birth of Venus*, in the Uffizi Gallery in Florence

Best Of.

Best Art Cities

Rome (▶ 35–60) – for 2,000 years of architecture, sculpture, painting and mosaics

Florence (▶ 118–124) – for the best of Renaissance art

Venice (▶ 100–104) – for a visually unique experience in a city built on water

Naples (▶ 146–147) – for an architectural mix of everything from Gothic to baroque

Siena (▶ 126–127) – for a perfectly preserved medieval city crammed with Gothic art

Ravenna (▶ 106) – for the world's finest Byzantine mosaics

Palermo (▶ 173) – for Norman, Byzantine, Romanesque and baroque

Best Coastal Areas

The Amalfi Coast (▶ 150–151) – towering cliffs, precipitous villages, green mountains and fabulous sea views

Gargano (▶ 155) – limestone coast, clear water, fishing villages and spring flora

Cinque Terre (▶ 82) – fishing and holiday villages on vine-planted cliffs

Costa Smeralda (▶ 175) – Sardinia's Emerald Coast, where natural beauty and translucent waters attract the rich

Riviera de Levante – jet-set resorts, cliff scenery and glitzy summer lifestyle

Best Cities for Shopping

Milan (▶ 74–75, 89) – big design names, street fashion and art galleries

Rome (▶ 65) – high fashion, department stores, specialist and artisan shopping

Turin (▶ 89) – trendy one-offs, designer clothes, chain stores and food

Florence (▶ 137) – leather goods, high fashion, jewellery, paper products and artisan workshops

Venice (▶ 111) – textiles, glass, masks, marbled paper

Best Italian Experiences

Try the regional food and wine
Browse in a food market
Join the evening *passeggiata*
Walk in the beautiful countryside
Enjoy an excellent cup of coffee in a bar
Take in at least one of Italy's great museums
Shop for clothes, knitwear, leather and crafts
Swim in the clear coastal waters

Detail in the Stanza dell'Incendio, Vatican Museums, Rome

Finding Your Feet

First Two Hours

Most intercontinental flights arrive in Rome's Fiumicino or Milan's Malpensa airports, while there is a much wider choice of entry points for inter-European flights. Ferries from Greece land at Ancona, Bari and Venice.

Arriving in Rome
Fiumicino

■ Scheduled international and internal flights land at Rome's main airport, Leonardo da Vinci, known as **Fiumicino** (tel: 06 65951, www.adr.it). The airport is 32km (20 miles) west of central Rome and has three termi-nals: A (domestic flights), B (domestic and international flights) and C (international flights). Facilities include a tourist information office, cash machines, foreign exchange desks (*cambio*), banks, a hotel reservation desk, car rental desks and restaurants.

■ **Taxis** to the city centre cost around €45, and take at least 30–40 minutes.

■ An **express rail service** operates to Stazione Termini, Rome's main train station and the focus of the bus and subway systems, between 7:37 am and 10 pm. The journey takes 30 minutes, and costs €8.80. Trains also go to Trastevere, Tiburtina and Ostiense. The terminal is near the main international terminal. **Validate your ticket** in one of the machines by the platform entrance before you travel.

■ Outside the train's operating hours, **CO.TRAL buses** link to Tiburtina rail-way station every 90 minutes, from outside the Arrivals hall. The journey takes around 45 minutes and costs €3.60.

Ciampino

■ **Ciampino**, Rome's second airport (tel: 06 794 941, www.adr.it), is 15km (9 miles) southeast of Rome on the Via Appia Nuova. Charter flights and some European low-cost scheduled flights land here, but there are few facilities.

■ **Taxis** to the city centre cost around €45 and take 30–45 minutes.

■ Ciampino town is the **nearest railway station**, linked to the airport by a 20-minute bus ride (€2.40)

■ There is **no direct bus route** into the centre of Rome, but between 6:30 am and 11 pm, CO.TRAL buses from the front of the airport build-ing go to the Anagnina Metro station (Line A) – around 25 minutes, €1.10. From here, subway trains link to Termini in about 20 minutes.

By Train

■ Most national and international train services arrive at Rome's **Termini railway station** (tel: 892021, www.trenitalia.com) on the eastern side of the city. Taxis wait outside the front entrance. Termini is on **two Metro lines** (A and B), and Rome's main bus terminal is beyond the taxi stands.

■ Some **long-distance routes and night trains** terminate at Ostiense (south of the centre of Rome) or Tiburtina (northeast of the centre) stations. During the day Metro trains run from Tiburtina (Line B) or Piramide, near Ostiense station (Line B); otherwise the best way into the city centre is by taxi.

Arriving in Milan (Milano)

- **Malpensa Airport** (tel: 02 748 5220; www.sea-aeroportimilano.it), 50km (31 miles) northwest of the city, is one of Europe's most modern airports. It has two terminals and facilities include tourist information, hotel reservation and car rental desks, bars, restaurants, shops and banks.
- A **taxi** into Milan costs around €75 and can take 35 minutes–1 hour.
- A **direct train** links the airport to Milano Nord railway station (6:30 am–1:30 am, €12, 40 minutes).
- **Shuttle buses** run to Stazione Centrale in Milan (5 am–10:30 pm, €5.50, 45–60 minutes).
- Milan's smaller city airport, **Linate**, 7km (4 miles) from the centre, also has full tourist facilities (tel: 02 748 5220, www.sea-aeroportimilano.it). A **taxi** into Milan costs around €25 and takes 15–25 minutes. The **ATM 73 bus** goes to Piazza San Babila (€1, 20 minutes).

Arriving in Venice (Venezia)

- **Marco Polo Airport** (tel: 041 260 9260, www.veniceairport.it) is on the northern edge of the lagoon, 7km (4 miles) from the city by water and 12km (7 miles) by road. Facilities include bureaux de change, banks, a post office, bars, restaurants and shops.
- **Land taxis** to Piazzale Roma cost around €20 and take 15–25 minutes.
- **Water taxis** (*taxi acquei*) into Venice cost around €70–€90 and take 20–35 minutes.
- There is also a **scheduled boat service** (Boat Alilaguna) every hour, via Murano and the Lido (€10, 70 minutes to the centre). The airport ATVO shuttle bus and ACTV bus number 5 both go to Piazzale Roma (€3, 20 minutes).

Arriving in Pisa/Florence (Firenze)

- **Galileo Galilei Airport** (tel: 050 849300, www.pisa-airport.com) is at Pisa, 91km (57 miles) west of Florence. Facilities include car rental desks, banks, a bureau de change, a bar, restaurant and shops. (Florence has its own small airport, Amerigo Vespucci, known as **Peretola**, with very limited flights.)
- A **taxi** into Pisa from Galileo Galilei Airport takes around 15 minutes and costs around €7. For Florence, allow 60–80 minutes and €120–€150.
- The **train service** into central Florence takes 75 minutes, via Pisa Centrale. (It is sometimes quicker to take a taxi to Pisa Centrale railway station, where there are additional trains to Florence.) The journey to Florence takes around 75 minutes, and tickets cost €4.85.
- A regular **CPT bus**, number 3, links the airport with central Pisa (50c, 10–15 minutes).

Arriving in Naples (Napoli)

- **Capodichino Airport** (tel: 081 789 6111; www.gesac.it) lies 8km (5 miles) northeast of the city. Aiport services include tourist information, a bank, a bureau de change, ATMs, restaurants and car rental.
- **Taxis** to central Naples cost around €20–€22 and take 20–30 minutes.
- There is **no rail link**. **CLP buses** (called ALIBUS, €3) go to Piazza Garibaldi and Piazza Municipio; bus number 35 goes to Piazza Garibaldi (€1, 20–30 minutes).

Getting Around

There are direct international rail connections to Austria, France, Germany, Spain and Switzerland. Internal flights are convenient but more expensive, and are the easiest way to reach Sicily and Sardinia. A comprehensive network of motorways and major roads covers the country, but avoid driving in the big cities, where congestion, lack of parking, narrow streets, one-way systems and occasional aggression are hazards.

Domestic Air Travel

■ Italy's national airline, **Alitalia** (www.alitalia.it) schedules regular flights between all main cities, including Milan, Naples, Palermo, Pisa, Turin, Venice and Verona. Their fixed-rate Visit Italy Pass (around €125, available when you book your Alitalia flight), offers a good deal if you plan up to three internal flights. Regional airlines like **Air One** (www.air-one.it) and **Meridiana** (www.meridiana.it) extend the range to smaller airports such as Bari, Bologna, Cagliari, Catania, Genoa and Florence.

Trains

■ Trains are run by the state railway company, **Trenitalia** (tel: 892021, www.trenitalia.com) and supplemented by a small number of private railway lines, which operate with identical systems.

■ The **Eurostar Italia (ES)** is a sleek, super-fast service that links the main Italian cities; advance booking is essential. **Intercity (IC)** high-speed trains connect cities and main regional towns; advance booking is recommended. **Treni Espressi (E)** and **Diretti (D)** connect major destinations within Italy, including some overnight services; sleeping accommodation should be booked in advance on Espressi. **Regionale (R)** are the local trains, which stop everywhere and can be very slow.

■ **Intercity Notte (ICN)** are the main long-distance overnight trains, offering a variety of ordinary carriages, Wagons-Lits and four-berth couchettes (*cuccetta*). Advance booking is essential; expect to pay a sleeper supplement of around €11–€38.

■ **Buy train tickets** at the railway stations, through FS (Ferrovie dello Stato) agents, or online at www.trenitalia.com. Fares are calculated according to the distance, with additional tickets and supplementary fares for faster services. Return (round-trip) fares (*andata e tornata*) are no cheaper than buying two single tickets (*andata*). It is essential to **reserve tickets for ES trains** in advance, and advisable to **book ahead** for any rail travel in the peak season between June and mid-September. Trains are divided into first and second class. **You must stamp your ticket** in the yellow machines on the platform before boarding the train.

■ If you are from Europe and plan to travel widely by train, the **Trenitalia Pass**, purchased before arrival, offers the best deal. Validated by a member of staff at any Italian station, it covers 4–10 specified days of travel within two months, and also gives discounts on some ferry routes. **Italy Flexi Rail Cards** offer a similar deal for visitors from the US and Canada. Under 26s can get a 20 per cent discount pass within Italy (*Cartaverde*), and over 65s the same (*Carta d'Argento*). For **Eurorail** passes, valid across Europe, visit www.raileurope.com.

Buses

■ There is no single national bus company for **long-distance routes**, but rather several small regional operators. Seat reservations are not generally available. Bus stations are usually next to train stations, and buses usually stop in the destination town's main square or *piazza*. Buy tickets on board or at the bus station.

■ **Local buses** serve outlying small towns and villages. They are usually timed to suit local needs such as school and working hours, and may be very limited at weekends and during school holidays.

Taxis

■ Government-regulated **taxis**, available from ranks or by telephone booking in all towns and cities, are usually either white or yellow. You'll pay a pick-up charge and a charge per kilometre, plus an extra charge for more people, items of luggage and travel in the evening or on Sundays. Charges should be listed on a **rate card** displayed inside the cab. Always check that the cab is licensed and the meter is running.

■ **Venice** has its own system of **water taxis** (white, with a cabin).

Domestic Ferries

■ **Ferries** link destinations within Sardinia and Sicily to the mainland; book ahead via a travel agent or online: www.traghettonionline.net/eng. Other **major islands** such as Elba, Capri and Ischia are linked by ferries and sometimes faster hydrofoils in high summer.

■ The **scenic lakes** of northern Italy, including Garda, Como and Maggiore, have their own ferries linking towns around the shores.

■ **Venice** has a waterborne transport network of *vaporetti* and the smaller, faster *motoscafi*. Run by ACTV, all craft are numbered on the side and follow set routes. Tickets are sold on the floating piers (*pontile*), or in shops showing the ACTV sticker, and must be validated at the machine on the pier before you board. *Traghetti* are gondola-ferries that cross the Canal Grande at seven fixed points; tickets cost 50c.

Driving

■ There is an excellent system of toll motorways/expressways (*autostrada*, marked A on maps and road signs) across Italy. **Key routes** include the A1/A3 down the western side of the peninsula from Milan to Bologna, Florence, Rome, Naples and Messina; the A14 down the eastern seaboard from Bologna to Táranto; and the A4 across the north from Turin to Venice and Trieste.

■ Other roads include main highways (*superstrade*, marked S), lesser highways (*nazionale*, marked N, and *strada statale*, marked SS), and minor country roads. In rural areas such as Tuscany you may also encounter hard-packed gravel roads known as white roads (*strada bianche*).

■ **If bringing your own car** to Italy, you must carry the following documentation in addition to your passport: a full, valid national driver's licence (with a translation, if not provided as part of the licence), certificate of motor insurance, and the vehicle's registration document (plus letter of authorisation from the owner if not registered in your name). Third party motor insurance is the **minimum requirement**, but fully comprehensive cover is strongly advised. Check that your **insurance** covers you against damage in transit, and that you have adequate **breakdown cover** (check with your motor insurer, broker or motoring club). You must also display an **international sticker** or distinguishing sign plate on the rear of the car by the registration plate. **Headlights** of left-hand drive cars must be adjusted for driving on the right. It is **compulsory to carry a warning triangle**, and spare bulbs, a first-aid kit and fire extinguisher are strongly recommended. If you're driving in **winter**, you may need winter tyres or snow chains.

Driving Know-How

- Drive on the **right** and give way to traffic approaching from the right unless directed otherwise.
- Drivers must be **18 or over**, and have a full licence.
- **Speed limits** are 50kph/31mph on urban roads, 110kph/68mph outside built-up areas and 130kph/81mph on *autostrade*.
- Use **dipped headlights** in non-urban areas **during the day**, and in towns or cities as well at night. Dipped headlights are **compulsory when driving in tunnels**, even if they are well lit.
- The **legal blood alcohol limit** is 0.05 per cent. If you drink, don't drive.
- **Tolls are charged** on most *autostrade*; foreign credit cards are not always accepted. Collect a ticket as you enter, pay as you leave. **Slip roads** onto *autostrade* are short; you may have to stop and wait for traffic to pass before you can join. Once on the *autostrada*, use only outer lanes for over-taking; be prepared to indicate and move over to let faster drivers past.
- **Fuel** (*senza piombo*) – unleaded (95 and 98 octane), diesel (*gasolio*) and LPG. At night look for a 24-hour (*24 ore*) filling station with automatic pump. These take €5, €10 and €20 notes, but may reject older ones.

Renting a Car

- Cars can be rented by drivers **over 21** who have held a full driver's licence for a year; note that some companies require a minimum age of **25**.
- For the **cheapest deals**, shop around and book ahead. Fly-drive packages may be less expensive.
- Most **major car rental firms** such as Budget, Avis and Hertz have outlets at airports, main railway stations and in large towns and cities through-out Italy. Most will let you return your car to other Italian cities and even other countries, but agree this ahead; there may be a surcharge.

Urban Transport

- Most big cities have efficient **integrated public transport systems**: buses, trams, local trains. Rome and Milan have subway rail systems (Rome has two lines, Milan four). **Tickets** are usually available from *tabacchi*, bars, news-stands and Metro stations, and must be validated for each journey by inserting into a machine on the vehicle or in the station.

Tourist Offices
Rome ✉ Via Parigi 5 ☎ 06 3600 4399; www.romaturismo.it 🕐 Mon–Fri 8:15–7:15, Sat 7:15–1:45 pm
Milan ✉ Via Marconi 1 ☎ 02 7252 4301/2/3 🕐 Mon–Sat 8:45–1, 2–6, Sun 9–1, 2–5
Venice ✉ Piazza San Marco 71f ☎ 041 529 8740 🕐 Mon–Sat 9:30–3:30
Pisa ✉ Piazza Duomo 1 ☎ 050 560464 🕐 Daily 9–7, Jun–Sep; Mon–Sat 9–6, Sun 10:30–4:30, Oct–May
Florence ✉ Via Cavour 1r ☎ 055 290 832/833 🕐 Mon–Sat 8:15–7:15, Sun 8:30–6:30
Naples ✉ Piazza Gesù Nuovo 🕐 Mon–Sat 9–7:30, Sun 9–2:30

Admission Charges
The cost of admission for museums and places of interest mentioned in the guide is indicated by the following price categories.
Inexpensive = under €2.5   **Moderate** = €2.5–€5   **Expensive** = over €5

Accommodation

There's a wide variety of accommodation throughout Italy, with a greater choice in the north and central regions than in the south. International hotel chains such as Best Western and Hilton are represented, and Italy has its own chains, including Jolly and Boscolo. There are fabulous luxury hotels in historic buildings, and chic small hotels, but for a more authentic experience of Italy you may like to try a family-run *pensione* or a rented villa or farmhouse.

Types of Accommodation
Hotels

- Hotels are inspected by regional authorities and are **grouped into five categories**, from one star (at the bottom) to five-star luxury hotels. Stars reflect the quality and variety of facilities, rather than character or comfort, and in one-star hotels you may have to share a bathroom with other guests. **Breakfast is generally included** in the price but may be poor, especially in simpler hotels, which may not have a restaurant. During high season in summer, resort hotels often require you to take half-board (breakfast and dinner) or full-board (all meals), and single travellers may have to pay full price for a double room if no singles are available.
- Usually family-run small hotels, *pensiones*, offer the best value if you're on a budget. Rooms are generally spotlessly clean and comfortable, if a little dated in style, and prices are fair. Inns – *locande* – used to be another good budget option, but these have mostly disppeared, and *locande* now refers to something more expensive and trendy.
- There are some great **luxury hotels** in Italy. The Orient Express group, owners of the famous train that runs from London to Venice, has three traditionally opulent hotels, including the Hotel Cipriani in Venice and the Hotel Splendido in Portofino (tel: 20 7805 5060, www.orient-express.com). For something ultra-stylish and modern, there are class acts such as the Gallery Hotel Art in Florence (tel: 055 27263, www.lingarnohotels.com/gallery/) or the Hotel de Russie in Rome (tel: 06 328881, www.roccofortehotels.com).

Rural Accommodation

- If you're exploring the countryside, look out for the yellow signs indicating *agriturisme* – redundant farm buildings that have been converted to offer accommodation, ranging from the simple to the luxurious. These venues are often in **beautiful rural locations** (especially in Tuscany and Umbria). Family rooms are sometimes available. Meals are usually offered, and include local produce.
- Local tourist offices can generally advise about *agriturisme* in their area. **For more details**, contact Agriturist, Corso V Emanuele 101, 00168 Roma, tel: 06 685 2342, www.agriturist.com. Agriturist have their own guide to farm stays in English, *Vacanza in Fattoria*, and the TCI has an annual publication, *Agriturismo e vacenze in campagna* (€20).

Self-catering

- Self-contained **villas and farmhouses** are widely available in towns, villages and country areas across northern Italy, Tuscany and Umbria, and offer particularly good value for families. Apartments and houses in the popular coastal resorts tend to be reserved well ahead by Italians themselves. Elsewhere, rental properties may be more difficult to find.

- Bookings made through **tour operators** may have the advantage of access flights and rental car included. If you're **touring independently**, local tourist offices also hold information for rental accommodation in their area, and should be contacted well in advance. See also www.holidayrentals.com and other websites.

Rifugi

- A network of **simply equipped mountain huts** *(rifugi)* is available if you are planning to hike or climb in the mountains. These are operated by the Club Alpino Italiano, but facilities are usually sparse.

Camping

- There are campsites all over Italy, especially down the Adriatic coast. They generally **open between April and September** and vary in the facilities they offer, from swimming pools and restaurants to simple basics. TCI publishes an annual guide, *Campeggio e Villaggi Turistici* (€20).

Finding a Room

- It's recommended that you **reserve accommodation ahead** in any of Italy's main tourist towns, whatever time of year you travel – or you may be disappointed. November, January and February are usually quieter months, but local festivals mean that any small town may fill up at short notice.
- **Confirm any reservation** immediately in writing, either by fax or e-mail, and if possible reconfirm bookings a few days before arrival.
- If you haven't reserved ahead, visit the **local tourist office**, which will have a list of accommodation and may be willing to book for you. In towns or villages without a tourist office, head for the main *piazza* or *centro storico*, where you're likely to find the greatest concentration of hotels. Yellow signs direct you to hotels on the margins of towns and villages.
- When you **check in**, you'll need to complete a registration form and leave your passport (don't forget to collect it at the end of your stay). Ask to see the room first, especially in cheaper accommodation. Noise can be a problem in any hotel when you want to sleep with the windows open for the cooler air, so it's worth asking for a room at the back or overlooking a central courtyard or garden.
- **Check-out time** is normally between 10 am and noon, but hotels will usually store your luggage until the end of the day on request.

Rates

- Accommodation prices are likely to **vary throughout the year** by up to 25 per cent, according to the season. Prices may be divided into high season (*alta*) and low season (*bassa stagione*), or the hotel may make the same charge all year round (*tutto l'anno*). Agree a price before you make a reservation. Rates are also required to be posted on the back of every bedroom door.
- Prices should **include any taxes**, but watch out for surcharges covering anything from an over-priced breakfast (*prima colazione*) you may not want to air-conditioning (*aria condizionata*).
- If you're travelling with a family, many hotels will put an **extra bed** in a room for an additional charge.

Prices
The following symbols refer to the average cost of a double room
€ under €100   €€ €100–€180   €€€ over €180

Food and Drink

Eating is a sensual pleasure that the Italians take seriously. Italian cookery falls into distinct regional styles according to what's locally available. Join in the daily search for the freshest food in markets and small shops – the discovery of local delicacies is likely to be a highlight of any visit.

What to Eat and When

- Many **bars open for breakfast** (*prima calzione*) at 7 or 7:30 am, serving strong coffee and pastries or croissants with sweet fillings such as jam or custard.
- Most **restaurants** open for lunch (*pranzo*) between 12:30 or 1 pm and 3 pm, and reopen for dinner (*cena*) at around 7:30 or 8 pm.
- A **full restaurant menu** is likely to include a starter (*antipasto*) consisting of a selection of cold meats and salami, or perhaps vegetable dishes or seafood. The first course (*il primo*) will probably be pasta, risotto or soup, which is followed by a portion of meat or fish served on its own (*il secondo*). Order vegetables (*contorni*) or a salad (*insalata*) separately. Puddings (*dolci*) or cheese (*formaggio*) usually round the meal off.
- If you want a **lighter meal** it is perfectly acceptable to select just the courses that appeal to you.

Where to Eat

- *Ristoranti* are formal, smart restaurants, often open only for dinner.
- The term *osterie* can refer to an old-fashioned restaurant serving home-cooked food, or a very well established, trendy eating place.
- For the best home-style cooking (*casalinga*), head for a *trattoria*. These are usually simple, family-run affairs, and may lack a written menu – just ask the waiter for the day's specials.
- The pizza was reputedly invented in Naples. Look out for *pizzerie*, which often serve pasta dishes, too. Some of the best pizzas come straight out of a wood-fired oven (*forno al legno*). For take-away pizzas, look for the sign *pizza al taglio*.
- Many **bars** serve freshly made snacks such as *pannini* (filled rolls, often served hot), *tramezzini* (sandwiches) and toasted sandwiches (*toast*). *Pannini* are also sometimes available from general grocer's shops (*alimentari*), and bakers (*forni*) sell flat bread made with oil and herbs (*foccace*) that also makes a good snack or basis for a picnic.
- *Távole calde* are snack bars that specialise in hot food, freshly prepared, while *rosticcerie* serve spit-roasted chicken and pasta and vegetable dishes to eat in or take away. Major international fast-food burger chains have branches in larger towns and cities.
- The Italians make some of the best ice cream in the world; find it at a *gelateria*, and look out for the home-made varieties (*produzione propria*). Ice cream is usually served in a tub (*coppa*) or a traditional cone (*cono*).

Paying and Tipping

- While larger restaurants in urban centres generally accept credit cards, many smaller ones expect to be paid **in cash**, so check ahead if necessary.
- In restaurants and *trattorie* a **cover charge** (*coperto*) will be added to your bill (*il conto*), including the bread served with your meal and the service itself. If the service is exceptional, you may like to leave your loose change or a tip of around 5 per cent.

Regional Menus

- With the exception of a few of the very largest cities, food is strictly regional in its style and presentation across the country. In **Rome and Lazio**, for example, you're likely to find offal on the menu, and strongly flavoured dishes such as *spaghetti aglio e olio* (with garlic and oil).

- In the **northwest**, try *osso buco* (slow-cooked veal), *risotto alla Milianese* (rice flavoured with saffron), polenta, and cheeses such as marscapone and Gorgonzola. Fragrant pesto (basil, cheese and pine-nut sauce) is a staple in the cuisine of Lombardy, while in Piemonte white truffles flavour pasta and risotto.

- The **northeast** is the home of Parma ham and Parmesan cheese, which you'll find served with rich sauces, and pasta stuffed with ricotta, spinach, pumpkin and varied meats. The food of Trentino-Also-Adige is altogether heartier, with spicy smoked meat (*speck*), dumplings and fruity puddings.

- In **central northern Italy**, look out for *crostini* (bread toasted in olive oil and served with different toppings), bean soups and meat grilled *alla Fiorentina*. Siena is the home of the chewy *panforte* (spiced fruit and nut cake), and *cantuccini* (hard almond biscuits for dipping into sweet wine) are also from the Tuscany region. Norcia, in Umbria, is famous for its prosciutto and salami.

- The **south** is the home of the pizza, but also of Mediterranean vegetables and delights such as *fiorilli* (courgette flowers, stuffed, battered and fried) and sweet pastries packed with ricotta cheese and candied fruit.

- Seafood is popular all **around the coast**, from simple, grilled *sarde* (sardines) to *seppie* (cuttlefsh) or perhaps *spaghetti alle vongole verace* (with clams).

Where and What to Drink

- You can get hot and cold drinks as well as alcohol and snacks in **bars**, which are open throughout the day from around 7 am. Local people tend to eat and drink standing up; you'll **pay a bit extra** to sit at a table, inside or out. In some city bars you may have to order and pay for your drink at the cash desk first, then show your receipt at the bar to receive it.

- **Bottled water** (*aqua minerale*) is usually drunk with every meal, and comes as still (*senza gas*) or sparkling (*con gas* or *frizzante*). For something refreshing on a hot day, try **freshly squeezed orange juice** (*spremuta di aranci*), or perhaps a fruity drink of crushed ice (*granita*). **Iced tea** (*té freddo*), flavoured with lemon or peach, is also popular.

- **White and red wine** (*vino bianco, vino rosso*) are widely drunk; for the house wine ask for either *vino de la casa* or *vino sfuso*. **Beer** (*birra*) is also widely available: Italian brands include Nostra Azzura and Moretti.

- **Spirits** may be taken before a meal (*aperitivi*) and/or after it (*digestivo*). The former include well-known brands such as Martini, Campari and Cinzano; the latter include fiery *grappa*. Local variations include lemon-flavoured Limoncello and almond-flavoured Amaretto.

- **Coffee** is generally served strong, and includes espresso (small and black), *cappuccino* (made with frothy milk) and *caffé con latte* (made with lots of milk). For something weaker, ask for a *caffé lungo* or *Americano*.

Prices
Expect to pay per person for a meal, excluding drinks:
€ under €20   €€ €20–€40   €€€ over €40

Shopping

Shopping in Italy can be a great experience, whether it's thumbing through the luxury goods and designer labels in the big cities of the north – Rome, Milan, Florence, Turin, Bologna – or exploring artisans' workshops down a backstreet in a small town just about anywhere.

Opening Hours

- **Opening times** are fairly standard across the country, but may vary according to the type of shop, the season and the location, so expect a few surprises. The regular opening times are from 8:30 to 1, and between 4 and 5:30 to 7 or 7:30, from Tuesday to Saturday.
- In **bigger towns and main tourist areas**, shops also open on Monday, and occasionally Sunday, and may remain open all day (*orario continuo*) rather than close for the siesta.
- **Food shops** may close on Monday afternoons or Wednesday afternoons.
- **Clothes shops** may not open until 10 am.
- During July and August, when many Italians take their holidays, **small shops may close** for a week or a month.
- Daily and weekly **markets** are a feature of cities and towns, and usually operate from around 8 am to 1 pm. They are a fun way to work out what the local delicacies are, and also an inexpensive source of clothing, bags and other items.

Payment

- Shops in towns, cities and major tourist areas usually accept payment by **credit or debit card**.
- For markets and smaller outlets, carry **euros in cash** with you.
- Visitors from outside the European Union can **reclaim IVA (sales) tax** on most major purchases. You'll need a *fattura* form from the shopkeeper, which must be shown with the receipts and stamped at customs, then returned to the shop by post for a refund.

What to Buy

- **High fashion** is a main focus for shopping in Italy, and you'll find the internationally known fashion houses and major chain stores in every large town and city. This is the home of designer names including Armani, Dolce & Gabbana, Fendi, Gucci, Prada and Versace, and fashionistas will find themselves spoilt for choice. Don't neglect what's underneath – some of the finest silk and satin underwear is found around Como and Milan.
- Shoes, belts, handbags and other **leather accessories** make good buys. Find them at bargain prices in markets as well as on the main streets.
- **Jewellery** is also a popular buy, and Italy is one of the great producers in the world. Production centres around Arezzo in Tuscany, but you'll find designer pieces and one-offs all over the country.
- **Crafts** vary according to the region, from coloured Murano glass and painted carnival masks in Venice to wooden inlay in Sorrento. Look out for ceramics and pottery, the carved olive wood of Tuscany, and exquisite handmade and marbled paper.
- Stock up on **Italian foods**, but beware of import restrictions that may affect what you can take back into your own country. Olive oil, pasta and most cheeses are generally safe bets, and wines and local spirits are good options, too.

Entertainment

There's plenty to keep you entertained in Italy, whether you're into summer *festas* or winter sports. Classical concerts are a good way to enjoy some of the country's finest churches, and almost every town has its own opera house where ballet and theatre are also staged. Italian cinema has its own following, and current Hollywood movies are usually dubbed into Italian. Tourist offices can usually tell you what's on and how to obtain tickets.

Music, Opera and Dance

- **Music festivals** are found across the country in summer, usually reflecting a conservative taste for the great composers and popular classics. Rock and jazz also feature, notably in the larger towns and cities.
- Italy is the **home of opera**, and joining an Italian audience for a show can be a great experience: opera-goers participate fully, interrupting the on-stage action to applaud favourite arias, and many houses have unofficial cliques attending every performance and controlling the crowd.
- **Verona's Arena** is the stunning venue for a world-class summer opera season from the end of June to the end of August, with popular favourites such as *Aida*, *Carmen* and *Madame Butterfly*. Advance reservation is essential (Via Dietro Anfiteatro 6/B, tel: 045 800 51 51; www.arena.it).
- **Traditional folk music** is performed at *festas*, and you may see national dance in costume as well.

Nightlife

- You'll have no trouble finding a **broad spectrum of nightlife** in Rome, Milan and other major cities. In summer, the focus shifts to coastal resorts such as Rimini, where crowds flock to the open-air bars and clubs.
- Nightlife in the cities starts to **take off at around midnight**. In rural areas, which rely more on local bars, everything may have closed down by 11 pm.
- Nightlife is **really about being seen**, so you'll find plenty of posing and not much hard-core drinking. There are no limited licensing hours.
- **Small clubs and music bars** are similar across the country. Many charge an entrance fee, which may include a free drink.
- The **gay scene is low-profile** in southern Italy, but in larger cities such as Florence, Rome and Milan there are plenty of bars and clubs. Check out gay listings for the whole country in the monthly publication *Babilonia*.

Sports and Outdoor Activities

- Italians are **passionate about soccer**. Most matches are played on Sunday afternoons from the end of August through to June, with a break over Christmas. Tickets are usually available from the venues, sports shops and agencies.
- **Watersports** are widely available around the coast and on the northern lakes. Resort beaches are usually divided into private sections (*stabilimento balnearo*), each with its own facilities including showers, toilets and sun loungers, and you'll have to pay to get in.
- The Alps are a **popular ski destination** for northern Italy in winter, and the Abruzzi Mountains are within easy reach of Rome and Naples. Smaller ski resorts are found all over the country, including Sicily and the Apeninnes, offering good low-key options for weekend breaks.

Rome

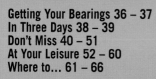

Getting Your Bearings

No other Italian city is as compelling as its capital. In this noisy, stylish and chaotic metropolis of over 4 million, modern institutions exist beside over 2,000 years of history. Nowhere else has as much to see spanning as many years, and it's this breadth, combined with its buzz and bustle, that gives Rome a magic matched by few other places.

Rome is built on seven hills and lies on either side of the Tevere (Tiber). The earliest settlement took place on the east bank, where you'll find the great classical monuments such as the Fori and Colosseo. Around them are the city's earliest Christian churches and the great basilicas, while further north medieval Rome, all narrow alleys and sun-dappled *piazze*, hugs the riverbank. Great Renaissance and baroque building schemes pushed north again, replacing ancient buildings with *palazzi*, squares, fountains and churches. Across the Tiber, the Città del Vaticano, powerbase of the Catholic Church, is an independent state, a tiny enclave packed with artistic treasures. Southwards, the riverside district of Trastevere is one of Rome's most vibrant neighbourhoods.

Exploring Rome is not easy; a month's sojourn would barely scratch the surface. Better to pick a few key sights and then soak up the atmosphere and feel the pulse of the city, stumbling on finds in obscure backstreets. Rome keeps many of her gems remarkably well hidden.

2 Musei Vaticani

Castel Sant'Angelo **6**

CITTÀ DEL VATICANO

1 PIAZZA SAN PIETRO

Basilica di San Pietro

Palazzo Corsini

Parco Gianicolense

Statue on Ponte Sant'Angelo

Above: The Vatican Museums
Previous page: Inside St Peter's

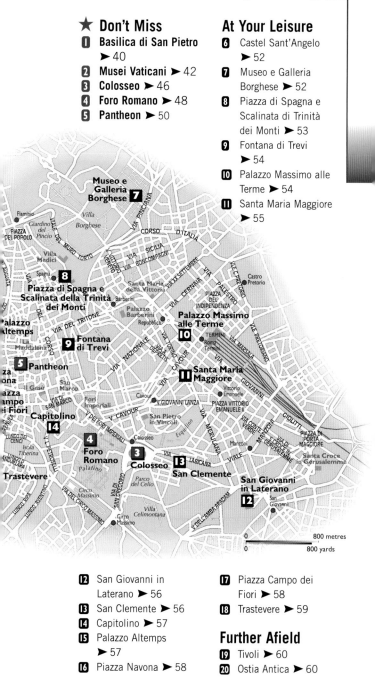

Three days is not long to spend in Rome, but with careful planning you should be able to experience the best of the Eternal City. Following a chronological journey through Rome's sights will help put the staggering scale of the city's history and its treasures in perspective.

Rome in Three Days

Day One

Morning

Start by exploring the heart of classical Rome at the **4 Foro Romano** (left, ➤ 48–49) and the **3 Colosseo** (➤ 46–47), before walking round the Monumente Vittorio Emanuele to the hill of the **14 Capitolino**, site of a beautiful square flanked by fine museums (➤ 57). If you want more Roman art, visit the **10 Palazzo Massimo alle Terme** (➤ 54–55), a 20-minute walk away up the Via Nazionale.

Afternoon

After lunch it's time for the one extant Roman structure still in use, the **5 Pantheon** (➤ 50–51), set in a glorious jumble of medieval streets. In the same area is the pick of Rome's fountains, the **9 Fontana di Trevi** (right, ➤ 54), from where it's a short walk to the **15 Palazzo Altemps** (➤ 57), a 16th-century palace showcasing the best of Roman sculpture.

Evening

Stay in the area for the evening; **16 Piazza Navona** (left, ➤ 58) is perfect for a drink, and that quintessential Roman *piazza*, the **17 Campo dei Fiori** (➤ 58), with its bars and restaurants, is ten minutes away.

Day Two

Morning

A day across the River Tiber starts in the **2 Musei Vaticani** (left, ➤ 42–45), the world's largest museum. Take your time to see the highlights before a late lunch near St Peter's Square.

Afternoon

Spend a couple of hours in and around the great **1 Basilica di San Pietro** (➤ 40–41), making sure you ascend the dome. Afterwards, walk down the Via della Concillazione to the **6 Castel Sant'Angelo** (➤ 52), with its fascinating interior and great views.

Evening

Head downriver to atmospheric **18 Trastevere** (below, ➤ 59).

Day Three

Morning

Begin the day with a trio of Rome's finest churches: ancient **13 San Clemente** (➤ 56) and the basilicas of **12 San Giovanni in Laterano** (➤ 56) and **11 Santa Maria Maggiore** (➤ 55).

Afternoon

After lunch, head for the verdant gardens of the Villa Borghese, home to the **7 Museo e Galleria Borghese** (right, ➤ 52–53), a small art museum that's one of the city's highlights.

Evening

Stroll through the park to emerge at the top of the graceful **8 Scalinata di Trinità dei Monti**, a sweeping stairway that leads down to the **Piazza di Spagna** (➤ 53). Early evening is a good time to hit the elegant shops around here, before heading off for dinner.

⓪Basilica di San Pietro

The Basilica di San Pietro (St Peter's) is the world's most famous church, an important place of Catholic pilgrimage, and Rome's most notable sight, even though it contains few important works of art.

History of the Basilica

The first known church on this site, raised in AD 326 over the shrine of St Peter, one of the Apostles, was crumbling by 1452. Pope Nicholas V commissioned a new version, and decades of false starts and alterations ensued. Building began in 1506 to a design by Bramante; Giuliano da Sangallo took over in 1516, and in 1546 Pope Paul III called in Michelangelo, who proposed a colossal dome. Though nearly complete when he died in 1564, this was changed in 1590 by Giacomo della Porta. In 1605, Carlo Maderno was asked for yet another redesign, and finishing touches were added by Bernini. The new church was finally consecrated in 1626.

Above: Crowds gather outside St Peter's to see the Pope

The Piazza and Basilica

Bernini's enormous Piazza San Pietro (1656–67) provides St Peter's grand setting, with two semicircular colonnades supported by 284 columns and crowned with 140 statues of saints.

New popes and sainthoods are proclaimed from the basilica's central balcony, and one of the façade's five portals, the Porta Santa (on the extreme right), is opened only during Holy Years (every 25 years). The central doors (1433–45) are among a handful of treasures retrieved from the old basilica.

Inside, the first impression is one of immense size: the church measures 185m (607 feet) long and 119m (390 feet) high at the dome, and can accommodate over 60,000 people.

Statuary and the Dome

The best-known statue in St Peter's is Michelangelo's *Pietà* (1498–9), which shows Mary cradling the dead Christ; it is now behind bullet-proof glass, since being vandalised in 1972.

Below: Detail of the ceiling inside St Peter's

Further down the church, the crossing is marked by the high altar and Bernini's bronze altar canopy, or *baldacchino* (1624–33). Behind you on your right as you face the canopy is a 13th-century statue of St Peter Enthroned, its right foot worn smooth by pilgrims' kisses.

In the apse beyond the high altar is Bernini's elaborate Cattedra di San Pietro (1656–65), a bronze canopy built to encase a throne reputedly used by St Peter (although probably dating from the 9th century).

At the end of the right-hand nave as you face the altar a lift and steps give access to the dome's first stage. From here, more steps lead to the higher drum and gallery, and a steeper, narrower staircase climbs to the very top of the lantern.

TAKING A BREAK

You will find several restaurants and eateries in the side streets off **Porta Angelica**.

Right: Marble *Pietà* by Michelangelo

Left: A member of the Swiss Guard

✚ 200 B3 ✉ Piazza San Pietro ☎ 06 6988 1662 🕐 Daily 7–7, Apr–Oct; 7–6, Nov–Mar
🚇 Ottaviano-San Pietro 🚌 40 or 62 to Via della Conciliazione; 64 goes close to Piazza San Pietro; 19, 23, 32, 49, 492, 990 to Piazza del Risorgimento 🎫 Basilica: free. Dome: moderate

BASILICA DI SAN PIETRO: INSIDE INFO

Top tips A **rigid dress code** forbids shorts, short skirts or skimpy tops. Women should cover their shoulders and men should dress with decorum.
• **Climb the dome** for one of the city's finest views.

2 Musei Vaticani

The Vatican Museums make up the world's largest museum complex. To get the most out of a visit, concentrate on the main highlights – the Museo Pio-Clementino, the Stanze di Raffaello (Raphael Rooms) and the Cappella Sistina (Sistine Chapel).

Museo Pio-Clementino and Galleries

Highlights here begin in the Gabinetto dell'Apoxyomenos, dominated by the *Apoxyomenos*, a Roman copy of a 4th-century BC Greek sculpture showing an athlete scraping the sweat, dust and oil from his body. The Cortile Ottagono, a small courtyard, contains classical masterpieces, most notably

Above: *Battle of the Milvian Bridge*, opposite the Stanza di Costantino

Left: Galleria delle Carte Geografiche – decorated with 16th-century map frescoes

the *Laocoön* (*c*50 BC), portraying a Trojan priest and his sons
fighting sea serpents. Beyond the adjacent Sala degli Animali
(ancient and 18th-century sculpted animals) is the Galleria
delle Statue. This contains the *Apollo Sauroktonos*, a Roman
copy of a 4th-century BC original showing Apollo about to
kill a lizard, and the *Candelabri Barberini*, a pair of 2nd-
century lamps discovered at the Villa Adriana in Tivoli
(▶ 60).

The **Galleria dei Candelabri** (candelabra) and the
Galleria degli Arazzi (tapestries) on the upper floor lead on
into the **Galleria delle Carte Geografiche**, decorated with
beautiful painted maps (1580s) of Italy and the Papal States.

Dispute of the Blessed Sacrament in the Stanza della Segnatura

Stanze di Raffaello

The four Stanze di Raffaello (Raphael Rooms) are almost
entirely covered in one of the painter's greatest fresco cycles,
commissioned by Pope Julius II in 1508 and completed by
Raphael's pupils after his death in 1520. To see them in the

Painting by Fra Angelico

order in which they were painted, begin with the **Stanza
della Segnatura** (1508–11), where four allegories represent-
ing Theology, Philosophy, Poetry and Justice contain a wealth
of allusion (it's worth buying a guide for detailed explana-
tions). Next comes the **Stanza di Eliodoro** (1512–14), with
the battle scenes of *The Expulsion of Heliodorus from the
Temple*; *Leo I Repulsing Attila*, whose central figure
(on a donkey) resembles Leo X; and *The
Deliverance of St Peter*, commemorating the
saint's escape from prison. The third room
chronologically is the **Stanza dell'Incendio**
(1514–17), whose main frescoes portray the
Coronation of Charlemagne, the *Oath of Leo III*,
the *Battle of Ostia* and the *Fire in the Borgo*.
Much of it was painted by pupils working to
Raphael's designs, as were the four principal
frescoes on the Emperor Constantine's life, in

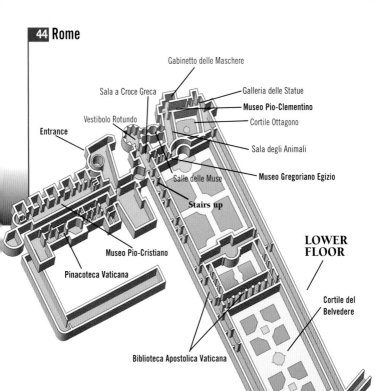

Gabinetto delle Maschere

Sala a Croce Greca

Vestibolo Rotundo

Entrance

Galleria delle Statue

Museo Pio-Clementino

Cortile Ottagono

Sala degli Animali

Salle delle Muse

Museo Gregoriano Egizio

Stairs up

LOWER FLOOR

Museo Pio-Cristiano

Pinacoteca Vaticana

Cortile del Belvedere

Biblioteca Apostolica Vaticana

Appartamento Bor

Cappella Sistina

the last room, the **Stanza di Costantino**
(1517–24). Before moving on, visit the nearby
Cappella di Niccolò V, a small chapel covered in
beautiful frescoes by Fra Angelico.

Cappella Sistina

The Sistine Chapel was built for Pope Sixtus IV
(1471–1484), and its lower walls were frescoed
between 1480 and 1483 by several notable artists
including Perugino, Domenico Ghirlandaio and Sandro
Botticelli. The ceiling was painted by Michelangelo
between 1508 and 1512, and his *Last Judgement* was
created between 1536 and 1541. Michelangelo's main
panels illustrate the Creation, Adam and Eve and
their fall, the Flood and Noah's drunkenness. Smaller sections illustrate prophets, sibyls, Old Testament characters and 20 *ignudi*
(nude youths).

   The Last Judgement (1536–41), covering the wall behind
the altar, shows God venting his judgement on cowering
mankind. The spared rise to Paradise on the left, while the
doomed sink to Hell on the right, and the dead rise from their
graves along the lower section. Christ stands at the centre,
surrounded by the Virgin, Apostles and saints. Look out for
the damned soul hugging himself as he awaits his fate.

TAKING A BREAK

Visit the Vatican Museums' café or try **Non Solo Pizza** (Via
degli Scipioni), a few blocks north of Piazza Risorgimento.

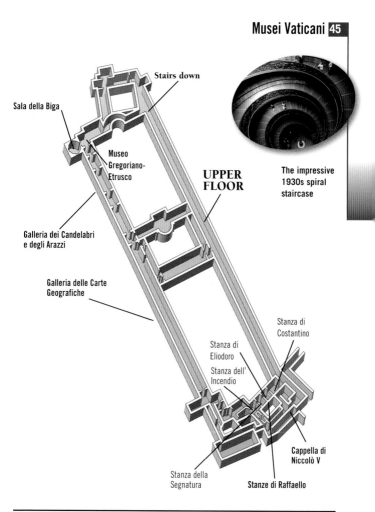

Stairs down

Sala della Biga

Museo Gregoriano-Etrusco

UPPER FLOOR

Galleria dei Candelabri e degli Arazzi

Galleria delle Carte Geografiche

The impressive 1930s spiral staircase

Stanza di Costantino

Stanza di Eliodoro

Stanza dell' Incendio

Cappella di Niccolò V

Stanza della Segnatura

Stanze di Raffaello

🕂 200 B4 ✉ Vaticano ☎ 06 6988 4947; www.vatican.va ⏰ Mon–Sat 8:45–1:45, Jan–Feb and Nov–Dec; Mon–Fri 8:45–3:45, Sat 8:45–1:45, Mar–Oct. Last Sun of month 8:45–1:45 (last ticket 1 hour before closing); closed on religious and public holidays ⓜ Ottaviano-San Pietro or Cipro-Musei Vaticani 🚌 19, 23, 32, 49, 492, 990 to Piazza del Risorgimento 💰 Expensive. Free last Sun of the month

MUSEI VATICANI: INSIDE INFO

Top tips Opening hours vary from year to year, as does the order in which you can walk around. The Sistine Chapel and Raphael Rooms are farthest from the museum entrance, and one-way systems are introduced at busy times.
• The Vatican Museums are **closed on Sunday except for the last Sunday of the month**, when admission is free. They open on Mondays, when most of Rome's state museums are closed.

③ Colosseo

Once the scene of gladiatorial combat, the Colosseum is now Rome's most majestic monument. To appreciate its scale, view it from the Colle Oppio, a park to the northeast, or the belvedere (Largo Agnes) immediately above the Colosseo Metro station exit.

Early Days

The Colosseum was begun around AD 70 by Emperor Vespasian on the former site of an ornamental lake. The marshy conditions required the laying of enormous drains, many of which survive. By the time of Vespasian's death in AD 79 the monument was finished to its third tier. Additions were made by his son, Titus, who inaugurated the Colosseum in AD 80 with celebrations that saw 100 days of festivities and the slaughter of 5,000 animals.

The completed structure had tiered seating and 80 exits, or *vomitoria*, allowing huge crowds to leave in minutes. A vast sailcloth roof, or *velarium*, supported by 240 wooden masts, could be unfurled to protect spectators from the elements.

Inside the Colosseum

Much of the seating and flooring has disappeared. A fire in AD 217 devastated the upper levels and wooden arena, and other fires and earthquakes over the next 400 years caused further damage. By the 6th century the arena was being used as workshops and a cemetery; by 1320 its south side had collapsed, and the stone was being ransacked. The desecration ceased in 1744, when Pope Benedict XIV consecrated the

View of the substructure below the arena floor

Arco di Costantino

Though overshadowed by the Colosseum, the Arch of Constantine (AD 315) is the city's largest and best-preserved arch. Most of its materials were taken from other buildings, including many sculptural reliefs probably removed from a monument to the victories of Marcus Aurelius in AD 176. Masons simply replaced his face with that of Constantine.

In places you can still see all four floors of the Colosseum

site in memory of Christians who were supposedly martyred there (in fact few if any Christians were killed in the Colosseum).

Today you can look down on the maze of tunnels and shafts through which animals and gladiators were brought to the stage from distant pens. The stage area could also be flooded for re-enacted sea battles.

Spectators were rigidly segregated. The emperor and Vestal Virgins faced each other in boxes at the lowest levels. Alongside them, on wide platforms, sat the senators. Above were knights and aristocrats, then Roman citizens (plebeians) and finally women, slaves and the poor. Some groups, such as soldiers, scribes and heralds, had separate sections; others – gravediggers, actors, retired gladiators – were banned altogether.

TAKING A BREAK

Aim for the less expensive bars and cafés in Via Cavour or the streets off Via di San Giovanni in Laterano to the east.

Right: Posing outside the Colosseum

🚩 202 A1 ✉ Piazza del Colosseo, Via dei Fori Imperiali ☎ 06 700 5469 🕐 Interior: daily 9–7:30, Apr–Sep; 9–6:30, Mar and Oct; 9–4:30, Nov–Mar. Last ticket 1 hour before closing Ⓜ Colosseo 🚌 30B, 75, 85, 87, 117, 175, 186 💶 Expensive. Combined ticket with Palatino

---

COLOSSEO: INSIDE INFO

Top tips View the Colosseum **after nightfall**, when it is spectacularly floodlit.
• The Colosseum's rather **hidden entrance** is on its southernmost side. From the entrance to the upper levels you can walk around part of the exterior away from the roaring traffic.

④ Foro Romano

The Forum, the heart of the Roman Empire for almost 1,000 years, is today a romantic jumble of ruins. Enjoy an overview from the terraces of the Campidoglio, reached from Piazza del Campidoglio; steps lead down to one of the Forum entrances, alongside the Arco di Settimio Severo.

Above: The Foro Romano, with the Colosseum in the background

Inset: Detail from the Tempio di Vesta

Exploring the Forum

The Forum's historical significance is overwhelming: you are, after all, walking in the footsteps of Julius Caesar, Nero, Caligula, Claudius, Hadrian and countless other resonant names from antiquity. Its site was originally the Velabrum, an inlet of the Tiber between the Capitoline and Palatine hills, where, according to legend, Romulus founded Rome in 753 BC. As Rome prospered the area was drained and developed until, in the 2nd century AD, shortage of space drove the focus of power to the Palatino, or Palatine Hill. As the empire declined much of the stone was plundered for Rome's medieval churches and palaces.

The Forum

To the left of the **Arco di Settimio Severo** a line of stones indicates the remains of the **Rostra**, or orator's platform, where Mark Antony reputedly appealed to the citizens after the assassination of Julius Caesar. The eight-columned **Tempio di Saturno**, to the south, is one of the Forum's oldest temples (around 497 BC). Turning away from the Capitoline Hill above, you pass the **Basilica Julia** on your right. South of the nearby **Tempio di Castore e Polluce** is the **Santa Maria Antiqua**, the Forum's primary Christian building, converted from a pagan monument in the 6th century.

Cutting through the site is the **Via Sacra**, once the principal thoroughfare. The large brick building ahead and to the right is the **Curia**, or Senate House, probably completed by Augustus in 28 BC. Before it the **Lapis Niger**, or Black Stone, is a black marble slab marking the site of a sanctuary to the god Vulcan. Past the **Tempio di Antonino e Faustina**, built in AD 141 by Emperor Antoninus to honour his wife, Faustina, is the **Tempio di Vesta** and **Atrium Vestae**, respectively the Temple and House of the Vestal Virgins, who tended the sacred flame symbolising Rome's continuity.

Beyond the Atrium on the left stands part of the **Basilica di Massenzio**, one of the Forum's most impressive monuments. Only one of its columns survives; it now stands in front of the church of Santa Maria Maggiore.

Below: Though little remains of the forum's former glory, this is still one of the city's most captivating and romantic sights

The last major monument before the Colosseum is the **Arco di Tito**, Rome's oldest triumphal arch, built in AD 81 by the Emperor Domitian to honour his brother Titus.

TAKING A BREAK

The nearest cafés are off Piazza del Campidoglio, east of the Colosseum, or in Via Cavour.

➕ 201 F2 ⊠ Entrances by Arco di Settimio Severo, Largo Romolo e Remo, by Arco di Tito and off Via del Teodoro ☎ 06 699 0110, 06 3996 7700 🕐 Forum and Palatino: Mon–Sat 9–1 hour before sunset, Sun 9–8; occasional later opening 🚇 Colosseo 🚌 75, 85, 117, 175, 810, 850 to Via dei Fori Imperiali 🎟 Forum: free. Palatino: expensive

FORO ROMANO: INSIDE INFO

Top tips Allow **up to two hours** to explore the site, more to see the Palatino, one of Rome's Seven Hills.

• The **most significant** among the ruins are the Curia, Arco di Settimio Severo, Tempio di Vesta and Basilica di Massenzio.

5 Pantheon

The Pantheon is one of Europe's best-preserved ancient buildings; its majestic outlines have remained virtually unchanged despite the passage of almost 2,000 years. Only at close quarters does its colossal scale become clear – few stone columns in Rome or elsewhere match the Pantheon's massive pillars.

Temple to Church

The Pantheon you see today was built by Emperor Hadrian between AD 118 and 125, superseding two previous temples. The reason for its excellent condition is its conversion to a Christian church in AD 608, when the Byzantine emperor Phocas presented the building to Pope Boniface IV. The building was covered in bronze and lead which, despite pillaging, helped preserve the dome and other surfaces.

Not all the building survived unscathed. Emperor Constans II plundered much of the bronze gilding in 663–7: most found its way to Constantinople and was melted down and minted. In 1626 Pope Urban VIII was persuaded by Bernini, the celebrated architect and sculptor, to remove some 200 tonnes of bronze gilding from the portico's wooden beams, most of which went to make Bernini's baldacchino, or altar canopy, in St Peter's (► 40–41).

Above: The Pantheon illuminated at night

Inset: Detail of Giacomo della Porta's fountain in Piazza della Rotunda

Dome and Interior

Looking up at the great coffered dome you will see a 9m (29-foot) hole, or *oculus*, in the middle of the ceiling. This was

The Pantheon's dome – one of the marvels of Roman engineering

part of Hadrian's design, allowing direct contemplation of the heavens. It is also a dramatic source of light, casting a powerful beam of sunlight into the marble-clad interior on sunny days and providing a beautiful glimpse of the starlit sky on clear evenings.

The dome is the Pantheon's greatest glory, measuring 44.4m (145 feet) in diameter – greater than that of St Peter's and exactly the same as the height of the building from floor to *oculus*. Its distinctive coffering, or *lacunas*, was made by pouring material into moulds, just one of the cupola's many engineering subtleties. The dome's skin becomes thinner as it approaches its apex – from 7m (23 feet) to just 1m (3 feet) thick – so reducing its overall weight, and progressively lighter materials are used: concrete and travertine at the base, volcanic tufa midway up, and featherlight pumice close to the *oculus*.

Around the walls are seven alternating rectangular and semicircular niches, originally for statues but now given over in part to the tombs of Italy's short-lived monarchy (1870–1946). The third niche on the left contains the tomb of the painter Raphael (1483–1520), who was exhumed in 1833 and reburied here in an ancient Roman sarcophagus.

TAKING A BREAK

The **Tazza d'Oro café** (Via degli Orfani 84, tel: 06 678 9792; closed Sun) just off Piazza della Rotonda serves some of Rome's best coffee, but you can't sit down and there is no view of the Pantheon.

➕ 201 E3 ✉ Piazza della Rotonda ☎ 06 6830 0230 🕐 Mon–Sat 8:30–7:30, Sun 9–6, public holidays 9–1 Ⓜ Spagna 🚌 116 to Piazza della Rotonda, or 30, 40, 46, 63, 62, 64, 70, 81, 87 and all other services to Largo di Torre Argentina 💲 Free

---

PANTHEON: INSIDE INFO

Top tips The Pantheon is sometimes **closed on Sunday afternoon**.
• **Come when it's raining** to see water pouring through the hole in the Pantheon's roof.

At Your Leisure

🢔 Castel Sant'Angelo

Castel Sant'Angelo's huge, dramatic bulwarks rise on the banks of the River Tiber east of St Peter's. This powerful monument started life in AD 130 as a mausoleum for Emperor Hadrian and his family. Its original name, *Hadrianium*, was changed to *Castellum Sancti Angeli* in honour of Pope Gregory the Great's vision of an angel while he was leading a procession through Rome in 590 to pray for the end to a bout of plague.

The circular design was copied from the Mausoleo di Augusto near the Capitoline Hill, itself probably based on Etruscan tombs. In AD 271 it was converted into a defensive fortress, which it remained for over 1,000 years; it also served as a prison.

On entering the castle, you walk along deep, subterranean passages, part of the original Roman-era mausoleum, then climb to the ramparts for excellent city views. Immediately below is the Ponte Sant'Angelo, a bridge adorned with ten statues of angels, sculpted to Bernini's design. The castle's various military and other exhibits are fairly dull, unlike the beautifully decorated

View of the Castel Sant'Angelo from Ponte Sant'Angelo

papal apartments and libraries in the labyrinth of rooms and passageways. Don't miss the frescoes in the papal apartments.

➕ 200 C3 ✉ Lungotevere Castello 50
☎ 06 681 9111 🕐 Tue–Sun 9–7
🚌 23, 34, 40, 49, 64, 70, 81, 87, 280, 492 💷 Moderate

🢖 Museo e Galleria Borghese

Though relatively small, the Borghese gallery and museum, housed in the peaceful Villa Borghese, is one of Rome's artistic jewels. Its collection is arranged over two floors, the lower devoted mainly to sculpture, the upper to paintings.

One of the gallery's most famous works, Antonio Canova's erotic statue of **Paolina Borghese** (1805) in the guise of Venus, greets you in the first room on the lower floor. So sensual was the sculpture that Paolina's husband forbade anyone to see it after its completion – even Canova.

Rooms II, III and IV contain sculptures by Gian Lorenzo Bernini. The principal sculpture shows **David**

(1623–4) hurling his slingshot stone at Goliath; his face is said to be a self-portrait of the sculptor. Next is his masterpiece, **Apollo and Daphne** (1624), which captures the moment Daphne turns herself into a laurel tree to escape the god. **Pluto and Persephone** (Proserpina in Italian; 1622) is renowned for the detail of Pluto's hand grasping Persephone's fleshy thigh. The six Caravaggio paintings in Room VIII include the **Sick Bacchus** (c1593), **David with the Head of Goliath** (c1609–10) and the **Madonna dei Palafrenieri** (1605–6).

The first main room upstairs contains the **Deposition** (1507) and several other works by Raphael, and there are fine paintings by Perugino, Andrea del Sarto, Correggio, Lorenzo Lotto, Bronzino and Giovanni Bellini.

➕ 202 A5 ✉ Piazza Scipione Borghese 5 ☎ 06 854 8577; www.galleriaborghese.it 🕐 Tue–Sun 9–7 🍴 Gallery café Ⓜ Spagna or Flaminio 🚌 52, 53, 910 to Via Pinciana or 116 to Viale del Museo Borghese 💶 Expensive

Bernini's *David* preparing to fight Goliath, in the Galleria Borghese

The Spanish Steps – a popular meeting place for visitors to Rome

🔟 Piazza di Spagna and Scalinata di Trinità dei Monti

The Piazza di Spagna is one of Rome's great outdoor salons, a beautiful square dominating the city's most elegant shopping district.

The Spanish Steps are the piazza's most celebrated sight. Properly known as the Scalinata di Trinità dei Monti, they comprise a majestic double staircase, cascading down the Pincio Hill from the church of Trinità dei Monti. Built between 1723 and 1726, they have been a favourite meeting place ever since.

Square and steps take their names from the Palazzo di Spagna, built in the 17th century as the Spanish Embassy to the Holy See. At the foot of the steps is the tiny Fontana della Barcaccia, the 'Fountain of the Rotten Boat', named after its centre-piece, a half-sunken boat with water spilling lazily from its sides. The baroque design – possibly based on an earlier Roman model – was probably a joint effort in 1629 by Pietro Bernini and his more famous son, Gian Lorenzo Bernini.

➕ 201 E4 ✉ Piazza di Spagna 🚌 119

❾ Fontana di Trevi

Throw a coin over your shoulder into this most beautiful of Italy's fountains and it is said that you will return to Rome.

The first major fountain was built in 1453 by Pope Niccolò V, who financed it by taxing wine. This led irate Romans to sneer that the pontiff had 'taken our wine to give us water'. The present fountain was begun by Pope Clement XII in 1732 and inaugurated 30 years later by Clement XIII. The design is attributed to Nicola Salvi, who draped the fountain over the entire wall of the Palazzo Poli, adding to its dramatic impact. The fountain's central figure represents Neptune, or Oceanus. In front stand two tritons (1759–62) by

Pietro Bracci: the one on the left as you face the fountain represents the stormy sea (symbolised by the agitated horse); the figure on the right blowing into a conch shell represents the sea in repose.

➕ 201 F3　✉ Piazza di Trevi
🚇 Barberini　🚌 52, 53, 61, 62, 63, 71, 80, 95, 116, 119, 175, 492, 630 to Via del Tritone　🎫 Free

❿ Palazzo Massimo alle Terme

The Palazzo Massimo alle Terme houses part of the Museo Nazionale Romano, a magnificent showcase for ancient Roman art. The gallery's first

Above: The Great Cloister of Santa Maria degli Angeli, part of the Museo Nazionale Romano, along with Palazzo Massimo

Below: The Trevi Fountain at night – one of Rome's highlights

two levels are devoted largely to sculpture, the top mostly to mosaics and a series of rare frescoed Roman rooms, moved from sites around the city. Art from the Republican era (late 2nd to early 1st century BC) features on the first level. The highlight of Room V is a statue of **Emperor Augustus** dressed as the *Pontifex Maximus* – note the exquisite detail of the toga.

The next level has an array of portraits, bas-reliefs, sarcophagi and statues, with work from the era of the Flavian emperors, Vespasian, Titus and Domitian (after AD 69), including the gallery's most famous statue, the **Discobolo Lancellotti**, or Lancellotti Discus-Thrower (mid-2nd century AD).

You can only visit the top level as part of a group or with a guide. Here you will find exquisite wall paintings removed from the Villa di Livia, which belonged to Livia Drusilla, mother of Emperor Augustus (reigned 27 BC–AD 14), and those from the Villa della Farnesina, uncovered in 1879. Sublime, detailed mosaics are exhibited on the same floor.

Above: The Cappella Sistina in the church of Santa Maria Maggiore

4 August, AD 356 and told him to build a church wherever snow fell the following day. Snow duly fell and the church was built. In truth, it was probably founded in the mid-5th century, on the site of an older building. Much has been added since then, not least its immense weight of decoration, but the original basilica-shaped plan survives. The magnificent coffered ceiling is gilded with the first gold brought from America. Colossal columns lead the eye upwards to a 5th-century 36-panel mosaic sequence depicting the lives of Moses, Isaac, Jacob and Abraham. The apse has a later but equally impressive mosaic depicting the *Coronation of the Virgin* by Jacopo Torriti (1295).

Among the interior's additions are the Cappella Sistina (1587, on the right as you face the altar) and the Cappella Borghese (1611, on the left). The high altar reputedly contains a relic of Christ's crib.

🔢 202 B3 ⊠ Piazza dei Cinquecento 67 ☎ 06 3996 7700 (recorded message in English) 🕐 Tue–Sun 9–7:45 🍴 Cafés in Piazza della Repubblica 🚇 Termini 🚌 64 and all services to Piazza dei Cinquecento, Repubblica 💶 Moderate; combined pass available

🔟 Santa Maria Maggiore

Santa Maria Maggiore is possibly the oldest of some 80 churches in Rome dedicated to the Virgin Mary. Its surroundings are not the prettiest, but its richly decorated interior is one of the most sumptuous in Italy.

According to legend, the church was built after the Virgin appeared to Pope Liberius in a vision on

🔢 202 B2 ⊠ Piazza di Santa Maria Maggiore and Piazza dell'Esquilino ☎ 06 483 195 🕐 Daily 7–7 🚇 Termini or Cavour 🚌 5, 14, 16, 70, 71, 75, 84, 105, 360, 649 💶 Free

Above: The 13th-century cloisters of San Giovanni in Laterano

12 San Giovanni in Laterano

Founded by Constantine in the 4th century, Rome's cathedral church housed the papal *cathedra* (throne) until the 19th century. The original church was destroyed by Vandals, and several subsequent versions were replaced or restored.

At the foot of the immense façade (1735) stands a statue of Constantine; to its right are bronze doors brought from the Forum's *Curia* (Senate House). The restrained interior (1646–50) is largely by Borromini, who retained the nave's ornate, gold-hued ceiling. The papal altar reputedly holds the skulls of saints Peter and Paul.

San Giovanni's real glory, however, is its tranquil cloister, where many of its variously shaped columns are adorned with exquisite Cosmati work (inlays of coloured stones and marbles).

✚ 202 C1 ✉ Piazza di Porta San Giovanni in Laterano ☎ 06 6988 6433 🕐 Church: daily 7–6:45. Cloister: daily 9–6 🍴 Cafés in Via di San Giovanni in Laterano 🚇 San Giovanni 🚌 3, 16, 81, 85, 87, 117, 218, 360, 590, 650, 714, 810, 850 🎟 Church: free. Cloister: inexpensive

13 San Clemente

The main body of this remarkable church, built between 1108 and 1184, boasts Rome's finest medieval interior. Among the paintings, pride of place goes to a Renaissance fresco cycle on the *Life of St Catherine* (1428) by the influential Florentine artist Masolino da Panicale (rear left aisle chapel). The star mosaic is the 12th-century *Triumph of the Cross,* which forms a majestic swathe of colour across the apse: note the 12 doves on the cross, symbolising the Apostles. Dominating the nave are

the choir screen's 5th- to 9th-century marble panels.

Steps from the rear descend to an earlier church, where traces of 5th-century frescoes survive, and down yet another level are the cast of a Mithraic altar, dedicated to a popular Roman cult, and remains of a Roman house and a granary or possibly workshops belonging to the imperial mint.

✚ 202 B1 ✉ Via di San Giovanni in Laterano ☎ 06 7045 1018 🕐 Church and excavations: Mon–Sat 9–12:30, 3–6, Sun 10–12:30, 3–6; closed during services 🚇 Colosseo 🚌 75, 85, 87, 117, 175 to Piazza del Colosseo or 85, 117, 850 to Via di San Giovanni in Laterano 🎟 Church: free. Excavations: inexpensive

🔢 Capitolino

The Capitoline Hill is the smallest but most important of Rome's original Seven Hills, though much is now obscured by the huge Monumento a Vittorio Emanuele II on **Piazza Venezia**. The hill once had two distinct crests: one to the north, the Arx, or Citadel, now the site of the church of Santa Maria in Aracoeli; and one to the south, the Capitolium. Between them lay an area called the Asylum, now occupied by **Piazza del Campidoglio**, a square bounded by Rome's town hall,

the Palazzo Senatorio and the Capitoline Museums.

From Piazza d'Aracoeli climb the ramp crowned by statues of Castor and Pollux. The equestrian statue of Emperor Marcus Aurelius at the heart of the piazza is a copy of the original in the Palazzo Nuovo, on your left. Steps between the Palazzo Nuovo and Palazzo Senatorio lead into **Santa Maria in Aracoeli**, first recorded in AD 574 and containing ancient columns, a beautifully decorated ceiling and fine frescoes.

Santa Maria in Aracoeli
🔼 201 F2 ⊠ Piazza d'Aracoeli ☎ 06 679 8155 🕐 Daily 9–12:30, 3–6:30
🚌 40, 44, 46, 60, 63, 64, 70, 75, 81, 85, 87, 175 and all other services to Piazza Venezia 💳 Free

Below: San Clemente's Mithraic Temple to the Eastern god Mithras

Palazzo Altemps, part of the Museo Nazionale Romano, is home to a remarkable collection of classical sculpture

🔢 Palazzo Altemps

Now part of the Museo Nazionale Romano complex, this 15th-century palace contains the cream of Rome's state-owned antiquities. Its airy central courtyard is flanked by statue-filled arcades. The collection's highlight, on the first floor, is the **Ludovisi Throne**, a 5th-century BC work illustrated with scenes including the birth of Aphrodite. Don't miss the superb helmeted head of **Mars** and the **Grande Ludovisi Sarcophagus**, a sculpture portraying a battle's victors (at the top), combatants (centre) and vanquished (bottom).

🔼 201 D3 ⊠ Piazza di Sant'Apollinare ☎ 06 683 3759 🕐 Tue–Sun 9–7 🚌 30, 70, 81, 87, 116, 492, 628 to Corso del Rinascimento 💳 Moderate

16 Piazza Navona

Piazza Navona, one of the city's baroque showpieces, is dominated by three fountains, a ring of ochre-coloured buildings and an almost constant throng of visitors, artists and stallholders. Its distinctive elliptical shape betrays its origins, corresponding almost exactly to the outline of the racetrack and stadium built on the site by Emperor Domitian in AD 86. All kinds of activities took place here over and above games and races. Sant'Agnese (Saint Agatha), a 13-year-old girl, was martyred here in AD 304 for refusing to renounce her Christian beliefs and marry a pagan. The simple oratory built on the site of her death was

Detail from Piazza Navona's Fontana del Nettuno

superseded in the mid-17th century by the present church of **Sant'Agnese in Agone** (Tue–Sat 9–noon, 4–7, Sun 10–1, 4–7) on the *piazza*'s western edge.

Gian Lorenzo Bernini designed the *piazza*'s central fountain, the **Fontana dei Quattro Fiumi** (1648), or Fountain of the Four Rivers. Its four major statues represent the four rivers of Paradise – the Nile, the Ganges, the Plate and the Danube – and the four known corners of the world: Africa, Asia, Europe and America.

From 1650 to the late 19th century the *piazza* was flooded and aristocrats were pulled around the artificial lake in gilded carriages, an echo of the *naumachia* – mock sea battles staged by the ancient Romans.

🚹 201 D3 ✉ Piazza Navona
🚇 Spagna 🚌 30, 70, 81, 87, 116, 492, 628 to Corso del Rinascimento or 40, 46, 62, 64 to Corso Vittorio Emanuele II

17 Piazza Campo dei Fiori

Campo dei Fiori (Field of Flowers), one of Rome's prettiest piazzas, is the site of a wonderful outdoor **market**, with palaces and houses providing the backdrop for a colourful medley of stalls selling fruit, flowers and fish.

In its earliest days the square really was a field of flowers: until the Middle Ages it formed a meadow that fringed the 1st-century BC Theatre of Pompey.

Many famous names are associated with the surrounding district: Lucretia Borgia was born locally, her brother Cesare was assassinated near by, and the artist Caravaggio murdered a rival after losing a tennis match in the square.

Today there's relatively little to see here apart from the market and characterful surrounding streets such as Via dei Cappellari (Street of the Hatters), a shadowy lane filled with furniture and other workshops.

🚹 201 D2 ✉ Piazza Campo dei Fiori
🚌 40, 46, 62, 64 to Corso Vittorio Emanuele II or 8, 63, 630, 780 to Via Arenula

Above: Café in Piazza di Santa Maria Trastevere
Left: Detail on house in Trastevere

The two main sights are the church of **Santa Maria in Trastevere** and the **Villa Farnesina**. The present church of Santa Maria in Trastevere dates from the 12th century. Its most arresting features are its façade mosaics which portray, among other things, the Virgin flanked by ten unidentified figures. From the church, walk northeast on Via della Scala and Via della Lungara to the Renaissance Villa Farnesina, built in 1511 for Agostino Chigi, a wealthy Sienese banker. Its highlight is the Loggia of Cupid and Psyche on the ground floor, adorned with frescoes (1517) designed by Raphael but largely painted by Giulio Romano and others.

🔞 Trastevere

Trastevere means 'over the Tevere', and refers to a quaint enclave of the city on the southern bank of the River Tiber (Tevere), an area that until recently was both the most traditional part of central Rome and the heart of its eating and nightlife district. Although no longer at the cutting edge, its cobbled streets and tiny squares are still good places for exploration and eating, either by day or by night.

Santa Maria in Trastevere
➕ 201 D1 ✉ Piazza Santa Maria in Trastevere ☎ 06 589 7332 ⏰ Daily 7:30 am–9 pm 🚌 H, 8, 630, 780 to Viale di Trastevere 🎟 Free

Villa Farnesina
➕ 201 D2 ✉ Via della Lungara 230 ☎ 06 6880 1767 ⏰ Mon–Sat 9–1 🚌 23, 280 to Lungotevere della Farnesina or H, 8, 630, 780 to Viale di Trastevere 🎟 Moderate

Further Afield

The Canopus at Villa Adriana, fringed with statues and fragments of columns

🔟 Tivoli

The two principal sights in the ancient town of Tivoli (Tibur), a popular day trip from Rome, are the Villa d'Este and the Villa Adriana.

The **Villa d'Este** began life as a Benedictine convent and was converted into a country villa in 1550. Its beautiful gardens feature the Viale delle Cento Fontane (Avenue of One Hundred Fountains), with its countless jets of water, Bernini's elegant Fontana del Bicchierone and the so-called Organ and Owl fountains, which – when they worked – reproduced the sound of an organ and the screech of an owl.

The **Villa Adriana**, probably the largest ever created in the Roman world, was begun in AD 125 and completed ten years later by Emperor Hadrian. Many of its treasures have long gone, but the site has a real sense of romance.

Villa d'Este

➕ 212 C2 ✉ Piazza Trento, Tivoli ☎ 0774 333 404 🕐 Tue–Sun 8:30–6:45, May–Aug; 8:30–6:15, Sep; 8:30–5:30, Oct; 8:30–4, Nov–Jan; 8:30–4:30, Feb; 8:30–5:15, Mar; 8:30–6:30, Apr 💶 Gardens: moderate

Villa Adriana

➕ 212 C2 ✉ Via di Villa Adriana, Tivoli ☎ 0774 382 733 🕐 Daily 9–6, summer; daily 9–3:30, rest of year 💶 Moderate

🔟 Ostia Antica

Ancient Rome's sea port is today an archaeological park west of the city, giving a fascinating impression of daily life in a Roman town. Ruins alongside the long street, the Decumanus Maximus, include shops, barracks, baths, inns, tombs, houses, Mithraic shrines and grain warehouses. On the right beyond the Porta Romana are the **Terme di Nettuno** (Baths of Neptune), best viewed from the stone stairs at the front. The **Thermopolium**, a Roman bar in Via di Diana, retains its original marble counter, wash basins, stove, shelves and benches.

➕ 212 C2 ✉ Via Romanogli 717, 000125 Ostia ☎ 06 5635 8099; www.itnw.roma.it/ostia/scavi 🕐 Tue–Sun 8:30–6, Apr to mid-Oct; Tue–Sun 8:30–5, Mar; Tue–Sun 8:30–4, Nov–Feb 💶 Inexpensive, under 18s free

Where to... Stay

Prices
Expect to pay per double room, per night
€ under €100   €€ €100–€180   €€€ over €180

Campo dei Fiori €€

This 2-star hotel could not have a better location, housed as it is in an ochre-coloured *palazzo* close to the central Piazza Campo dei Fiori, one of Rome's most colourful and pleasant squares (▶ 58). The 27 rooms vary considerably in size and decoration – most are rather small – but all are clean and appealing, though those at the front can be noisy. Only 12 have bathrooms. The hotel has a bar but no restaurant and no lift or air-conditioning. From the roof terrace there are fine views over the city centre.

➕ 201 D2   ✉ Via del Biscione 6
☎ 06 6880 6865; fax: 06 687 6003

Celio €€–€€€

The elegant, 3-star Celio, housed in a 19th-century *palazzo*, appeals on several counts: its intimacy (it has just ten rooms); its comfort and aesthetics; and its location, in a reasonably quiet street close to the Colosseum, which makes it ideal for exploring the area. All the rooms are tastefully decorated and frescoed with scenes inspired by Renaissance and baroque painters. The bathrooms have mosaic floors and rooms on the upper floors have Jacuzzis.

➕ 202 B1   ✉ Via dei Santi Quattro
35c   ☎ 06 7049 5333; fax: 06 7096
6377

Eden €€€

Ranked among Rome's three or so top hotels, the 5-star Eden has style, old-fashioned luxury and a relaxed atmosphere. It has been a popular choice with celebrities for more than a century, attracting European royalty and stars of film and stage. Despite renovation the Eden has retained its distinctive and sumptuous decoration, antique furniture and marble bathrooms, and all rooms have satellite TV and internet access. The Terrazza restaurant is superb, and there are spectacular views from the roof terrace.

➕ 201 F4   ✉ Via Ludovisi 49
☎ 06 478 121; fax: 06 482 1584;
www.hotel-eden.it

Grande Hotel de la Minerva €€€

The 5-star Minerva occupies an historic 17th-century palace, immediately behind the Pantheon and Church of Santa Maria Sopra Minerva and close to the city's major shopping areas. The service is excellent, the facilities are the equal of – and often superior to – similarly starred hotels, and little can beat the view as you step from the hotel's front door. Rooms are equipped with air-conditioning, minibar, trouser press, satellite TV and internet access.

➕ 201 E3   ✉ Piazza della Minerva
69   ☎ 06 695 201; fax: 06 679 4165;
www.hotel-invest.com

Hotel Imperiale €€–€€€

Just a short walk from Piazza di Spagna, Piazza Barberini and the Fontana di Trevi is the Hotel Imperiale. Rooms overlooking the Via Vittorio Veneto offer a good view of this famous city street, but can be a little noisy. All are decorated in warm colours and have satellite TV, air-conditioning, shower and Jacuzzi. There are two restaurants – one inside, the other in a conservatory on Via Vittorio Veneto.

➕ 201 F4   ✉ Via Vittorio Veneto 24
☎ 06 482 6351;
www.alfagroup.net/loan

Hotel d'Inghilterra €€€

Palazzo Torlonia, built by the wealthy Torlonia family in the 15th-century, was turned into a grand hotel around 1850. With its opulent common areas, period furniture and oriental carpets, precious Neapolitan paintings and fine collection of prints and pictures, it offers a real taste of luxury. Past guests have included the Hungarian composer Franz Liszt and American writer Ernest Hemingway. Not all of the 105 rooms are as spacious as they could be – those on floors four and five tend to be larger. The hotel is conveniently located in a quiet side street close to the shopping district around Via Condotti.

✚ 201 E4 ⊠ Via Bocca di Leone 14
☎ 06 699 81; fax: 06 6992 2243;
www.hotelinghilterraroma.it

Navona €€

Despite its 1-star rating, the Navona's position is unbeatable – just a minute from Piazza Navona,

in a quiet side street away from the hustle and bustle of the city. The vast majority of its rooms have been renovated to a standard that makes a nonsense of its lowly star rating. The English-speaking Italio-Australian owners have worked hard to create a pleasant, friendly atmosphere, and the only drawbacks are the poor breakfast (take it in a nearby bar instead) and the hefty supplement charged for air-conditioning. Parts of the building, which was erected over the ancient Baths of Agrippa, date back to the 1st century AD. English poets Keats and Shelley once occupied the top floor. Credit cards are not accepted.

✚ 201 D3 ⊠ Via dei Sediari 8
☎ 06 686 4203; fax: 06 6880 3802;
www.hotelnavona.com

Scalinata di Spagna €€€

What you pay for a room in this hotel wouldn't get you a bigger room elsewhere, but it wouldn't get you a setting quite as romantic – the hotel sits at the top of the Spanish Steps

looking down over Keats' house and the Piazza di Spagna. Some of the 16 traditionally furnished rooms are small, but all are charming, as are the old twisting stair-cases and secret little roof garden. The hotel does not have a restaurant. Reservations must be made months in advance as the rooms here are highly sought after.

✚ 201 F4 ⊠ Piazza Trinità dei Monti 17 ☎ 06 679 3006; fax: 06 6994 0598; www.hotelscalinata.com

Teatro di Pompeo €€–€€€

In Rome you walk through history, but in this hotel you can sleep in it as well. Situated on a quiet square just north of the Campo dei Fiori, the hotel occupies the site of the ancient Teatro di Pompeo (Theatre of Pompey), dating from the 1st century BC. Parts of the original building can still be seen in the remarkable rough-stone vaulted dining room and elsewhere. History aside, this is a pleasant hotel thanks to a welcoming owner and modest

size – just 13 rooms. The attic rooms with their beamed ceilings and terracotta floors are some of the nicest. Avoid the less charming annexe. Rooms are equipped with TVs and air-conditioning.

✚ 201 D2 ⊠ Largo del Pallaro 8
☎ 06 6830 0170; fax: 06 6880 5531;
www.hotelteatrodipompeo.it

Trastevere €–€€

The small, friendly, family-run Trastevere is the best of only a handful of hotels, inexpensive or otherwise, in the lively, old-fashioned Trastevere district (▶59). Though the rooms are quite small, they have bright, modern bathrooms, terracotta floors and wood panelling. Four private apartments with kitchens are good value if there are more than two of you or if you are spending a longer period of time in the city. It can be noisy at night.

✚ 201 D1 ⊠ Via Luciano Manara 24
☎ 06 581 4713; fax: 06 588 1016;
www.hoteltrastevere.it

Where to...
Eat and Drink

Prices
Expect to pay for a three-course meal for one, excluding drinks and service
€ under €20   €€ €20–€40   €€€ over €40

Antico Caffè Greco €

Rome's most famous café was founded in 1740 and has played host to the likes of Casanova, Wagner, Lord Byron and Shelley. Though it may no longer be the city's best café, it is still worth the price of a cappuccino to enjoy the venerable interior and savour its historic atmosphere.

➕ 201 E4 ⊠ Via Condotti 86 ☎ 06 679 1700 ⊛ Daily 8 am–9 pm

Babington's €–€€

Babington's was founded by two British spinsters at the end of the 19th century and has had the look and feel of a British tea room ever since. You can sip fine teas and nibble dainty cakes here, but their high prices reflect its smart Piazza di Spagna location.

➕ 201 E4 ⊠ Piazza di Spagna 23 ☎ 06 678 6027 ⊛ Wed–Mon 9–8:30

Café Café €

A tiny, one-room café-restaurant just seconds from the Colosseum with a cosy, ochre-coloured interior, serving good cold snacks, with one or two hot dishes daily. Perfect for lunch, tea, coffee or a glass of wine.

It's also popular for Sunday brunch, and a good choice for vegetarians and vegans.

➕ 202 A1 ⊠ Via dei Santi Quattro (Coronati) 44 ☎ 06 700 8743 ⊛ Tue–Sun 10 am–1 am; closed Aug

Il Convivio €€€

The bill may be a shock, but it probably compares well with the city's other top-class restaurants, and here at least you're assured of a memorable meal with good service in intimate surroundings. The menu changes according to season and the inclinations of the chef, combining a dash of traditional Roman cuisine with creative Italian-based cooking. The wine list is one of the best in Rome.

➕ 201 D3 ⊠ Vicolo dei Soldati 31 ☎ 06 686 9432 ⊛ Lunch: Tue–Sat 1–2:30. Dinner: Mon–Sat 8–10:30; closed 1 week in Aug

Leoncino €

Other *pizzerias* in the city may be better known, but Il Leoncino, just a couple of blocks west of Via del Corso, offers the authentic Roman *pizzeria* experience. Pizzas are made behind an old marble-topped bar and cooked in wood-fired ovens.

➕ 201 E3 ⊠ Via del Leoncino 28, off Piazza San Lorenzo in Lucina ☎ 06 687 6306 ⊛ Lunch: Mon–Fri 1–2:30. Dinner: daily 7–midnight

Margutta €–€€

Margutta has been in business for many years, which is no small achievement given that it is a vegetarian restaurant, something that until recently was barely known in Italy. The stylish dining area is airy and filled with modern art; the food is always imaginative and the wines, beers and ciders are all organic. At lunch there's a good set-price, all-you-can eat buffet menu. You can also have tea or a snack in the bar area.

➕ 201 E4 ⊠ Via Margutta 118 ☎ 06 3265 0577 ⊛ Daily 12:30–3:30, 7:30–11

Myosotis €€

The vivid modern dining rooms and light, innovative cooking at Myosotis are a departure from Rome's often rather traditional and decoratively uninspired restaurants. Service is amiable, the atmosphere relaxed and the prices reasonable. Menus change with the season, but almost always include Roman classics such as *spaghetti alla carbonara* and a selection of fish.

➕ 201 E3 ☒ Vicolo della Vaccarella 3–5 ☎ 06 686 5554 ⏱ Tue–Sat 12:30–3; dinner Mon–Sat 7:30–11; closed 3 weeks in Aug

Nerone €–€€

Nerone, less than a minute's walk from the Colosseum, is the perfect spot for an inexpensive and relaxed *trattoria* meal. *Antipasti* (starters) here are especially good – you can choose from Roman and Abruzzese specialities. In summer you can sit outside at a few tables on the pavement with a corner of the Colle Oppio park just across the road.

➕ 202 A2 ☒ Via delle Terme di Tito 96 (corner of Viale del Monte Oppio) ☎ 06 481 7952 ⏱ Mon–Sat noon–3, 7–11

Otello alla Concordia €€

In summer you need to book well in advance to secure a table in the courtyard-garden of this attractive restaurant. The interior is almost as pleasant: a long, plain room with a wonderful old wooden ceiling. Food is thoroughbred Roman – house special *spaghetti all'Otello* offers a classic Italian tomato and basil sauce.

➕ 201 E4 ☒ Via della Croce 81 ☎ 06 679 1178 ⏱ Mon–Sat 12:30–3, 7:30–11

La Rosetta €€€

Rome's best and most central fish and seafood restaurant is just a few steps from the Pantheon and Italian Parliament (it's politicians' favourite). Prices are high but meals are memorable and the elegant setting is perfect if you want to dress up. Reservations are essential at this popular venue.

➕ 201 E3 ☒ Via della Rosetta 8–9 ☎ 06 686 1002 ⏱ Lunch: Mon–Fri noon–3. Dinner: Mon–Sat 8–11:30

Taverna Angelica €€

This, the best mid-range restaurant within easy reach of St Peter's, lies on the south side of a tiny piazza in the heart of the Borgo. The modern interior is minimalist, and the cooking light, innovative and biased towards fish and seafood. The wine list is good, and includes some by the glass. Be sure to book.

➕ 200 C3 ☒ Piazza delle Vaschette 14a ☎ 06 687 4514 ⏱ Dinner only: daily 7:30–midnight; closed 3 weeks in Aug

La Terrazza €€€

La Terrazza is the Michelin-starred restaurant of the Eden hotel (▶ 61), and combines modern Mediterranean cooking with a magnificent city view from its terrace dining room. The food here is always excellent, sometimes exceptional. Simpler dishes might include smoked scallops with a salad of wild leaves and asparagus, or sea bass with black olives and oregano. Service is very formal. Prices are rather high, but there are special lunch and set-price menus.

➕ 201 F4 ☒ Via Ludovisi 49 ☎ 06 478 121 or 06 4781 2752 ⏱ Daily 12:30–2:30, 7:45–9:30

Dal Toscano €€

This lively restaurant, just east of the entrance on Via Germanico between Viale Ottaviano and Via Vespasiano, is convenient for the Vatican Museums. It's also popular with locals and families, so booking is recommended, at least in the evenings. Dishes include the thick *bifstecca alla fiorentina* (T-bone steaks), *ribollita* (hearty vegetable soups), and other staples of Tuscany.

➕ 200 B4 ☒ Via Germanico 58–60 ☎ 06 3972 5717 ⏱ Tue–Sun 12:30–3, 8–11; closed 1 week in Dec and 2 weeks in Aug

Where to...
Shop

The Eternal City might not be in the same shopping league as London, Paris or New York, and even in Italy it takes second place to Milan, yet Rome has plenty of top designer stores, as well as countless specialist shops and many interesting markets. The area around Piazza di Spagna is particularly good for bespoke tailoring. Note that many small businesses take their annual two-week break in August so shops may be closed at this time.

The largest concentration of designer, accessory and luxury goods shops is found in the grid of streets surrounding Via dei Condotti, Rome's version of London's Bond Street or New York's Fifth Avenue. Look out particularly for **Gucci** (No 8), **Valentino** (No 13), **Max Mara** (No 17–19a), **Trussardi** (No 49–50), **Armani** (No 76) and **Prada** (No 94).

Less expensive clothes and shoe shops line several key streets, notably Via del Corso – which you'll often packed on Saturdays – Via del Tritone and Via Nazionale. Shoes and clothes are generally good buys, as are food, wine, leather goods, accessories such as gloves, leather goods, luxury items and fine antiques.

Other, smaller streets have their own specialities: antiques and art galleries, for example, on Via de Coronari, Via Giulia, Via del Babuino, Via di Monserrato and Via Margutta; paper and wickerwork on Via Monterone; and religious ephemera and clothing on Via dei Cestari. Via del Governo Vecchio and Via dei Banchi Nuovi are both dotted with second-hand stores, jewellers and small artisans' workshops, and Trastevere has its share of small craft, antiques and speciality shops, but is not a major shopping area.

Rome does not offer much in the way of one-stop shopping: it has only one or two department stores in the centre. The best of these is **Rinascente**, Largo Chigi 20, near the corner of Via del Tritone and Via del Corso, which sells a mainly high-quality selection of clothes, accessories, lingerie and general household and fashion items.

The city has several fine markets, notably the picturesque Campo dei Fiori (every morning except Sunday), the bigger and more prosaic Piazza Vittorio Emanuele (central Rome's main market, Monday to Saturday), and the famous Sunday flea market at Porta Portese, southwest of the centre near Porta Sublicio in Trastevere. It is said to be the largest flea market in Europe, with around 4,000 stalls selling anything and everything from antiques to organic food. The market gets extremely crowded by mid-morning, so arrive early for the best buys (it finishes at 2 pm). Be aware, though, that this market is particularly popular with pickpockets. Credit cards are not accepted.

Most shopping for food is still done in tiny neighbourhood shops known as *alimentari*. These general shops sell everything from olive oil and pasta to basic toiletries. They usually have a delicatessen counter, where you can have a sandwich (*panino*) made up from the meats and cheeses that are on display.

Rome's shop assistants have a reputation for aloofness, especially in smarter boutiques. If they pretend you don't exist, ignore them or politely ask for help: the phrase is *mi può aiutare, per favore?*

Don't be tempted to bargain – prices are fixed. Prices may drop in sales: look for the word *saldi*.

Where to...
Be Entertained

You won't find a great deal of world-class classical music, opera, ballet and other cultural entertainment in Rome, but there is fine jazz and church music, and a sprinkling of good clubs and live music venues.

Information

Information on most cultural activities and performing arts can be obtained from the main visitor centre and information kiosks around the city. The listings magazine *roma c'è* (www.romace.it) is an invaluable weekly publication with details of classical and other musical events, theatre, dance, opera, nightclubs, current museum and gallery opening times, shopping,

restaurants and much more: it also has a summary of key events and galleries in English at the back. It can be obtained from most newspaper stands and bookstores. The English-language *Wanted in Rome* (www.wantedinrome.com) is published every other Wednesday.

If you understand some Italian, listings can be found in *Time Out Roma* (Thursdays); *Trovaroma*, a 'what's on' insert in the Thursday edition of *La Repubblica* newspaper; or daily editions of newspapers such as *Il Messaggero* (which has a detailed listings supplement, *Metro*, published on Thursdays).

Tickets

The following ticket agencies are useful. They charge a commission, usually about 10 per cent: **Orbis**

(Piazza dell'Esquilino 37, tel: 06 482 7403; information only over the phone – if you want tickets you must visit in person); **Hello Ticket** (tel: 800 907 080; www.helloticket.it). Tickets for jazz, classical and other concerts and events are available from **Ricordi** music store, Via Cesare Battisti 120 (tel: 06 679 8022). **Chartanet** is an online booking service (www.chartanet.it) for opera, some concerts and theatre productions.

Nightlife

Discobars are popular across the city – smaller than clubs but with room to dance as well as drink and talk. Long-established gay bars and clubs include **Alibi** (Via Monte Testaccio 67, tel: 06 574 3448) and **Hangar** (Via in Selci 69, tel: 06 488 1397). Other clubs such as **Piper** (Via Tagliamento 9, tel: 06 855 5398) often have gay nights.

Admission prices for most clubs are high, but entry often includes your first drink. Some clubs or bars

call themselves private clubs, which means you have to fill out a (usually free) membership card. Remember that many clubs close during summer or move to outdoor or seaside locations beyond the city.

Classical Music

Two organisations in central Rome are the **Associazione Musicale Romana** (Via dei Banchi Vecchi 61, tel: 06 686 8441), which stages chamber concerts in early spring at various venues, and the **Oratorio del Gonfalone** (tel: 06 687 5952), which has its own orchestra and choir who usually perform in Via del Gonfalone and specialise in chamber recitals. Contact visitor centres for details of Rome's excellent programme of summer concerts in venues all over the city.

Cinema

Trastevere has one of Rome's few English-language cinemas, the three-screen **Pasquino** (Piazza Sant'Egidio 10, tel: 06 581 5208).

Northwest Italy

Getting Your Bearings

Northwest Italy is blessed with a beguiling mix of mountains and hills, wild and cultivated landscape, lakes and coastline – beautiful countryside that balances the fast pace of life in its prosperous and historic cities. Here, big city pleasures and civilised small-town life lie within easy reach of stunning scenery and outdoor pursuits – a winning combination.

Three main cities form a triangle within the region. In the northeast is Milano (Milan), a rich, grey, industrious northern city. Southernmost is Genova (Genoa), Italy's largest port and home to a stunningly revamped harbour and superb *palazzi*, churches and museums. To the northwest is Torino's (Turin's) elegant baroque townscape. North of Turin lies the Parco Nazionale del Gran Paradiso, a swathe of breathtaking mountainous terrain.

The Cinque Terre, a string of tiny coastal villages, extends beneath precipitous, vine-planted cliffs south of Genoa. The Italian Lakes region has drawn visitors for centuries. Partly lying in the northeast region, easternmost Lago di Garda is the largest of the lakes, but most hearts are won by Como, with its mix of natural beauty and the creature comforts of trendy lakeside resorts, or by Maggiore, whose waters are studded with the idyllic Borromean islands. West and south of the lakes are medieval Bergamo, set in the Alpine foothills, and Mantova (Mantua), whose Palazzo Ducale is one of the region's architectural masterpieces.

Previous page:
Rocca
Scaligera, Lake
Garda

Left: Desenzano
del Garda, Lake
Garda's largest
town

Left: Detail of Casa Fontana Silvestri, Milan

Basilica di San Giacomo, Bellagio

View towards Isola Bella on Lake Maggiore

You will need to be selective in the great swathe of land that makes up northwest Italy. There's so much natural beauty in the region that it's worth concentrating on the countryside, and visiting just a couple of the main cities for a cultural and urban balance. An alternative to constant travelling might be to base yourself for two nights on lakes Maggiore or Como, within easy reach of Milan and Bergamo, following this with a couple of nights in the Cinque Terre, a train-ride from Genoa.

Northwest Italy in Five Days

Day One

Morning
Start your trip with a day in the **❶ Parco Nazionale del Gran Paradiso** (► 72–73), heading south from Aosta to Cogne and the Giardino Alpino Paradiso at Valnontey.

Afternoon
Spend the afternoon tackling at least part of one of the mountain walks from Valnontey.

Evening
Return to the Valle d'Aosta and head up the Val Savarenche to spend the night.

Day Two

Morning
Head down the A5, picking up the A4 for **❷ Milano** (► 74–75). Get your bearings by visiting the Piazza del Duomo and Duomo (left).

Afternoon
After lunch, visit the Pinacoteca di Brera or the Castello Sforzesco before viewing Leonardo da Vinci's *Last Supper* at Santa Maria delle Grazie.

Evening
Take a stroll in the Quadrilatero d'Oro, Milan's classy shopping area, before a drink in the Galleria Vittorio Emanuele II and a relaxed dinner.

Day Three

Morning

Leave Milan and head north on the A4 to spend a couple of hours exploring 6 **Bergamo** (➤ 81).

Afternoon

After lunch drive north on the SS639 to 3 **Lago di Como** (➤ 76–77); stay in Bellagio, Tremezzo or Menággio (right).

Evening

Take an early evening boat trip, before a lakeside stroll and dinner.

Day Four

Morning

Drive south along the lake to Como, then join the A9 and A4 to head west to 4 **Mantova** (➤ 78–79), reached via the A22.

Afternoon

Visit the Palazzo Ducale, the Duomo and the churches before heading for the Palazzo Tè. Return for a drink in the Piazza delle Erbe before dinner.

Day Five

Morning

Either head north for a relaxing day exploring 7 **Lago di Garda** (➤ 82), or take the A22, A1 and A15 back to the east coast, arriving in the 8 **Cinque Terre** (➤ 82) in time for lunch.

Afternoon

Spend the afternoon on the beach or take the train up the coast to explore 9 **Genova** (right, ➤ 83).

❿Parco Nazionale del Gran Paradiso

Italy's first national park is also its loveliest. This former hunting reserve of the House of Savoy is ranged around the 4,084m (13,400-foot) Gran Paradiso massif, the only mountain over 4,000m (13,125 feet) completely within Italy. It offers incredible panoramas, wonderful walking territory and rare wildlife and alpine flowers.

In 1920 Vittore Emanuele III of Savoy bequeathed 2,100ha (5,190 acres) of the reserve to the state so that the natural environment, flora and fauna could be preserved. Two years later the Parco Nazionale Gran Paradiso was established. It now covers 70,000ha (172,970 acres), stretching across the Valle d'Aosta and Piedmont, and linked with the Vanoise National Park, over the border in France. The scenery takes in snowcapped peaks and glaciers, mountain slopes, flower-filled alpine pastures, waterfalls and forests of larch, pine and fir.

Bearded vulture in flight

Wildlife

One of the great attractions of the park is the fauna, notably the *stambecco* (ibex), chamois and marmots. Numbers of ibex, more or less extinct in the rest of Europe, have risen to

Scenery in the national park includes high pastures and fast-flowing streams

around 3,500, and they continue to thrive. They are best spotted in the pastureland of the Gran Piano di Noasca. A beautiful path connects the Gran Piano with Nivolet, giving fine views of the Orco Valley. Birds to be seen here include the bearded vulture, royal eagle, ptarmigan and crossbill.

Resorts

The most interesting approach to the park is from the Valle d'Aosta and the north. **Cogne**, half an hour from **Aosta**, makes a good excursion base. From **Valnontey**, near here, one of the park's best walks leads to the mountain *rifugi* (refuges) of Vittorio Sella and Sella Herbetet (allow a full day). **Valsavarenche**, southwest of Aosta, is the main village in the Val Savarenche, and a base for summer walkers.

Below: The village of Cogne in the Valle d'Aosta

Locana has an exhibition on traditional and modern trades in the Valle Orco, and there are displays in **Ceresole Reale** and **Ronco Canavese** on the ibex; in **Degioz** on animals of prey, notably the lynx (extinct in the park), and in **Rhêmes Notre-Dame** on the bearded vulture and other birds of prey.

Late spring is best for alpine flora; autumn is the mating season for the ibex and chamois; winter is ideal for cross-country skiing. The busiest periods are August and summer weekends.

TAKING A BREAK

Vecchio Ristoro in Aosta (Via Tourneuve 4; closed Jun) offers excellent cooking and the best of Valle d'Aosta wines.

Tourist information

✚ 204 B3 ✉ Via Umberto 1, Noasca (near the town hall) ☎ 0124 901070; www.parks.it/parco.nazionale.gran ⏰ Daily 9–12:30, 2–7

PARCO NAZIONALE DEL GRAN PARADISO: INSIDE INFO

Top tips The **Giardino Alpino Paradiso**, Valnontey, south of Cogne, has a varied landscape of rocks, marshland, peat moors, small lakes and streams, and supports around 2,000 species of European flora and non-European alpine flora. June is the best time to visit (tel: 0165 74147, open daily, mid-Jun to mid-Sep).

• During summer many visitor centres organise **activities, films and trips for children**. Noasca (Valle Orco), tel: 0124 901070; Ceresole Reale (Valle Orco), tel: 0124 953186; Rhêmes Notre-Dame (Valle di Rhêmes), tel: 0165 936193; Locana (Valle Orco), in the deconsecrated church of San Francesco, tel: 0124 83459; Degioz (Valsavarenche), tel: 0165 905808.

2 Milano (Milan)

From its beginnings as a Celtic settlement on the Lombardy plain, Milan has grown to become Italy's second city and economic powerhouse. For most visitors Milan means chic Italian fashion, world-famous opera and stylish bars and restaurants, but the city also boasts splendid art collections and monuments, and it provides an excellent base for tours to the nearby lakes Maggiore and Como and the historic cities of Bergamo, Brescia, Cremona and Pavia.

Milan was rebuilt in modern style after heavy World War II bombardment, but standing out among the trendy stores and modern office blocks are two gems: the Duomo, Europe's most striking example of northern Italian Gothic architecture; and the Pinacoteca di Brera, a 17th-century *palazzo* housing one of Italy's finest collections of paintings.

The Piazza del Duomo, at the city's heart, is dominated by the **Duomo**, the third largest church in Europe after St Peter's in Rome and Seville's cathedral. Crowned with a forest of statues, spires and pinnacles, it was begun in 1386 and took nearly 500 years to complete. The dazzling pinkish-white marble façade measures 174m (570 feet) long and 68m (223 feet) wide; the interior is, in contrast, quite bare, but is lit by exquisite stained-glass windows. The view from the roof, weather permitting, extends as far as the Alps.

North of the cathedral lies the **Galleria Vittorio Emanuele II**. This famous belle-époque, glass-roofed shopping arcade, lined with stylish shops and expensive cafés and restaurants, has been a popular meeting place since it was built in 1867 and is known as Il Salotto di Milano (Milan's drawing room). A walk through the Galleria leads to Piazza della Scala and the world's most famous opera house, **Teatro alla Scala**. The opulent gilt and velvet auditorium, which seats over 2,000, is under restoration until 2005.

The **Pinacoteca di Brera**, further north, is the city's main art gallery, which has a wide-ranging collection extending to the 20th century. Perhaps its best-loved work is the heartbreaking *Dead Christ* by Andreas Mantegna, with its unusual use of perspective.

West of the Brera district is **Castello Sforzesco**, begun by the Visconti family in the 15th century and enlarged by the Sforzas. It now houses a superb collection of art and archaeology, including Michelangelo's unfinished sculpture, the *Pietà Rondanini*.

The 15th-century church of **Santa Maria delle Grazie** is home to the city's single most famous work of art – Leonardo da Vinci's *The Last Supper*, a fragile fresco covering the refectory of the adjoining convent. Only 25 people are admitted at a time, and visits are restricted to 15 minutes.

TAKING A BREAK

Try **Cantina della Vetra** on Piazza Vetra (➤ 87) for good hearty food.

➕ 207 E4
Tourist Information Office
✉ Via Marconi 1 ☎ 02 72524301/2/3; www.milanoinfotourist.com
🕐 Mon–Sat 8:45–1, 2–6, Sun 9–1, 2–5

Top and bottom left: Figures on the exterior wall of the Duomo

Duomo
✉ Piazza del Duomo ☎ 02 86463456 🕐 Daily 9–7

La Scala
✉ Corso Magenta ☎ 02 4691528 🕐 Daily 9–6 (museum open; theatre closed until 2005) 💲 Moderate

Above: Eating out in the Galleria Vittorio Emanuele II

Pinacoteca di Brera
✉ Via Brera 28 ☎ 02 722631 🕐 Tue–Sat 8:30–7:30 💲 Expensive

Castello Sforzesco
✉ Piazza Castello ☎ 02 6208 3940; Museo 02 88463701 🕐 Tue–Sun 9–5:30 💲 Free

Far left: The Magnificent marble façade of the Duomo

Santa Maria delle Grazie
✉ Piazza Santa Maria delle Grazie ☎ 02 89421146 🕐 Tue–Sun 8–7:30; book at least 2 days in advance 💲 Expensive

MILANO (MILAN): INSIDE INFO

Top tip: The big-name fashion, accessory and luxury shops cluster in the **Quadrilatero d'Oro** (Golden Rectangle), an area bounded by Via della Spiga, Via Borgo Spesso, Via Monte Napoleone and Via Sant'Andrea.

❸ Lago di Como

Lake Como, Italy's deepest lake (also known as Lake Lario), is famous for the natural beauty of its setting, framed by a ring of plunging mountains. This was a popular destination for the Lombard nobility in the 18th century, and in the 19th it inspired poets, composers and scholarly travellers, including Flaubert, Tennyson, Stendhal, Goethe, Shelley and Rossini. Today visitors still flock here for the lush surroundings, gardens, villas and breathtaking views afforded by the boat trips.

Como's Three Lakes

Although it is smaller than Maggiore and Garda, Como's distinctive inverted 'Y' shape gives it the longest shoreline. The lake's three branches are roughly equal in length (about 25km/16 miles). Lecco inhabitants call their eastern arm Lake Lecco; the western arm is Lake Como, and the northern section is sometimes referred to locally as Lake Cólico, after the town in the northeast. All three meet at Punta Spartivento, the 'Point that divides the Wind'.

Como's Towns and Villas

The car ferry service at the centre of the lake links Menággio, Varenna, Bellagio and Cadenabbia, but there are various options for boat trips on the lake, all offering spectacular views of the picturesque villages, most of which are invisible from the coast road.

Above: Small boats at rest on the lake

Como sits at the end of the western arm of Lake Como. Its historic centre is still called the 'walled city' though most of the walls have disappeared. The pleasant waterfront is lined with cafés and promenades, and close by is the splendid 15th-century Renaissance-Gothic Duomo. Como's other fine monuments include the 13th-century Broletto (Court of Justice), San Fedele church and the Romanesque Basilica of Sant'Abbondio.

North of Como, at **Tremezzo**, is Villa Carlotta, one of the most spectacular 18th-century residences on the lake, best known for its gardens of azaleas and rhododendrons.

Below: Bellagio with its charming setting and beautiful villas is easily the prettiest village on the lake

Bellagio, sitting at the tip where the two lower arms of the lake meet, is the most attractive village, with pretty views and narrow streets. It is famous for its villas, in particular Villa Serbelloni (gardens open to visitors), Villa Melzi d'Eryl and Villa Giulia.

Visitors to **Cernobbio** are drawn to Villa d'Este, a masterpiece of opulent design, while the bustling resort of **Menággio** offers fine excursions into the surrounding mountains.

Varenna, with its medieval centre, lovely lakeside setting and views, also makes an excellent base.

Tourist information

🕂 207 E5 ✉ Piazza Cavour 17, Como ☎ 031 3300111; www.lakecomo.com ⓘ Mon–Sat 9–1, 2–6

Villa Carlotta

✉ Via Regina 2, Tremezzo ☎ 0344 40405; www.villacarlotta.it ⓘ Daily 9–6, Apr–Sep; 9–11:30, 2–4:30, Mar, Oct 💵 Expensive

Villa Serbelloni

✉ Via Roma 1, Bellagio ☎ 031 951551 ⓘ Visitors to gardens only; guided visits daily 11 and 4 💵 Expensive

Villa d'Este

✉ Via Regina 40, Cernobbio ☎ 031 3481; www.villadeste.it ⓘ Open to hotel guests

LAGO DI COMO: INSIDE INFO

Top tips Sports include windsurfing, trekking and rock-climbing.
• **Ferries and hydrofoils** operated by Navigazione Lago di Como cover the entire lake (www.navigazionelaghi.it). There is also a good (pedestrian) ferry service between Como and Cólico, with reduced services in winter.
• There is a **lakeshore bus service**, but this is less dependable than the ferries.

4 Mantova (Mantua)

The charming walled city of Mantua is surrounded on three sides by marshy lakes formed by the River Mincio. Under the patronage of the Gonzaga family between 1328 and 1708 it became one of Europe's greatest Renaissance courts, graced with fine palaces and squares.

Piazza Sordello

At the heart of the city is Piazza Sordello, bordered by the Palazzo Ducale and the Duomo (Cattedrale di San Pietro). The vast and lavishly decorated **Palazzo Ducale** complex was once occupied by the Gonzaga family. Its earliest sections are the Palazzo del Capitano and the adjacent Magna Domus, founded by the Bonacolsi family, rulers of Mantua from 1271 to 1328. One of the highlights is the Camera degli Sposi (Bridal Chamber), with its cycle of frescoes (1474) by Mantegna.

Top: Mantua stands on the edge of Lake Inferiore

The **Duomo** was rebuilt in the 16th century following designs by Giulio Romano (c1492–1546), who was also responsible for the rich interior. Reliquaries from the cathedral (gold, silver and Gonzaga jewels) can be seen in the **Museo Diocesano** on nearby Piazza Virgiliana.

Above: In the grounds of the Palazzo Ducale

Piazza Broletto and Piazza delle Erbe

From Piazza Sordello an archway leads to Piazza Broletto with its tall **Torre Civica** (Civic Tower) and **Palazzo del Podestà**. From here a medieval passageway takes you to the inner court; beyond this is Piazza delle Erbe, the loveliest of the three squares and (with Piazza Sordello) the scene of the Thursday morning market. Major art exhibitions are staged in the hall of the 13th-century **Palazzo della Ragione**, whose Torre dell'Orologio has a splendidly complex clock face.

East of Piazza Broletto is the **Teatro Accademico** (1769), an elegant little theatre, whose tiered wooden boxes are decorated with frescoed landscapes.

Below: The colonnaded portico of the 13th-century Palazzo Ducale

Piazza Mantegna
The **Basilica di Sant'Andrea** is a major Renaissance landmark, designed by Leon Battista Alberti (1404–72). Don't miss the funerary chapel of Andrea Mantegna (first chapel on the left).

Palazzo Tè
This exuberant villa, south of the centre, was decorated in the mannerist style by Giulio Romano for Federico Il Gonzaga's mistress, Isabella Boschetti. Frescoes adorning the rooms range from the Gonzagas' life-size horses to erotic murals of Psyche. The *tour de force* is the Sala dei Giganti (Room of the Giants), depicting Jupiter's victory over the Titans.

TAKING A BREAK
Piazza Sordello is full of *gelaterias*, cafés, *trattorias* and modern restaurants.

🞦 208 A2

Tourist office
✉ Piazza Mantegna 6 ☎ 0376 328253/4; www.aptmantova.it 🕐 Mon–Sat 8:30–12:30, 3–6

Palazzo Ducale
✉ Piazza Sordello ☎ 0376 382150 🕐 Tue–Sat 8:45–7:15, Sun 9–2; closed Mon
💲 Expensive

Cattedrale San Pietro (Duomo)
✉ Piazza Sordello ☎ 0376 320220 🕐 Daily 8–12, 3–7 💲 Free

Museo Diocesano
✉ Piazza Virgiliana 55 ☎ 0376 320602 🕐 Daily 9:30–12, 2:30–5, Apr–Jun, Sep–Oct: Thu, Sat, Sun (same hours), Jul–Aug; Sun only (same hours), Nov–Mar 💲 Moderate

Basilica di Sant'Andrea
✉ Piazza Mantegna ☎ 0376 328504 🕐 Daily 7:30–12, 3–7 💲 Free

Teatro Accademico Bibiena
✉ Via Accademia 47 ☎ 0376 327653 🕐 Tue–Sun 9:30–12:30, 3–6 💲 Inexpensive

Palazzo Tè
✉ Viale Tè ☎ 0376 323266 🕐 Tue–Sun, 9–6, Mon 1–6 💲 Expensive

At Your Leisure

5 Lago Maggiore

Lake Maggiore, also known as Verbano, is Italy's second largest lake after Garda. Fabulous villas, mansions, hotels and gardens along the shores of this long, narrow expanse of water – whose northern section lies in Switzerland – have attracted visitors since the 17th century.

Left and below: Isola Bella, the best known of the three Isole Borromee (Borromean Islands)

The highlight of any visit is the Gulf of Borromeo, with its jewel-like islands – Isola Bella, Isola Madre and Isola dei Pescatori – and spectacular mountain scenery. Lying just off Stresa, on the western shore of the lake, they are easily accessible by boat.

Isola Bella, nearest the shore, was transformed from a simple fishing island into an island-palace by the illustrious Borromeo family. In the 17th century Count Carlo III built a baroque *palazzo* with gardens spread out over ten terraces for his wife, Isabella d'Adda, after whom the island is named. **Isola dei Pescatori** (Fishermen's Island) is occupied by a fishing village where brightly coloured *lucia* (traditional boats) line up in the harbour. **Isola Madre** (Mother Island) is the largest of the three. The Borromeo family built a single villa here, surrounded by magnificent parkland.

Many attractive towns are set on the lake's shores: **Stresa**, with fabulous views of the Borromean islands;

Arona, best known for its colossal statue of San Carlo Borromeo (1538–84); **Pallanza**, home to the Villa Taranto and one of world's leading botanical gardens; **Baveno**, nestling below its beautiful pink granite mountain; **Angera**, whose main draw, the

impressive Rocca Borromeo, towers over the town; and **Lesa**, which boasts the lake's best Romanesque church, San Sebastiano.

From the summit of **Monte Mottarone**, behind Stresa (accessible by cable-car) there's a view of no fewer than seven lakes.

Tourist information

➕ 205 D3 ✉ Piazza Marconi 16, PO Box 17, 28838 Stresa ☎ 0323 31308 🕐 Daily 9–12:30, 3–6:30, summer; Mon–Sat 10–12:30, 3–6, winter 🚆 Trains from Milan 🚌 Buses from Verona ⛴ Boats to Borromean Islands every 30 minutes in high season. Ferries to other lakeside destinations (Angera, Stresa, Pallanza, Intra)

6 Bergamo

Just an hour by train from Milan is Bergamo, with its beautiful bell towers and domes, cobbled alleys, medieval and Renaissance monuments and one of Italy's loveliest Renaissance squares. The medieval upper town (Città Alta), on the hill, has been perfectly preserved; the lower town (Città Bassa), connected by funicular railway, is decidedly more modern.

The main sights cluster in the upper town's Piazza Vecchia and Piazza del Duomo. On Piazza Vecchia's south side stands the white marble **Biblioteca Civica** (Civic Library), designed by Vicenzo Scamozzi in 1594. Closing the northern end of the square is the arcaded, late 12th-century **Palazzo della Ragione**, Italy's oldest town hall (largely rebuilt after a fire in the 16th century). The *palazzo*'s arches lead to Piazza del Duomo, where the **Duomo**, on the left, pales into significance against the Renaissance porch of the **Basilica di Santa Maria Maggiore** and the lavish façade of the **Capella Colleoni**, a masterpiece of Lombard Renaissance architecture.

From Piazza Vecchia, Via Colleoni leads to the 14th-century **Cittadella**, built by Venetians to defend the Città Alta and now housing the **Museo di**

Piazza del Duomo, in Bergamo's Città Alta (Upper Town)

Scienze Naturali and the **Museo Civico Archeologico**.

The lower town's chief landmarks are the **Galleria Accademia Carrara**, one of Italy's richest collections of art, with works by Bellini, Botticelli, Canaletto and Mantegna, to name a few; **Teatro Donizetto**, the neoclassical memorial of composer Donizetti, born here in 1798; and the **Church of San Bartolomeo**.

Tourist office
➕ 205 E3 (Upper Town) ✉ Vicolo dell'Aquila Nera 2 ☎ 035 242226 (Lower Town) ✉ Viale Vittorio Emanuele 20 ☎ 035 210204; www.apt.bergamo.it

Basilica di Santa Maria Maggiore
✉ Piazza Duomo ☎ 035 223327 🕐 Daily 9–12:30, 2:30–6, Apr–Oct; weekdays 9–12:30, 2:30–5, Sun, hols 9–1, 3–6, Nov–Mar. No visits during religious services 🎟 Free

Galleria Accademia Carrara
✉ Piazza dell'Accademia, 82/A ☎ 035 399643 🕐 Tue–Sun 10–1, 3–6:45, Apr–Sep; Tue–Sun 9:30–1, 2:30–5:45, Oct–Mar; closed Mon, 1 Jan, Easter, 25 Dec 🎟 Inexpensive

7 Lago di Garda

In the 19th century European aristocrats, politicians and *literati* were
lured to Garda, the largest Italian
lake, by its healthy climate, and
villas and resorts duly sprang up.
Among the lakeside towns **Sirmione**
is the prettiest, its well-preserved
13th-century castle half submerged
in the waters, and **Desenzano del
Garda** is the most important on the
southern shores, with an old tree-
lined harbour and fine buildings.

Saló is worth a visit for its fine
Gothic cathedral and pastel-painted
houses, and **Riva del Garda**, at the
lake's northern tip, is a hotspot for
windsurfers.

After Sirmione, **Malcesine** is
Garda's most delightful village, with
a fine view of the castle from its
beach.

Garda itself has strong Venetian
associations. Two of its most impressive buildings are the Palazzo dei
Capitani, once occupied by the
ruling Captains of the Lake, and Villa
Albertini, a romantic, castle-like
mansion.

A cable-car climbs to Monte
Baldo, the long ridge dominating
Lake Garda's eastern shore.

Tourist office
✚ 208 A3 ✉ Lungolago Regina
Adelaide 3, 37016 Garda ☎ 045
6270384; www.aptgardaveneto.com
🕒 Mar–Oct

The 13th-century Rocca Scaligera broods
over Sirmione's little harbour

8 Cinque Terre

The stunning coastline of the Cinque
Terre (Five Lands) is named after the
quintet of fishing villages clinging
precariously to the steep cliffs that
descend to the sea. **Monterosso** is
the largest, with a port usually filled
with brightly painted fishing boats.
Vernazza, arguably the most beautiful of the five, is a charming tangle of
tiny streets and avenues, and has a
fine 14th-century parish church with
an octagonal bell tower. From here
it's an easy drive to **Corniglia**, the
smallest of the villages, perched high
above the sea. In **Manarola**, where
steep cobbled lanes lead down to the
sea, the streets are too narrow for
cars, but a car-park is provided.
From here the Via dell'Amore
(Lovers' Lane) leads to **Riomaggiore**,
which has a good selection of hotels
and restaurants.

Tourist information
✚ 207 E2 ✉ Via Seggino,
Monterosso ☎ 0187 817506;
www.aptcinqueterre.sp.it 🕒 Daily
9–12, 3–6, Jun–Sep only 🚂 La
Spezia–Monterosso line 🚢 Apr–Oct
Navigazione Golfo dei Poeti operates a
regular boat service linking all villages
except Corniglia. Summer ferries
and catamarans from Genova to
Cinque Terre

9 Genova (Genoa)

The birthplace of Christopher Columbus (in 1451) is often regarded as a traffic-ridden, chaotic town, but beyond its unattractive outskirts there is a rich art and architectural heritage with a wealth of historical palaces, churches and museums to explore. Its harbour received a major revamp by architect Renzo Piano before EXPO 92, and now has museums, galleries, a theatre, an opera house, an excellent market and shops.

In addition to the handsome, early 13th-century **Cattedrale di San Lorenzo**, with its black-and-white striped marble façade, there are

of the New World 500 years earlier, contains a Caribbean coral reef, the Red Sea Tank, seals, penguins, sharks and dolphins.

Museum cards are available from the Palazzo Ducale ticket office, aquarium, main railway station and other locations.

Tourist information
🔁 207 D2 ⊠ Porto Antico, Ponte Spinola ☎ 010 2530671; www.comune.genova.it

Cattedrale di San Lorenzo
⊠ Piazza San Lorenzo ☎ 010 2471831 🕐 Mon–Sat 9–12, 3–6; Museo del Tesoro, guided visit only 🖐 Moderate

Genoa's fame was built on the seafaring exploits of its sailors and its medieval trading prowess

several 16th-century palaces, built when Genoa's power was at its peak. The **Museo Civico**, in 16th-century Palazzo Bianco, exhibits work by Rubens, Van Dyck, Antonello da Messina, Caravaggio and Murillo, and the 16th- to 18th-century Palazzo Spinola houses the **Galleria Nazionale**, crammed with furniture, frescoed ceilings and works by Van Dyck, Antonello da Messina, Rubens and Pisano. Genoa's Royal Palace, **Palazzo Reale**, has ornate apartments with frescoed and stuccoed ceilings and a superb hall of mirrors.

Acquario di Genova, the state-of-the-art aquarium opened for EXPO 92 to celebrate European discovery

Museo Civico di Palazzo Bianco
⊠ Via Garibaldi 11 ☎ 010 5572013 🕐 Tue–Fri 9–7, Sat–Sun 10–6 🖐 Moderate, free on Sun

Galleria Nazionale
⊠ Via San Luca ☎ 010 2705300 🕐 Tue–Sat 8:30–7:30, Sun 1–8 🖐 Inexpensive

Palazzo Reale
⊠ Via Balbi 10 ☎ 010 2710201 🕐 Tue–Wed 9–1:30, Thu–Sun 9–7 🖐 Inexpensive

Acquario di Genova
⊠ Ponte Spinola, Porto Antico ☎ 010 2345678; www.acquariodigenova.it 🕐 Mon–Fri 9:30–7:30 (last admission 5:30), Sat, Sun, hols 9:30–8:30 (last entrance 6:30) 🖐 Expensive

Turin's 19th-century Mole Antonelliana is visible from all over the city

Nazionale del Risorgimento, which highlights Turin's pivotal role in the Unification of Italy (1861).

Galleria Civica d'Arte Moderna e Contemporanea (GAM) holds 15,000 works of art, mainly by Italian artists, with the emphasis on the Piedmontese schools.

The **Mole Antonelliana**, symbol of the city, towers 167m (548 feet) high. During the 19th century it was one of the world's tallest buildings. Inside is an outstanding museum of cinema.

Turin is set to host the Winter Olympic Games in 2006, which has prompted the construction of a new metro system.

🔟 Torino (Turin)

Visitors to Turin are invariably surprised by this handsome city. Although primarily an industrial city – in 1899 Giovanni Agnelli founded the Fiat motor company here – it has in recent years become an important cultural centre, with a plethora of contemporary art museums, galleries and major exhibitions, and is renowned as the home of the *Sindone*, better known as the **Turin Shroud**. Housed in the **Capella della Sacra Sindone**, next to the 15th-century **Duomo**, the shroud, believed by some to have wrapped the body of Christ, is rarely on show, yet continues to attract the faithful.

The **Museo Egizio**, the world's third most important Egyptian museum after Cairo's and London's, and the **Galleria Sabauda**, with its exceptional collection of paintings, are both housed in the vast, baroque Palazzo dell'Accademia delle Scienze, and rank as two of Turin's greatest attracions.

The **Palazzo Carignano**, birthplace of Vittorio Emanuele II in 1820, houses the **Museo**

Tourist information
🛈 206 B4 ✉ Piazza Castello 161
☎ 011 535181/53590

Museo Egizio
✉ Via Accademia delle Scienze 6
☎ 011 5617776 🕐 Tue–Sun 8:30–7:30
✋ Expensive

Galleria Sabauda
✉ Via Accademia delle Scienze 6
☎ 011 547440 🕐 Tue–Sun 8:30–7:30
✋ Moderate

Museo Nazionale del Risorgimento
✉ Via Accademia delle Scienze 5
☎ 011 5621147 🕐 Tue–Sun 9–7 (last entrance 6) ✋ Moderate

Galleria Civica d'Arte Moderna e Contemporanea (GAM)
✉ Via Magenta 31
☎ 011 5629911
🕐 Tue–Sun 9–7
✋ Moderate

Mole Antonelliana
✉ Via Montebello 20
☎ 011 8125658
🕐 Tue–Sun 9–8, Sat 9–11 ✋ Moderate

Statue of Emanuele Filiberto, Duke of Savoy, Piazza San Carlo

Where to... Stay

Prices

Expect to pay per double room, per night

€ under €100   €€ €100–€180   €€€ over €180

MILANO (MILAN)

Baviera €€

The central Baviera is a ten-minute walk away from the Stazione Centrale rail station and the glitzy Monte Napoleone shopping street. Rooms have large springy beds, en-suite bathrooms and big colour televisions.

✚ 207 E4 ☒ Via Castaldi 7 ☎ 02 659 0551; www.hotelbaviera.com

Carlyle Brera Hotel €€–€€€

The Carlyle Brera is a cut above the usual business hotel, with its fine breakfasts, free bicycle rental and high-speed internet access terminals. Large, soundproofed windows light the modern and comfortable bedrooms.

✚ 207 E4 ☒ Corso Garibaldi 84 ☎ 02 29003888; fax: 01 29003993; www.brerahotels.com

Hotel Michelangelo €€€

This is Milan's most convenient hotel for getting in and out of the city – trains and buses to the two major airports leave from just outside, and the huge Stazione Centrale rail station is visible from many of the hotel's windows. Many bedrooms have a Jacuzzi and other mod cons, all surrounded by a gleaming wooden finish.

✚ 207 E4 ☒ Via Scarlatti 33 ☎ 02 675 51; www.milanhotel.it

Hotel Speronari €

One of Milan's best-located hotels, just off Via Torino. The grand Piazza Duomo and Galleria Vittorio Emanuele shopping areas are just a few minutes' walk away. Rooms are rather small but clean and tidy, and about half have en-suite facilities. The hotel fills up with business guests during Milan's many international trade fairs so it's best to make reservations ahead.

✚ 207 E4 ☒ Via Speronari 4 ☎ 02 8646 1125; fax: 02 72003178

BELLAGIO

Grand Hotel Villa Serbelloni €€€

The Grand Hotel certainly lives up to its name, with marble-floored halls and luxurious lounges. Most rooms have Roman columns, views over the lake and ancient tiled floors.

✚ 205 E3 ☒ Via Roma 1 ☎ 031 950 216; fax: 031 951 529; www.villaserbelloni.it

MANTOVA (MANTUA)

Rechigi €€

The interior of this modern hotel near the centre of the old city is decorated with polished marble, interesting lighting and contemporary art. The bedrooms are comfortable and well equipped, though the bathrooms are rather compact. The hotel's good breakfasts, location close to the Palazzo Ducale and friendly staff make it a good choice.

✚ 208 A2 ☒ Via Calvi 30 ☎ 0376 320781; fax 3762 220291; www.rechigi.com

COMO

Albergo Firenze €€

Just a two-minute walk away from the lake, the Firenze has a cosmopolitan feel. The multilingual staff are very friendly and helpful, and most of the rooms have parquet floors, lake views and modern décor. Breakfast is served buffet style, with bowls of buns and spreads to complement the plates of cheese and ham.

✚ 207 E5 ⊠ Piazza Volta 16 ☎ 031 300 333; fax: 031 300 101; www.albergofirenze.it

BERGAMO

Agnello d'Oro €

The antique-laden Agnello d'Oro looks over a tiny square in a quiet street in the Città Alta. Dine in style in the attached restaurant, which teems with objets d'art. Book ahead for one of the old-style bedrooms, with en-suite bathroom.

✚ 205 E3 ⊠ Via Gombito 22 ☎ 035 249 883; fax: 035 235 612

STRESA

Grand Hotel des Iles Borromees €€€

This luxurious hotel was made famous by Ernest Hemingway, one of whose characters stayed here in the World War I epic *A Farewell to Arms*. In addition to rooms with giant beds, lake views and elegant bathrooms, the hotel offers lots of entertainment – choose from golf, sailing, riding and much more.

✚ 205 D3 ⊠ Corso Umberto I 67 ☎ 0323 938 938; fax: 0323 32405; www.borromees.it

LEVANTO

Villa Margherita €

This bed-and-breakfast occupies a restored classic Italian villa in the village of Levanto in the Cinque Terre. Rooms are spacious, with original tiled floors and high ceilings, and some have a balcony. There are no lifts, but the owners will happily carry your luggage for you.

✚ 207 E5 ⊠ Via Trento e Trieste 31 ☎ 0187 807212

GENOVA (GENOA)

Hotel Acquaverde €

The inexpensive Hotel Acquaverde is midway between the Porto Antico area and the Piazza Principe train station, just a short walk from the Via XX Settembre shopping area. Rooms are spacious, if slightly dated. An outside terrace is available for guests for sunbathing from March to October. Drivers can use the hotel's private parking area nearby.

✚ 207 D2 ⊠ Via Balbi 29 ☎ 010 26 5427; fax: 010 246 4839; www.hotelacquaverde.it

Jolly Hotel Marina €€€

Genoa's most luxurious hotel gleams with modern variations on wood, steel and glass décor. Breakfast and dinner are often served on a wooden deck built over the harbour, with great views of the sea. All rooms are equipped with every modern convenience, and all are soundproofed. The American flag inside the hotel flies in honour of George W Bush, a former guest.

✚ 207 D2 ⊠ Molo Ponte Calvi 5, Porto Antico ☎ 010 25 391; fax: 010 251 1320; www.jollyhotels.com

Hotel Canelli €

A centrally located, low-budget option, in a pretty side street off the Via Garibaldi shopping thoroughfare. Rooms are ample; most have an en-suite shower. There is no restaurant inside the hotel, but there are plenty of eateries near by.

✚ 206 B4 ⊠ Via San Dalmazzo 7 ☎ 011 546 078

Starhotel Majestic €€–€€€

A highly recommended and thoroughly modern choice near Turin's Porta Nuova rail station and just a short walk from the city's historic centre. A wealth of services includes laundry, movies on demand, babysitting, an air and rail ticket booking service and a full range of international newspapers. The attached restaurant matches its contemporary luxury.

✚ 206 B4 ⊠ Corse Vittorio Emanuel II 54 ☎ 011 539 153; fax: 011 534 963; www.starhotels.it

Where to...
Eat and Drink

Prices
Expect to pay for a three-course meal for one, excluding drinks and service
€ under €20   €€ €20–€40   €€€ over €40

MILANO (MILAN)

Aimo e Nadia €€€
Delicious central Italian food is served at high prices, cooked by award-winning chef Signor Aimo and his wife, Nadia. Dishes are often laced with fresh herbs or delicacies from all over Italy. Home-made pasta with fresh eggs and truffles makes a delightful starter, while veal with truffles, flash-grilled swordfish steaks and beef tartar are some of the heavier options.

🚹 207 E4 ☒ Via Montecuccoli 6
🕿 02 416 886 🗓 Mon–Fri 12:30–3,
8–10; Sat 8–10

Cantina della Vetra €€
One of the few top-drawer real Italian restaurants by the Porta Ticinese shopping area, near the imposing San Lorenzo ruins. Giant slabs of lasagne, stew, hearty pastas and grilled meats will fill you up at lunch. A selection of opened wines sits ready for sampling by the glass doorway.

🚹 207 E4 ☒ Piazza Vetra 5 🕿 02
8940 3843 🗓 Daily noon–3, 7:30–1;
closed Sat lunch

Chandelier €€–€€€
Nouvelle cuisine features foie gras, truffles, grilled sturgeon, clams and figs among a bewildering number of fresh ingredients. Great cocktails. Chandeliers of all shapes, sizes and styles are suspended from every conceivable surface; most are for sale. Bright young things and arty types make up the majority of the clientele.

🚹 207 E4 ☒ Via Broggi Giuseppe 17
🕿 02 2024 0458 🗓 Tue–Sat 7–11

Da Gaspare €€
With refreshingly low prices for normally pricey seafood, Da Gaspare stands head and shoulders above the rest of Milan's fish restaurants. It is small, uncomfortable and often terribly noisy but the regulars keep flooding back for the daily specials, all of which are dictated by what's on offer at the local fish market. Order l'antipasti misto and a tray of starters will appear including grilled squid, shellfish in oil and boiled octopus. Larger dishes include salmon carpaccio and grilled swordfish for around €15.

🚹 207 E4 ☒ Via Correggio 39
🕿 02 4800 6409 🗓 Thu–Tue
noon–2:30, 7–11

Mauro il Bolognese €€
A wide variety of local dishes in a city known for its wonderful, rich food. Every one bursts with seasonal delights such as mushrooms, truffles, soft fruit and tomatoes. Pasta in thick sauces is the menu's mainstay. Choices range from ultra-thin spaghetti with grilled Italian sausage to tagliatelle with meat and olive stew.
Swordfish, chicken and beef served with olives, hard cheese and nuts make up some of the larger courses. There is alfresco dining in the pretty courtyard from May to September.

🚹 207 E4 ☒ Via Lombardini 14
🕿 02 8372 886 🗓 Wed–Sun
noon–2, 8–10:30; Tue 8–10.30

Ottimofiore €€
Sicilian specials are on offer at this simple, family-run eatery near

Milan's funky Brera district. Fresh, tangy bites serve as the *antipasti* including crunchy whitebait, anchovies steeped in olive oil, goats' cheese and sun-blushed tomatoes. Swordfish, monkfish and tuna grace the main menu, and there's a small selection of unpretentious Sicilian house wines.

➕ 207 E4 ⌂ Via Bramante da Urbino 2 ☎ 02 3310 1224 ◷ Mon–Sat 12:30–3, 8–11

COMO

Il Palazzo €€

Il Palazzo is rather plain in appearance, on a secluded square off the Via Indipendenza, but its menu bursts with hearty regional specialities that are very reasonably priced. Choices include fish stew, seared beef fillet and a *carpaccio* appetiser. The four-course set meal option is excellent value.

➕ 207 E4 ⌂ Piazzolo Terragni 6, 22100 Como ☎ 031 272 186 ◷ Thu–Tue noon–2:30, 7–11

BERGAMO

Airoldi €

A solid option for light lunches, dinners and drinks in the lower section of Bergamo's two-tier town centre. Daily chalkboard items include steaks, pastas with sauce and lasagne. Prices are even lower if you choose one of the set options.

➕ 205 E3 ⌂ Viale Papa Giovanni XXIII 18 ☎ 035 244 423 ◷ Mon–Sat 7 am–11 pm

Donizetti €–€€

The pick of Bergamo's many fine restaurants in the historic Città Alta area. Dishes are typical of northern Italy, with truffle-laden risotto, breasts of game and local cheeses. Eat in the rustic restaurant area or in the delightful courtyard. Many guests come to sample the hundreds of wines in the restaurant's two vast cellars.

➕ 205 E3 ⌂ Via Gombito 17 ☎ 035 242 661; www.donizetti.it ◷ Daily noon–3, 7–11

GENOVA (GENOA)

La Madaleine €–€€

One of Genoa's coolest little bars, as well as a modern Italian snack bar and eatery. Bright walls, funky objets d'art and young, discerning diners give the establishment a fashionable edge. Lunch and evening meals are healthy and light. Choose from seared tuna steaks, *linguine alla Genovese* and lasagne. There are Italian beers on draught, or try one of the bottles of wine sitting on the bar.

➕ 207 D2 ⌂ Via Maddalena 103 ☎ 010 246 5312 ◷ Mon–Sat noon–late

TORINO (TURIN)

L'Albero di Vino €–€€

A fine Piedmontese restaurant that changes its menu from season to season. Summer brings outside dining on the Piazza della Cosolata with light pastas and grilled meats on the menu. In winter the fare –

including beef, mountain lamb and thick stews – is served in the snug dining alcoves. The wine list features several hundred Italian wines, with prices stretching right up to €250 per bottle. Many are sold by the glass.

➕ 206 B4 ⌂ Piazza della Cosolata 9 ☎ 011 521 7578 ◷ Tue–Sat noon–3, 7:30–midnight

La Badessa €€

One of Turin's premier restaurants, set within a 300-year-old Piedmontese palace, complete with old masters, gold furnishings and true medieval style. Game, meat and vegetables are provided directly from a network of local monasteries. The small, pricey wine list includes the deep red Barolo, one of the region's finest. Book in advance for tables on Friday and Saturday evenings.

➕ 206 B4 ⌂ Piazza Carlo Emanuele II 17 ☎ 011 835 940; www.labadessa.com ◷ Tue–Sat 12:30–2:30, 8–11, Mon 8–11

Where to...
Shop

The hard-working, high-spending northwest has some of Europe's greatest shopping. You'll find the best of the best in Milan and Turin, but even smaller towns offer terrific retail therapy, from smart fashion outlets to local handicrafts and specialities.

Wherever you are, it's worth trawling the daily food markets for presents with a difference, or the weekly general markets, where there's a wonderful assortment of everything from pots and pans to rip-off designer knitwear.

Milan's main and most expensive shopping area is the **Quadrilatero d'Oro** – the Golden Rectangle – which is centred around **Via Monte Napoleone**. Here you'll find the big fashion houses, antiques shops, glittering jewellers and art galleries. If you're a budget-conscious fashionista it's worth checking out the *blochisti*, huge warehouses selling last season's lines at half price; you'll also find designer cut-price goods at the Saturday morning market on the **Viale Papiniano** – but get there early.

Northwestern towns have the pick of Italy's department stores and high street fashion chains. **La Rinascente** and **Coin** have floors full of men's and women's fashion, accessories and homeware; cheaper, but still distinctly Italian, are **Upim** and **Standa**, worth a browse to fill a gap in the holiday wardrobe and good for cosmetics and body-care products. There's a strong presence

everywhere of fashion chains such as **Max Mara**, **Benetton**, **Sisley** and **Stefanel**, with delicious and affordable underwear offered by **Intimissimi**, and true luxury available at **La Perla**. Leather goods are an excellent buy – shoes, bags, belts and luggage – and if you're looking for something quirkier, **Mandarina Duck**'s funky bags and luggage are sure to fit the bill.

In the smaller towns there are usually artisan workshops producing traditional and beautiful pieces – look out for gilded picture frames and mirrors, sleek tableware and quintessentially Italian throws and cushions in sumptuous velvets and brocade.

Among book shops **Feltrinelli** is the biggest chain, and stocks beautiful picture and art books, a good range of English-language paperbacks and scenic calendars for the year ahead (on sale as early as March).

Chocoholics should head for **Turin**, where even the chocolate

shops are a work of art, and your selection will be elegantly gift-wrapped on the spot.

If you're staying by the sea, the boutiques in the **Cinque Terre** (Five Lands) villages (▶ 82) are great places for swimwear and laid-back, fun holiday clothes. Locally made ceramics are popular and you'll also find tiny shops devoted to fishing and diving gear and enough children's toys to keep the most restless kid happy.

In the lakeside towns along Como, Maggiore and Garda, it's the same story – plenty of shopping with a local twist. At **Como**, it's silk that takes pride of place: the town is an excellent place for scarves, wraps and fabric.

To the west, up in the mountains of the **Parco Nazionale del Gran Paradiso**, there's a plethora of outdoor and wintersports shops; Italy makes some of the world's best walking boots and, for skiers, the range of sleek and chic skiwear is very tempting.

Where to...
Be Entertained

As northern Italy's richest and fastest-paced city, it's hardly surprising that Milan tops the bill in terms of entertainment. Many visitors come to Milan for one reason only – to hear opera at La Scala, one of the world's most famous opera houses. The season runs from December to July and you'll need to book well in advance; outside this period, you can often hear concerts at La Scala.

Other evening options might include the cinema; Milan has several showing arthouse and mainstream movies in their original languages. For clubbing and live music, among the best in Italy, head for the streets around the **Brera, Navigli** and **Ticinese** quarters, where the hippest clubs are based. Thursday is the optimum night. For more information, check with the tourist office.

The nightlife in **Turin** may not be as lively as Milan's, but there's still plenty on offer. Head towards the **Murazzi** area by the embankment to find the best. If you want to listen, rather than dance, September is the big month, when the **Settembre Musica** festival features classical, modern, jazz and world music. Turin is also home to the **RAI National Symphony Orchestra**, a prestigious institution funded by the state-run broadcasting corporation. It performs at the Lingotto centre, a stunning Renzo Piano conversion of a Fiat factory. Turin's opera house in the **Teatro Regio** is considered one of the best in the country. Winter is a good time for Turin, particularly the six weeks around Christmas when the **Illuminazione,** a 20km (12-mile) long, state-of-the-art display lights shopping streets, *piazzas* and walkways beside the River Po.

Genoa has a lively music and club scene; find out more in the local daily, *Il Secolo XIX,* or the summer-only listings magazine, *Genova by Night.* The main opera house is the **Teatro Carlo Felice,** on Piazza de Ferrari (www.carlofelice.it). You will find some good bars and cafés close by for pre- or post-performance refreshments.

Away from these main centres, evening entertainment is far lower key, though you'll find summer concerts, late-night bars and resort clubs throughout the area – ask at local tourist offices about what's on.

Sports enthusiasts are well served throughout the year all over the northwest. Winter sees the skiing season in the resorts around the **Parco Nazionale del Gran Paradiso,** particularly northwest of Aosta, around **Courmayeur,** which has some of the best skiing in the Alps. Within the park itself the accent is more on cross-country skiing, with miles of well-kept trails running through woodlands and splendid scenery.

Summer offers plenty to do both along the coast and around the lakes. Watersports are a good bet, particularly on **Lake Como. Como, Lake Garda** and **Lake Maggiore** all have areas where you can swim. Walking or riding in the hills above all three lakes is a delight, with well-marked trails and stupendous views – use the local buses to gain your height.

West, on the coast, the **Cinque Terre** is summertime paradise, with swimming, snorkelling, diving and boat trips all on offer.

Northeast Italy

Getting Your Bearings

Flat and fertile, misty in winter and parched in summer, the valley of the River Po slashes across southern northeast Italy. This is prime agricultural country, whose produce has made the region rich and funded the construction of the splendid cities and towns. Northwards, the land rises, vine-covered hillsides giving way to the dramatic eastern Alps. This is the northern edge of Italy, where German language and culture predominate; east again, the towns of Friuli-Venezia-Giulia stand on the brink of Slavic central Europe.

Left: View of Monte Pelmo in the Dolomites

Previous page: Monte Cimone della Pala

Every year millions of visitors are seduced by the lagoon settlement of Venice. Reached by water and served by boats, this is a city apart, whose beauty never fails to work its magic. Its nearest urban neighbour is mainland Padova (Padua), a great university town famous for its Giotto frescoes. West lie Verona, a rose-red, prosperous city that boasts one of the world's greatest Roman arenas, and Vicenza, an architectural showcase for the neoclassical genius of Palladio.

Below: *St Augustine in his Study by Vitore Carpaccio, Scuola di San Giorgio degli Schiavoni, in Venice*

South of here Bologna, an historic city with its feet firmly in the 21st century, dominates the flatlands of Emilia Romagna; its northern neighbour, Parma, is the birthplace of the world-famous cheese and ham. Eastwards lie the Adriatic and the quiet town of Ravenna, once capital of the Roman Empire and home to the world's greatest Byzantine mosaics. Far to the north, the jagged pinnacles and dramatic peaks of the Dolomites provide the back-drop for year-round outdoor activities.

★ **Don't Miss**

At Your Leisure

Vipiteno

Malles Venosta

Merano

Dobbiaco

A22 **E45**

Bressanone/
Brixen

*Parco
Nazionale
dello
Stelvio*

TRENTINO-
ALTO-
ADIGE

Arabba

Cortina d'Ampezzo

Bolzano

Tolmezzo

A23

Tarvisio

Dimaro

Predazzo

1 **Dolomiti**

Gemona del Friuli

Madonna di
Campiglio

Mezzolombardo

*Parco
Nazionale delle
Dolomiti
Bellunesi*

FRIULI-
VENEZIA
GIULA

E55

Trento

Roncegno

Belluno

Udine

A22

Feltre

Vittorio
Veneto

Pordenone

A23

Gorizia

Storo

Bassano
del Grappa

Conegliano

Oderzo

A28 **A4 E70 E55**

Monfalcone

A4 E70

Schio

A27

Treviso

Portogruaro

Grado

Trieste

Vicenza

Cittadella

A4

Caorle

Lignano
Sabbiadoro

Verona

4

VENETO

**Padova
(Padua)** 5

Mira

3 **Venezia
(Venice)**

Lido di Jesolo

2

Soave

Villafranca
di Verona

Legnago

Monselice

Piove
di Sacco

Chioggia

Ostiglia

Rovigo

SS12

Mirandola

Bondeno

Adria

SS309

Mesola

A13

Ferrara

arma

Carpi

Cento

Codigoro

**eggio
milia**

Casina

Modena

Altedo

Comacchio

Lido di Spina

A1 E35

7 **Bologna**

Marina di
Ravenna

A-ROMAGNA

Sasso Marconi

Lugo

6 **Ravenna**

A1 E35

Imola

A14 E45

Cervia

orretta Terme

Loiano

Faenza

Forlì

Rimini

Rocca San
Casciano

Cesena

Bagno di
Romagna

0 ———————— 60 km
0 ———————— 40 miles

Above: Fresco
detail in the
Baptistery in
Parma

Verona's
amphitheatre

There's a choice in the northeast between glorious mountain country and superb urban centres, with incomparable Venice topping the list. You could get the best of both by simply splitting your time between the Dolomiti and Venice itself, or drive through the best of the mountains, leaving extra days to explore the region's other towns. Ravenna, with its Byzantine mosaics, lies off the main circuit; one option is to start there and cut down time in Bologna and Parma. Bear in mind, too, that Bologna is a major city, so you might want to bypass it and head straight for Padova.

Northeast Italy in Five Days

Day One

Morning
Start in Parma, then take the A1 southeast to **7 Bologna** (➤ 106).

Afternoon
Spend the afternoon in Bologna, before heading north on the A13, to arrive in **5 Padova** (Basilica di Sant'Antonio, right, ➤ 105).

Evening
Get your bearings with a late evening stroll through the heart of Padova.

Day Two

Morning
Visit the Scrovegni Chapel then drive up the A4 to **4 Vicenza** (➤ 105) and take in the best of this small city before lunch.

Afternoon and Evening
Head west on the A4 to **2 Verona** (➤ 98–99), arriving in time to visit the Arena, Castelvecchio and San Zeno, before an evening around the Piazza delle Erbe and the Piazza della Signori.

Day Three

Morning and Afternoon

From Verona head north up the A22 into the **① Dolomiti** (left, ➤ 96–97), stopping for a quick glimpse of lovely Trento. At Bolzano head west through the mountains on the Grande Strada delle Dolomiti, a spectacular mountain road that gives you a taste of the very best of the high peaks and fertile valleys. It's a long drive, but the best way to sample the area when time is short.

Evening

Spend the night in Cortina d'Ampezzo.

Day Four

Morning

Leave early for **③ Venice** (➤ 100–104), picking up the A27 at Ponte delle Alpi. Leave your car in one of the mainland car parks before crossing the causeway into the city.

Afternoon

Spend the afternoon relaxing in Venice, perhaps taking a *vaporetto* down the Grand Canal (right).

Evening

Stroll the streets for dinner near one of the city's *campi*.

Day Five

Morning

Head for the Piazza San Marco to visit the Basilica di San Marco, the Campanile and the Palazzo Ducale.

Afternoon

Take in some of Venice's splendid art and architecture; choose between the Accademia, the Collezione Peggy Guggenheim, the Ca' Rezzonico and the Ca' d'Oro

Evening

Spend the evening shopping and relaxing over dinner.

❶ Dolomiti

Nothing in the Alps can quite compare with the beauty and
splendour of the Dolomites, whose surging peaks and precipitous rock walls set them apart from gentler ranges. In the
northwest of Trentino-Alto-Adige and the Veneto regions the
mountain activities include skiing, high-altitude hiking and
rock-climbing. Throw in fertile green valleys, flower-strewn
meadows, delightful villages filled with wooden houses and
sweet air and you've got the recipe for one of Europe's great
outdoor experiences.

The incredible shapes and rock formations that are the hallmark of the Dolomites were created by compression, upheaval
and the weathering action of wind, ice and storms. The lower
slopes are wooded or covered in alpine pasture, used for
summer grazing, while the valley bottoms are also used for
grazing or the cultivation of vines and apples.

The 20th century saw the development of the massifs into
a recreational playground, with ski centres dotted throughout
the mountains. Pistes cater for all levels of expertise, and the
valleys have good cross-country skiing, sledging and tobog-
ganing. The summer walking is among the finest in Europe,
with a network of scenic trails accessed by cable-cars and lifts
and linked by *rifugi alpini* (mountain refuges), open from the
end of June to the end of September. They all provide food,
drink and accommodation.

**Val di Funes,
northeast of
Bolzano**

North of Belluno are the Italian-speaking Cadore
Dolomites, whose main resort, **Cortina d'Ampezzo**, was the
venue for the 1956 Winter Olympics. Set in a ring of splendid
peaks, with great winter skiing, it comes at an unsurprisingly
high price.

Trento and **Bolzano** are the main towns in the western
Dolomites and you can reach the mountains from either. The
Dolomiti di Brenta, west of Trento, is the most famous

DOLOMITI: INSIDE INFO

Top tips Visit the small **local tourist offices** to collect information and talk to the staff.
• If you're planning to walk **invest in a good map** (Kompass maps are excellent) and make sure you're properly equipped.
• A few **basic German phrases** can be very useful.

Monte Lagazuoi, west of Cortina d'Ampezzo

massif in the west, and is a good place to start hiking – **Madonna di Campiglio** makes the best base as many walks start close to the town. The Val di Sole and the Val di Non are the main valleys here.

East of Bolzano the stunning Val di Fassa is at the heart of the old Ladino culture. There's an exhibition at the **Castel de Tor Museum**, which is dedicated to preserving this unique culture of the Dolomite valleys. Ladino is still spoken today and each valley retains its own unique dialect and distinct traditions. To the west rises the Catinaccio/Rosengarten massif, one of the most dramatic of all the ranges. The Val Sugana is another fertile valley (cherries this time), dotted with castles and pretty villages and overshadowed by superb peaks.

✚ 208 C4
Tourist information offices
✉ Piazzetta San Francesco 8, Cortina d'Ampezzo ☎ 0436 3231 🕔 9–12:30, 3–7, Dec–Mar; 9–12:30, 3–6, Apr–Sep; Mon–Sat 9–12, Oct–Nov; www.infodolomiti.it

✉ Piazza Marconi 5, Molveno ☎ 0461 586086 🕔 Mon–Sat 9–12:30, 3–6:30; Sun 9:30–12:30

✉ Via Roma 18, Vigo di Fassa ☎ 0462 764093 🕔 Mon–Sat 8:30–12:15, 3:30–7; Sun 10–12:30

❷ Verona

Beautiful Verona, tucked into a bend of the River Adige 50km (30 miles) from Vicenza, has more than its fair share of fine monuments, spanning the centuries since Roman times.

The City Centre

Piazza Brà, the largest square, is dominated by the 1st-century **Arena**, one of the world's largest Roman amphitheatres and now the venue for Verona's summer opera season. From the Arena, the pedestrianised Via Mazzini leads to the Piazza delle Erbe, site of a morning market since medieval times and lined with loggias, town houses and Renaissance palaces. From here head down Via Cappello for a glimpse of the **Casa di Giulietta** (Juliet's House). Its balcony was added in 1935, but Shakespeare did base his tragedy *Romeo and Juliet* on real families, the Cappelli and the Montecchi, who probably came from Vicenza.

Behind the Piazza delle Erbe are the Piazza dei Signori and the adjoining courtyard of the Mercato Vecchio, whose medieval and Renaissance buildings, loggia and staircase were once the focus of public life. The 12th-century, candy-striped **Palazzo della Ragione**, linking the Piazza delle Erbe with the Signori, is dominated by the **Torre dei Lamberti**. On the piazza's east side are the **Arche Scaligeri** (Scaligeri Tombs), Gothic funerary monuments to the Scaligeris, Verona's medieval ruling family, in particular Cangrande I.

Top: Piazza delle Erbe, the city's heart and social meeting place

Inset: Detail on the fountain of Madonna Verona, Piazza delle Erbe

The splendid tomb of Cangrande I

Going North

North lies **Sant'Anastasia**, Verona's largest church, built between 1290 and 1481, and the **Duomo** (Cathedral). The reconstructed Roman bridge, **Ponte della Pietra**, crosses the river to the ruins of the Roman theatre, used for summer plays, ballet and music.

Going West

Heading along the river you come to the **Castelvecchio**, medieval seat of the Scaligeri, now housing the **Civico Museo d'Arte**. A short walk leads to the basilica of **San Zeno Maggiore**, northern Italy's finest Romanesque church, where the hauntingly lovely *Madonna and Saints* by Andrea Mantegna (1431–1506) hangs over the high altar.

TAKING A BREAK
Try **Caffè Coloniale** (Piazza Viviani 14/c).

⊞ 208 B2

Tourist Information Office
✉ Via degli Alpini 9 (Piazza Brà) ☎ 045 806 86 80, 045 800 08 61 🕐 Mon–Sat 9–7, Sun 9–3

Arena
✉ Piazza Brà ☎ 045 800 51 51 🕐 Tue–Sun 8:30–6:30, Mon 1:45–6:30, except during opera season (Jul–Aug), Tue–Sun 9–3:30 💷 Inexpensive

Casa di Giulietta
✉ Via Cappello 23 ☎ 045 803 43 03 🕐 Tue–Sun 8:30–7:30, Mon 1–7:30 💷 Moderate

Torre dei Lamberti
✉ Piazza dei Signori, Cortile Mercato Vecchio ☎ 045 803 27 26 🕐 Tue–Sun 9:30–7:30, Mon 1:30–7:30 💷 Inexpensive

Sant'Anastasia
✉ Corso Sant'Anastasia 🕐 Mon–Sat 9–6, Sun 1–6 💷 Inexpensive

Duomo
✉ Piazza del Duomo 🕐 Mon–Sat 10–5:30, Sun 3:30–5:30 💷 Inexpensive

Castelvecchio and Civico Museo d'Arte
✉ Corso Castelvecchio 2 ☎ 045 594 734 🕐 Tue–Sun 8:30–7:30, Mon 1:30–7:30 💷 Moderate

---

VERONA: INSIDE INFO

Getting there Hourly **Intercity** trains from **Venice** take around 90 minutes.
• Buses to the city centre stop **outside the railway station**; buy your ticket in the station and validate it on the bus.

Top tip Invest in the **three-day Verona Card**.

③ Venezia (Venice)

Beautiful Venice, a city built on water, is one of the world's greatest sights. Created on a series of islands in a lagoon, with narrow canals threading their way past architecture spanning over 800 years, it's a city made for walking. Take in the big set pieces, such as San Marco and the Grand Canal, but leave time for wandering at will, and combine your walks with Venice's water buses, the *vaporetti*, to see the best of this unique city.

Around the Piazza San Marco

The Piazza San Marco is the heart of Venice, a huge expanse surrounded by gracious 16th- and 17th-century arcaded buildings and dominated by the **Basilica di San Marco**. From its **Campanile**, a replica of the 1514 original, which collapsed in 1902, there are superb views over the city and lagoon. The basilica itself, built between 1063 and 1094 to house the body of St Mark, Venice's patron saint, is topped by five domes, each embellished with mosaics; there are over 4,000sq m (43,050 square feet) of them within the building. Other treasures include a bronze four-horse Roman chariot group, a city symbol, dating from the 2nd century AD.

South of San Marco is the **Palazzo Ducale** (Doge's Palace), an opulent complex of state rooms, courtyards and corridors that was the seat of the Venetian government in the Republic's heyday. Highlights include the Scala d'Oro, leading to the Doge's Apartments, the Sala del Maggior Consiglio, decorated by Tintoretto, and the famous **Ponte dei Sospiri** (Bridge of Sighs), which leads across a canal to the prison cells.

Top: Piazza San Marco

Along the Grand Canal

To take in much of the rest of the best of Venice, hop on a No 1 *vaporetto* at the station end of the Grand Canal and enjoy the parade of glorious buildings along its banks. Look out first for the **Palazzo Vendramin-Calergi**, on your left, now the winter home of the city's Casino, and the magnificent **Ca' Pesaro** on the right, designed by Baldassare Longhena in 1652. Further down to the left is the beautiful **Ca' d'Oro**, Venice's most famous Gothic *palazzo*, now housing an excellent small museum.

Ahead lies the **Rialto bridge**, built between 1588 and 1591 and the **Rialto markets**, selling the freshest of fish, fruit and vegetables. Next comes the 17th-century **Ca' Rezzonico**, on the left, housing a museum of 18th-century life, and opposite, the **Palazzo Grassi**, venue

Top: The Grand Canal in front of the Rialto bridge

Above: The Ca' d'Oro – one of the ciy's finest examples of a Gothic *palazzo*

Right: A *ferro* on the prow of a gondola

for some of Venice's most prestigious exhibitions. Alight at the **Accademia** to visit this world-famous art gallery, where the history of the city's painting can be traced through works by Bellini, Tintoretto, Veronese, Giorgione, Carpaccio, Titian and Tiepolo. A short stroll from here is the **Collezione Peggy Guggenheim**, a stunning collection of 20th-century art amassed by the millionairess and displayed in her former home. A few minutes' walk takes you to the church of **Santa Maria della Salute**, designed in 1631 by Longhena. It signals the end of the Grand Canal and the opening up of the busy Basin of St Mark.

Tintoretto's ceiling painting *Glory of St Roch* in the Scuola Grande di San Rocco

Bottom: Cannaregio remains a remarkably untouched backwater

Other Venice Highlights

Much of the best of Venetian art is found in the city's churches. Santa Maria Gloriosa dei Frari, in the *sestiere* (ward) of Dorsoduro, and SS Giovanni e Paolo, in Castello, make good starting points. The **Frari**, built by the Franciscans in 1250, is a lofty Gothic church housing a glorious *Assumption of the Virgin* (1518) by Titian above the main altar, the *Madonna di Ca' Pesaro* by the same artist, and a serene *Madonna and Child* by Giovanni Bellini. Near the side entrance is the **Scuola Grande di San Rocco**, headquarters of a charitable guild, where a cycle of 54 paintings by Tintoretto, painted over 23 years, shows scenes from the Old and New Testaments.

Across the city at Castello is **SS Giovanni e Paolo**, built for the Dominicans between 1246 and 1430 and containing fine Renaissance sculpture. Other churches to enjoy include the **Madonna dell'Orto** in the *sestiere* of Cannaregio, with more paintings by Tintoretto, who was buried here. The nearby **Ghetto** is the historic Jewish *campo* and area, from which all ghettoes took their name. Venice is full of *campi*, many the heart of distinctive neighbourhoods, so be sure to leave time to explore some of them – Campo Santa Margherita, Campo Santo Stefano, Campo Santa Maria Formosa, Campo San Polo and Campo San Giacomo dell'Orio are the pick of the bunch. Take time, too, to stroll along the quaysides beside the lagoon – the **Zattere** is the best place to experience a glorious Venetian sunset.

The Lagoon Islands

The 518sq km (200 square-mile) lagoon is scattered with dozens of islands, some supporting bustling communities, some utterly deserted. To sample the best, head for the northern lagoon and the three contrasting islands of Murano, Burano and Torcello.

Below: Statues of the Apostles on the façade of Madonna dell'Orto

Murano has long been famous for glass; it was here that the Republic established the city furnaces in 1291. Many of its numerous glass factories offer tours and demonstrations, and the Museo Vetrario traces the industry's history.

A 40-minute boat trip north from here is **Burano**, a tiny island with a little fishing fleet and brilliantly painted houses. Fresh fish is served in its restaurants and shops sell Burano's traditional handicraft, gossamer-fine lace.

Another five minutes on the *vaporetto* brings you to remote **Torcello**, home to the lagoon's oldest building, the **Basilica di Santa Maria Assunta**. Torcello was Venice's earliest settlement, occupied from the 5th century by mainlanders fleeing the barbarians as Rome fell. Its

Right: Gondola trip on the Grand Canal

population was decimated by malaria and today the only signs of its past glory are two churches, the 11th-century **Santa Fosca** and the **Basilica**, where superb mosaics portray a Byzantine *Virgin and Child* and the *Last Judgement*.

VENEZIA (VENICE): INSIDE INFO

Top tips Invest in a *vaporetto* **pass**, valid for 24 hours, 72 hours or seven days. Validate it in the yellow box on the landing stage the first time you use it.
• Try **getting off the main routes**; you may get lost but you'll see the genuine city.

➕ 209 D2

Tourist Information Office
✉ Piazza San Marco 71 ☎ 041 529 87 40 🕐 Daily 9–3:30 🚊 Vallaresso

Basilica di San Marco
✉ Piazza San Marco ☎ Pala d'Oro: 041 522 56 97 🕐 Mon–Sat 10–4:30, Sun 1–4:30
🚊 Vallaresso, San Zaccaria ✋ Pala d'Oro: inexpensive

Campanile
✉ Piazza San Marco ☎ 522 40 64 🕐 9–7:30 🚊 Vallaresso, San Zaccaria ✋ Expensive

Palazzo Ducale
✉ Piazza San Marco ☎ 041 271 59 11 🕐 Daily 9–7, Apr–Oct; daily 9–5, Nov–Mar
🚊 Vallaresso, San Zaccaria ✋ Expensive

Ca' d'Oro
✉ Calle della Ca' d'Oro ☎ 041 523 87 00 🕐 Mon 8:15–1:30, Tue–Sun 8:15–7:15 🚊 Ca' d'Oro
✋ Moderate

Ca' Rezzonico
✉ Fondamenta Rezzonico ☎ 041 241 01 00 🕐 Wed–Mon 10–6 🚊 Ca' d'Oro ✋ Expensive

Accademia
✉ Campo Carità ☎ 041 522 22 47 🕐 Mon 8:15–2, Tue–Sun 8:15–7:15 🚊 Accademia
✋ Expensive

Collezione Peggy Guggenheim
✉ Palazzo Venier dei Leoni, Fondamenta Venier ☎ 041 240 54 11 🕐 Wed–Mon 10–6
🚊 Accademia, Salute ✋ Expensive

Santa Maria della Salute
✉ Campo della Salute ☎ 041 523 79 51 🕐 Daily 9–12, 3–6 🚊 Salute ✋ Sacristy: inexpensive

Museo Vetrario, Murano
✉ Fondamenta Giustinian 8, Murano ☎ 041 739 586 🕐 Tue–Thu 10–6 🚊 Murano
✋ Moderate

Basilica di Santa Maria Assunta, Torcello
✉ Torcello ☎ 041 270 24 64 🕐 Tue–Sun 10:30–5:30 🚊 Torcello ✋ Moderate

Santa Maria Gloriosa dei Frari
✉ Campo dei Frari ☎ 041 272 86 11 🕐 Mon–Sat 9–5:30, Sun 1–5:30 🚊 San Tomà
✋ Inexpensive

SS Giovanni e Paolo
✉ Campo SS Giovanni e Paolo ☎ 041 523 59 13 🕐 Mon–Sat 8–6; Sun 3–6 🚊 Ospedale
✋ Free

Scuola Grande di San Rocco
✉ Campo San Rocco ☎ 041 523 48 64 🕐 Daily 9–5:30, Apr–Oct; daily 10–5, Nov–Mar
🚊 San Tomà ✋ Moderate

Madonna dell'Orto
✉ Campo Madonna dell'Orto ☎ 041 719 933 🕐 Mon–Sat 10–5, Sun 3–5 🚊 Orto
✋ Inexpensive

At Your Leisure

4 Vicenza

Vicenza is a place of green spaces and architectural gems, many designed by Palladio, who was born here. Dominating the central Piazza dei Signori is Palladio's dazzling **Basilica** and his Loggia del Capitaniato. The main draw, though, is his masterpiece, the **Teatro Olimpico** (Olympic Theatre), Europe's oldest indoor theatre, which opened in 1585 and has an astonishing *trompe l'oeil* backdrop.

Vicenza is ringed by Palladian villas, the most famous of which is the **Villa Capra** or La Rotonda.

Detail from the façade of Vicenza's dazzling Basilica di Sant'Antonio, showing the *Virgin and Child*

University, where Galileo worked for 20 years. Further south, the **Basilica di Sant'Antonio** is one of Italy's most important pilgrimage churches.

Tourist Information Office
🏛 208 C2 ✉ Stazione Ferroviaria ☎ 049 875 20 77; www.turismopadova.it 🕐 Mon–Sat 9–6, Sun 9–noon

Tourist Information Office
🏛 208 C2 ✉ Piazza Matteotti 12 ☎ 0444 320 854 🕐 Daily 9–1, 3–6

Basilica
✉ Piazza dei Signori ☎ 0444 323 681 🕐 Tue–Sun 10–7 💶 Moderate

Teatro Olimpico
✉ Piazza Matteotti 11 ☎ 0444 222 800 🕐 Tue–Sun 9–7, Jun–Aug; 9–5, rest of year 💶 Expensive

Villa Capra
✉ Via Rotonda 29 ☎ 0444 321 793 🕐 Tue–Sun 10–noon, 3–6, mid-Mar to Oct 🚌 8 💶 Expensive

5 Padova (Padua)

This historic university city witnessed the earliest stirrings of Renaissance art in Giotto's frescoes, which he painted in the **Cappella degli Scrovegni** between 1303 and 1305. Padua's three main *piazze*, delle Frutta, delle Erbe and dei Signori, host daily markets; the extraordinary building between delle Frutta and delle Erbe is the 13th-century **Palazzo della Ragione**. Other fine buildings include the

Cappella degli Scrovegni and Musei Civici
✉ Piazza Eremitani 8 ☎ 049 820 45 51 🕐 Daily 9 am–10 pm 💶 Expensive

Palazzo della Ragione
✉ Piazza delle Erbe ☎ 049 820 50 06 🕐 Tue–Sun 9–7 💶 Moderate

Basilica di Sant'Antonio
✉ Piazza del Santo ☎ 049 878 97 22 🕐 6:30 am–7:45 pm, Apr–Oct; 6:30 am–7 pm, rest of year 💶 Free

An elegant canal encircles Padua's Prato della Valle

Left: Mosaic in Ravenna's Mausoleo di Galla Placidia

Below: Bologna's Neptune Fountain

dominated by the **Basilica di San Petronio**. Northeast of Piazza Maggiore are the *torri pendenti* (leaning towers), survivors of the 180 or so original medieval towers. Via Zamboni leads past **San Giacomo Maggiore**, with its magnificent chapel, to Bologna's principal art gallery, the **Pinacoteca Nazionale**. The excellent **Museo Civico Archeologico** is east of San Petronio.

6 Ravenna

The early Christian mosaics in Ravenna – the Roman Empire's western capital from about AD 402 – are some of the world's finest. The most important adorn the walls of the **Basilica di San Vitale**, the **Mausoleo di Galla Placidia** and the **Basilica di Sant'Apollinare Nuovo**, and contain some of the earliest images of Christ's baptism, the Virgin, saints, martyrs and apostles.

Tourist Information Office
➕ 211 E5 ✉ Via Salara 8–12
☎ 0544 35404; www.turismo.ravenna.it
🕐 Mon–Sat 8:30–7, Sun 10–4

Basilica di San Vitale
✉ Via Fiandrini ☎ 0544 215193
🕐 Daily 9–7 💶 Combined ticket: expensive

Mausoleo di Galla Placidia
✉ Via Fiandrini ☎ 0544 541688
🕐 Daily 9–7 (book tickets in advance 1 Mar–15 Jun) 💶 Inexpensive

Basilica di Sant'Apollinare Nuovo
✉ Via di Roma ☎ 0544 219518
🕐 Daily 9–7 💶 Combined ticket: expensive

7 Bologna

Bologna's medieval core is crowded with churches, monuments, museums and one of Europe's oldest universities. Its main squares are Piazza del Nettuna and Piazza Maggiore,

Tourist Information Office
➕ 210 C5 ✉ Piazza Maggiore 1
☎ 051 246541 🕐 Daily 9–8

Basilica di San Petronio
✉ Piazza Maggiore ☎ 051 225442
🕐 Daily 7:30–1, 2:30–8 🎫 Free

Museo Civico Archeologico
✉ Via dell'Archiginnasio 2 ☎ 051 2757211 🕐 Tue–Sat 9–6:30, Sun 10–6:30 💶 Moderate

Pinacoteca Nazionale
✉ Via Belle Arte 56 ☎ 051 4209411
🕐 Tue–Sun 9–7 💶 Moderate

8 Parma

Parma is renowned for its *prosciutto* (Parma ham) and *parmigiano* (Parmesan cheese), but also offers designer shops, fine buildings and works of art. Its lovely 11th-century **Duomo** features Corregio's *Assumption* fresco (1534). The **Palazzo della Pilotta** houses the Galleria Nazionale, the Museo Archeologico Nazionale and the Renaissance Teatro Farnese. Across the river is the delightful **Parco Ducale**.

Tourist Information Office
➕ 208 A1 ✉ Via Melloni 1
☎ 0521 218889

Palazzo della Pilotta
✉ Piazzale della Pilotta 15
☎ 0521 233309
🕐 Tue–Sun 8:30–2 💶 Combined ticket: expensive

Where to... Stay

Prices
Expect to pay per double room, per night
€ under €100 €€ €100–€180 €€€ over €180

DOLOMITI

Schloss Korb €€–€€€
If you fancy spending the night in a castle there's no better choice than this atmospheric 13th-century pile in the hills near Bolzano. Rooms are furnished in an old-world style to match their setting. No credit cards.

✚ 208 B4 ⊠ Missiano, Strada Castel d'Appiano 5, Bolzano (Bozen) ☎ 0471 636 000; fax: 0471 636 033 Ⓧ Closed Nov–Easter

VERONA

Il Torcolo €–€€
Overlooking a quiet square a block away from Piazza Brà, Il Torcolo is a friendly hotel with a relaxed atmosphere. Its style is simple elegance, its rooms well equipped. Breakfast is served on the terrace during summer months. Parking available.

✚ 208 B2 ⊠ Vicolo Listone 3 ☎ 045 800 7512; www.hoteltorcolo.it

Victoria €€€
The Victoria is a mix of top-class facilities, ostentation and history. Rooms are in the older section, beyond the lobby, and some have traces of medieval and even Roman mosaics and frescoes. All are fully equipped (TV, phone, safe, minibar, whirlpool bath on request), and there is a sauna and solarium. Garage parking available for a price.

✚ 208 B2 ⊠ Via Adua 8 ☎ 045 590 566; www.hotelvictoria.it

VENEZIA (VENICE)

Agli Alboretti €
Close to the Accademia, on a quiet tree-lined street, Agli Alboretti is a good choice if you want to be in a tranquil but artistic neighbourhood. The 25 rooms are modest in size but are nicely furnished, with windows overlooking the garden or street. All have shower or bath, air-conditioning and TV; there is no lift. The hotel is popular with British and American visitors, who enjoy dining in the charming restaurant downstairs.

✚ 209 D2 ⊠ Dorsoduro 884, Rio Terrà Antonio Foscarini ☎ 041 523 0058 🚏 Accademia

Cipriani €€€
The Cipriani sits in verdant luxury, looking back at San Marco from across the water. Step out of the Cipriani launch (always on call from the San Marco pier) and find lush gardens, exquisitely decorated rooms, personalised service, a world-class restaurant, a giant pool – and an atmosphere that is relaxing yet stimulating, formal yet intimate. A really great hotel for those who can afford it.

✚ 209 D2 ⊠ Giudecca 10 ☎ 041 520 7744 🚏 Zitelle

Locanda San Barnaba €€
An attractive, small hotel, in a converted 16th-century *palazzo* on the narrow street that runs between Campo San Barnaba and the Ca' Rezzonico *vaporetto* stop – far from the madding tourist crowd. Each of the rooms has a theme and is individually decorated with antique furniture, frescoes and parquet floors. Some overlook a leafy garden. Air-conditioning and private bathrooms in all rooms.

✚ 209 D2 ⊠ Dorsoduro 2486, Calle del Traghetto ☎ and fax: 041 241 1233; www.locanda-sanbarnaba.com 🚏 Ca' Rezzonico

Metropole €€€

Many of the Metropole's rooms overlook St Mark's Basin; others look on to the tree-shaded inner gardens. It is filled with the owner's personal antique collections: marble statues draped with velvet and ivy adorn the comfortable Venetian Salon, where tea is served. Buffet breakfasts and dinners (open to the public) are served in the garden in summer. Private boat landing and car-parking is available.

✚ **209 D2** ⊠ **Castello 4149, Riva degli Schiavoni** ☎ **041 520 5044; www.hotelmetropole.com** 🚉 **San Zaccaria**

San Zulian €€

Two minutes' walk from Piazza San Marco, yet tucked away in a tranquil non-touristy street, this comfortable hotel has been remodelled with charm and some nice detailing: parquet floors, colourful painted Venetian furniture, Persian carpets, exposed beams in the rooms under the roof. All rooms have private bathrooms and air-conditioning.

✚ **209 D2** ⊠ **San Marco 534/5, off Campo San Zulian** ☎ **041 522 5872; fax: 041 523 2265** 🚉 **Vallaresso, San Zaccaria**

VICENZA

Cristina €–€€

This central hotel is family-run with parking and well-equipped guest rooms – though some are more spacious than others, so you may want to view before booking. The public areas are comfortable and elegant.

✚ **208 C2** ⊠ **Corso SS Felice e Fortunato 32** ☎ **0444 324 297; fax: 0444 543 656** 🔒 **Closed 24 Dec–2 Jan**

PADOVA (PADUA)

Majestic Toscanelli €€–€€€

Set in the Ghetto district, within easy reach of the city's main sights, it offers fully equipped guest rooms plus extras such as childminding services, and welcomes visitors in style to a lobby kitted out in neo-Georgian and Venetian baroque fashion.

✚ **208 C2** ⊠ **Via dell'Arco 2** ☎ **049 663 244; www.toscanelli.com**

Sant'Antonio €

With low prices the Sant'Antonio also has the advantage of a good setting, looking over the stone bridge on the town's northern boundary. Some of the rooms have started to look rather faded, but all are spacious and welcoming; some have private bathrooms. The hotel has a bar and a lift, and pets are allowed.

✚ **208 C2** ⊠ **Via San Fermo 118** ☎ **049 875 1393; www.hotelsanantonio.it**

BOLOGNA

Orologio €€€

You can enjoy peace and quiet even in the city centre at this fine hotel opposite the Palazzo Comunale.

Rooms are tastefully decorated and offer a good range of facilities (TV, hairdryer, safe, internet access), and a few look out on to the city's medieval towers. Pets are allowed and garage parking is available.

✚ **210 C5** ⊠ **Via IV Novembre 10** ☎ **051 231 253**

PARMA

Verdi €€–€€€

For a taste of 19th-century extravagance the Verdi is an excellent choice. Inside the pink villa on the outskirts of the Parco Ducale is a wealth of antiques, artworks, elaborate Persian carpets, delicate china and flamboyant chandeliers. The bedrooms are roomy, comfortable and well furnished, with stylish, marble-lined bathrooms. Meals at the restaurant are pricey but good. Private parking is available.

✚ **208 A1** ⊠ **Via Pasini 18** ☎ **0521 293 539; fax: 0521 293 559; www.hotelverdi.it**

Where to...
Eat and Drink

Prices

Expect to pay for a three-course meal for one, excluding drinks and service

€ under €20   €€ €20–€40   €€€ over €40

DOLOMITI

El Filò €–€€

Game is the speciality at this restaurant in central Molveno, set in a medieval building. For main meals you can sample the *cervo* (venison) or *cinghiale* (wild boar), or opt for Trentino recipes such as *gnocchi alle artiche* (potato dumplings with nettle sauce); alternatively, you can just choose one of the light snacks.

🕇 208 B4 ⊠ Piazza Scuole 5, Molveno 🕾 0461 586 151 🕲 Daily 12–2, 7–10.30, Jun–Oct; Fri–Sun 12–2, 7–10.30 rest of year

VERONA

Trattoria alla Colonna €

You won't have to spend much to enjoy superb local dishes at this restaurant near Piazza dell'Erbe – there's a fixed-price menu at €13. It's popular with residents and visitors alike for meals such as rabbit and *bigoli* pasta, and for its Veneto wines. The place gets packed from about 9 pm. The colonna in its title refers to a column in the middle of the dining room.

🕇 208 B2 ⊠ Largo Pescheria Vecchia 4 🕾 045 596718 🕲 Mon–Sat 12–2:30, 7.30 pm–2 am

VENEZIA (VENICE)

Ai Gondolieri €€€

Ai Gondolieri, close to the Peggy Guggenheim collection, is unusual among Venetian restaurants – it serves no fish! Instead, it offers an enticing range of traditional meat, game, vegetable and cheese dishes from the Veneto hills. Try the duck, lamb or beef cooked with wild herbs and salt-kissed vegetables, artisan-made cheeses, fine Italian wines and delicious desserts.

🕇 209 D2 ⊠ Dorsoduro 366, Fondamenta Venier 🕾 041 528 63 96 🕲 Wed–Mon noon–3, 7–10; closed for lunch Jul–Aug 🚢 Accademia

Bar Algiubagiò €

While you are waiting at the Fondamenta Nuove *vaporetto* stop for a boat to the islands, drop in and have a great sandwich or a snack at this bar. There is an enterprising selection of *tramezzini* (half-sandwiches) and rolled sandwiches, to eat at the tables inside or out, or to take away. Fillings include peppers, mortadella and roast pork (*porchetta*). There are also ice-creams in summer.

🕇 209 D2 ⊠ Cannaregio 5039, Fondamenta Nuove 🕾 041 523 60 84; www.algiubagio.com 🕲 Daily 6:30 am–8:30 pm 🚢 Fondamenta Nuove

Caffè Florian €€€

The Caffè Florian was opened as a coffee house in 1720, and the present building has a series of rooms dating from 1859, all frescoes, mirrors and polished wood. Marble tables and upholstered chairs spill on to the arcade and *piazza*, where an orchestra serenades cocktail-hour and evening drinkers. Have an *aperitivo*, a cocktail, a pot of tea or a sinfully rich *cioccolata calda con panna* (hot chocolate with whipped cream).

🕇 209 D2 ⊠ Piazza San Marco 56/59 🕾 041 520 56 41; www.caffeflorian.com 🕲 Sun–Fri

10 am–11 pm, Sat 10 am–midnight, Mar–Nov: Thu–Tue 10 am–11 pm, rest of year 🚊 San Marco

Harry's Bar €€€

One of the most famous bars in Venice, if not the world, is tucked down a narrow street a stone's throw from the Piazza San Marco. There's no terrace and the service can be offhand, but customers come more for the ambience than for the food. In summer, sample one of Harry's cocktails, the legendary Bellini, a delicious mix of peach juice and sparkling *prosecco*, along with a savoury snack, such as *polpette* (fried meatballs). You can also choose from a three-course set menu or the à la carte menu. Ernest Hemingway spent a lot of time propping up the bar, and assorted film stars and socialites still come here.

➕ 209 D2 ⊠ Calle Vallaresso, San Marco 1323 ☎ 041 528 57 77 🕘 Daily 10.30 am–11 pm 🚊 San Marco

VICENZA

Antica Trattoria Tre Visi €–€€

First-class local ingredients, used in their proper season, are the hallmark of this friendly restaurant, which serves Venetian dishes in a delightful 15th-century building. Favourites include *porca l'Orca in pignatti con fungi*, goose with wild mushrooms, and *bigoli al radicchio di treviso con accioghe*, *Treviso radicchio* with home-made pasta and anchovies.

➕ 208 C2 ⊠ Corso Palladio 25 ☎ 0444 324 868 🕘 Tue–Sat 12:30–2:30, 7:30–10:30, Sun 12:30–2:30

BOLOGNA

Cesari €

Cesari has been run by the same family for more than three decades and is only a short walk south of the city's central square. Bolognese specialities are the order of the day, with home-made treats such as white truffle with celery and Parmesan among the regular items, plus more daunting dishes such as *ravioli di coniglio* (rabbit pasta). Home-grown wines are also on offer, along with a lengthy list of other labels. Reservations essential.

➕ 210 C5 ⊠ Via de' Carbonesi 8 ☎ 051 237 710; www.da-cesari.com 🕘 Mon–Sat 12:30–3, 7:30–10:30; closed Sat, Jul–Aug

PADOVA (PADUA)

Anfora €–€€

Based in the Ghetto area near the Piazza dell'Erbe, this little restaurant is popular with students and a laidback young crowd. Local ingredients are used to produce delicious and reasonably priced dishes such as the fish of the day; *zuppe di vognole e cozze* (clam and mussel soup) or *tagliatelle ai porcini* (wild mushroom pasta).

➕ 208 C2 ⊠ Via Soncin 13 ☎ 049 656 629 🕘 Mon–Sat 12:30–3, 8–10:30

Fantoni €

It's an easy walk from the city centre to this cheerful *trattoria*. Local dishes are the staple of the daily-changing menu; home-made pasta and wines are a regular feature, with fresh fish served from Thursday to Saturday. No credit cards.

➕ 210 C5 ⊠ Via del Pratello 11 ☎ 051 236 358 🕘 Tue–Sat 12–2.30, 8–10:30, Mon 12–2:30; closed Aug

PARMA

Santa Croce €–€€

Come here to taste Parma ham as it should be – perhaps as part of the mixed plate of *salumi*. Regional food with an inventive touch is served in three dining rooms. Seasonal fare might include autumn *cappone* (capon), and desserts include mousse and *semifreddi*. Extensive international wine list.

➕ 208 A1 ⊠ Via Pasini 20 ☎ 0521 293 529 www.ristoratori.it/santacroce 🕘 Mon–Fri 12:30–2, 8–10, Sat 8 pm–10 pm; closed 3 weeks in Aug

Where to... Shop

You can count on excellent shopping throughout the northeast, whether in the major cities of Bologna, Verona and Venice or in the smaller towns.

You'll probably spend time browsing the Venetian shops, where you'll find a winning combination of mainstream shopping and the city's own specialities. Despite being relatively small, Venice has branches of all the main designer stores, so head for the streets around **Vallaresso**, west of St Mark's Square, to track down **Armani, Missoni, Prada, Gucci, Bottega Veneto** and the like. The best places to hunt for mid-range shops are the streets on either side of the Rialto bridge, home to a swish **Benetton**, the **Coin** department store and plenty of one-off clothes and accessories shops.

What makes shopping special, though, are the Venetian speciality stores, where the accent is on glass, paper goods and masks. Masks are on sale everywhere, but many are imported, cheap fakes; for the real thing choose a workshop, where you'll be able to buy masks you've seen being made. Glass, too, is everywhere, and the same caveat applies; for something special, prices will be high. The biggest names are **Vennini** and **Pauly**. Beautiful, hand-made marbled paper, made up into address books, folders, waste-paper baskets and lots more, is available all over Venice, and local shops also have fabulous ranges of accessories for the home – tasselled key-fobs, desk furniture, cushions and throws. Fabrics, generally, are superb – you'll find fabulous pleated Fortuny-style silks, rich velvets and brocades. Look out also for gondola paraphernalia – hats, striped shirts and hand-carved oar-locks.

Away from Venice, the region's best shopping is found in Bologna, Padova and Verona, all large cities with demanding consumers. **Bologna**'s main shopping area is along and around the Via dell'Indipendenza, though there are wonderful shops throughout the city. For visitors the great buys here are food products – the city's *salumerie* and *gastronomie* (delicatessens) are among the finest in Italy.

Padua, too, is big on food shops, and with its big student population is noted for funky fashion, jewellery and accessory stores and excellent book shops.

To experience the best of Italian provincial shopping, head for **Verona**, a city that's big and rich enough to attract serious shops, but small enough to make for stress-free shopping. Via Mazzini, lined with expensive and tempting stores, runs from the Arena to the central Piazza dell'Erbe – concentrate on this area, where the range of shops is excellent and there's the bonus of a superb market.

If you're visiting **Parma** look out for more wonderful food stores where you can buy both *prosciutto di Parma* (Parma ham) and *parmigianino* (Parma cheese) on their home ground.

Up in the mountain towns of the Dolomiti, shopping takes on a distinctly Austrian twist. **Bolzano** and **Merano** are both good shopping centres, where you'll find both mainstream shops and local delights such as *loden* jackets and coats, embroidered wool cardigans, *dirndl* skirts and *broderie anglaise*, and marvellous thick, felt, cork-soled slippers for Alpine winter evenings. Food, too, has an upland touch – mountain liqueurs, wild-flower honey and *speck*, the local cured ham, make excellent presents to take home.

Where to...
Be Entertained

Northeast Italy is strong on culture of every type, with cities like Bologna, Verona and Venice all boasting plenty in the way of theatre, concerts and, above all, opera.

The best summertime opera venue has to be **Verona**, where, from June to August, you can hear your favourite operas in the sublime setting of the Roman Arena (www.arena.it); you'll need to book this well in advance – and take a cushion!

Venice itself has plenty going on throughout the year; the biggest, longest shindig is the **Carnevale** (www.carnevale.venezia.it), running for two weeks before the start of Lent, when the whole city is crowded with partying costumed and masked figures. The city's other great entertainments are the traditional festivals, particularly **Il Redentore** in July, with a pontoon bridge across the Giudecca and spectacular fireworks, and the splendidly costumed **Regata Storica** in early September. There's highbrow culture every two years when the **Biennale Internazionale d'Arte** showcases the best of modern art, and an annual **International Film Festival** (www.mostradelcinema-divenezia.com) running for two weeks in September. You can hear opera during the winter months at the splendidly rebuilt Fenice (Phoenix) opera house, which true to its name, has risen from the ashes once more, and regular concerts are held throughout the year, often in beautiful churches. There's live classical music and occasional opera on offer too in towns like Padua, Ravenna, Parma and Vicenza.

If you're more into nightlife and generally letting your hair down, the northeast's summer clubbing scene and Italy's answer to Ibiza is Rimini, a huge resort with miles of beaches and buzzing clubs (www.riminifiera.it or www.riminiturismo.it).

Don't overlook gentler evening entertainment – there's nothing nicer than strolling through atmospheric streets, or sitting in a *piazza* or waterfront café and drinking in the sheer beauty of night-time Italy. If you're staying off the beaten track, this may be your only option.

Away from the cities there's plenty to do if you're looking for fresh air and exercise. The obvious place to go is the Dolomiti mountains, whose high peaks and valleys offer year-round outdoor fun. Come in winter for skiing, snowboarding, cross-country skiing and winter walking on waymarked trails, or head here in summer, when you can experience some of Europe's best high-altitude walking and hiking. Lifts and gondolas give easy access to the mountains, which are criss-crossed by beautifully kept and waymarked trails, offering superb walking for every taste and ability. Down in the valleys there are more trails, which you can also explore on horseback from local stables.

The coast offers good sports facilities in the shape of floodlit tennis courts, golf courses, riding in fragrant pinewoods and all sorts of water sports. Sailboarding and windsurfing are popular and you can rent equipment and arrange tuition in the larger resorts.

Whatever you choose to do, make local tourist offices your first port of call to pick up information on what's on and how to find it.

Central Italy

Getting Your Bearings

Rolling hills, farms and villas, hilltop villages, grapevines, olive groves and cypresses – the Italian dream is a reality in the Tuscan and central Italian landscapes. Here, in the birthplace of the Renaissance, are natural beauties, ease of life and more artistic treasures than anywhere else in Europe.

Firenze (Florence), capital of Tuscany, is the hub of the region, packed with sublime art and crammed with visitors all year. North of Florence, two cities draw the crowds: Pisa, famous for its cathedral complex and leaning tower, and prosperous Lucca, where solid walls enclose a core of medieval treasures. South of Florence is San Gimignano, with its clutch of medieval towers and ancient, flower-hung streets. Near by, set in glorious countryside, is Siena, Florence's historic rival and a perfectly preserved medieval city that contains the Campo, arguably Italy's loveliest *piazza*. The country south from here is dotted with hill towns, and east lies landlocked Umbria, the green heart of Italy, whose splendid capital is historic Perugia. Neighbouring Assisi, birthplace of St Francis, overlooks fertile fields of vines and sunflowers. To the west are the lower-key delights of Orvieto, set on a volcanic crag, while Umbria's southern gem is Spoleto, gateway to the central Apennines. To the north, from medieval Gubbio, roads cut through the Apennines to the region of the Marche, whose art capital, Urbino, preserves one of the most perfect of all Renaissance palaces.

Viareggio

Lucca

Pisa

Marina di Pisa

Livorno

Cecina

San Vincenzo

Isola di Capraia

Piombino

Isola d'Elba

Portoferraio

Golfo di Follonica

Porto Azzu

Isola Pianosa

Left: Palazzo Pitti, viewed from the Boboli Gardens

Previous page: Michelangelo's *David* in Florence

Detail of fresco in San Damiano Church, Assisi

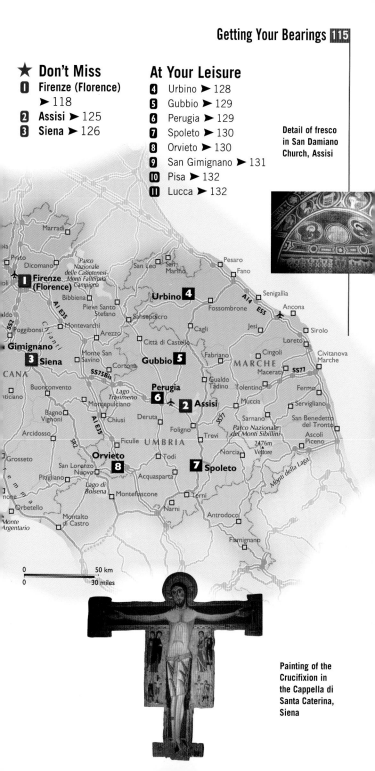

Painting of the Crucifixion in the Cappella di Santa Caterina, Siena

To visit the best in central Italy in five days, you will have to cut down on the time spent in each place. Alternatively you could bypass Pisa and Lucca in the north, and Orvieto and Spoleto in the south – freeing up more time for Florence and the wonderful landscape of Tuscany and Umbria. Another option would be to ignore the tourist honeypots – with the exception of Florence – and concentrate on lower-key towns such as Lucca, Orvieto, Spoleto, Gubbio and Urbino.

Central Italy in Five Days

Day One

Morning
Spend time in **10 Pisa** (➤ 132), visiting the **Campo dei Miracoli**, then drive north to **11 Lucca** (➤ 132) in time for lunch.

Afternoon
Take in Lucca's main sights, leaving time for a walk along the walls and a glimpse of the **Piazza Anfiteatro**, before taking the A11 southeast to **8 Florence** (➤ 118–124).

Evening
Take an evening stroll around the **Piazza della Signoria** and over the **Ponte Vecchio** (detail of façades, right).

Day Two

Morning
Aim to visit the **Duomo** complex (left) early before heading to pick up your pre-booked ticket at the **Uffizi**.

Afternoon
After a late lunch take in another of Florence's main sights – perhaps the **Accademia**, **Bargello** or **Palazzo Pitti** – before heading south on the SS2 to **9 San Gimignano** (➤ 131).

Evening
Explore the picturesque streets of San Gimignano, at their best without the daytime visitors, before a leisurely dinner *al fresco*.

Day Three

Morning
After visiting the **Collegiata**, drive into **3 Siena** (➤ 126–127) and head for the **Campo** (right) and **Palazzo Pubblico**.

Afternoon
Visit the **Duomo** and surrounding museums before heading through the best of southern Tuscany (➤ 185–187) to **8 Orvieto** (➤ 130).

Evening
Settle in then take a stroll and a drink at one of the bars overlooking the floodlit Duomo.

Day Four

Morning and Afternoon
Take in Orvieto's top sights before heading east; visit either **6 Perugia** (➤ 129) or **7 Spoleto** (➤ 130) before arriving in **2 Assisi** (➤ 125) in the early evening.

Evening
Wander around Assisi, soaking up the town's beauty and peaceful atmosphere.

Day Five

Morning
An early start means a crowd-free visit to the Basilica before heading north to **5 Gubbio** (➤ 129) for lunch.

Afternoon and Evening
Drive through the Apennines to **4 Urbino** (below, ➤ 128), arriving in time to visit the Palazzo Ducale and the Duomo.

⓪ Firenze (Florence)

Set on the banks of the River Arno among gentle hills, Florence and its artistic treasures epitomise the flowering of the Renaissance. The late 14th and 15th centuries saw an explosion of creativity and a return to the principles and styles of the classical world. In no other city can the development of Renaissance art be traced so comprehensively in such a relatively small space.

Duomo, Museo dell'Opera del Duomo, Battistero, Campanile

Construction on the present **Duomo** (cathedral), which replaced an earlier version, was completed in 1436, when Filippo Brunelleschi added the largest dome since classical times. The ornate green-and-white marble exterior is a superb contrast to the austerity within. Two equestrian wall monuments to famous *condottieri* (mercenaries) are the work of Andrea del Castagno and Paolo Uccello, but the finest treasures are now in the **Museo dell'Opera del Duomo**, behind the Duomo. Here you'll find Ghiberti's bronze Baptistery doors (1452), which Michelangelo dubbed the 'Gates of Paradise'. Outside, the 11th-century **Battistero** is entirely encased in coloured marble; parts probably originally date from the 6th and 7th centuries. Its three sets of bronze doors, by Andrea Pisano (1330s) and Ghiberti, are reproductions of the originals kept in the museum. Look up to take in the dome's rich mosaics (1225) – Florence's only mosaic cycle.

Above: Brunelleschi's magnificent dome

Left: *The Venus of Urbino* by Titian, in the Uffizi Gallery

Opposite stands the **Campanile**, designed by Giotto in 1334, redesigned in 1337 and decorated with red, green and white marble, sculpture and reliefs. Climb the 414 steps for panoramic views.

Galleria dell'Accademia

Founded as part of an art school in 1784, this is home to the world's most famous sculpture, Michelangelo's *David*, designed as a symbol of republican liberty for the Piazza della Signoria in 1501. The figure of young David preparing to fight Goliath made the 26-year-old sculptor's name. The Accademia has five

Taking a break at the Uffizi

other superb Michelangelo sculptures: four unfinished *Slaves* and a statue of *St Matthew*, all commissioned for Pope Julius II's tomb in Rome. Other rooms showcase Florentine 13th- and 14th-century paintings and a collection of musical instruments.

Galleria degli Uffizi

The huge building which once held the government offices (*uffizi*) now contains the world's most important collection of Renaissance paintings, mainly acquired by the ruling Medici family and bequeathed to Florence in 1737. Early works represent the move from stylised Byzantine art to Renaissance realism, epitomised by Giotto's *Maestà* and the *Adoration of the Magi* by Gentile da Fabriano. Then come the glories of the Renaissance, with a beautiful Filippo Lippi *Madonna and Child with Angels* (1465) contrasting with Piero della Francesca's *Portrait of the Duke and Duchess of Urbino*. The

The Doni Tondo by Michelangelo, in the Uffizi

next rooms (10–14) have major works by Sandro Botticelli – *Primavera*, symbolic of the rebirth of spring, and the tender *Birth of Venus*. There are two early pictures by Leonardo da Vinci: the serene *Annunciation* and the *Adoration of the Magi*, crammed with symbolism and character studies. The octagonal Tribuna room

The courtyard of the Museo Nazionale del Bargello

contains Bronzino portraits and classical sculpture, including the *Medici Venus* (1st century BC). In Room 25 you'll find Michelangelo's *Doni Tondo* (1504), the only easel painting he completed. Mannerist paintings are housed in Room 27 and elsewhere there are pictures by Bellini and Veronese, Tintoretto and Caravaggio, Rubens, Rembrandt and Van Dyck.

Museo Nazionale del Bargello

The Bargello, built in 1255 as the seat of the city government, is the city's sculpture showcase. From the arcaded Gothic courtyard, decorated with the coats of arms of Florence's Podestà (chief magistrate), enter the great hall, where Michelangelo's *Bacchus* is the star turn. Here too, is his *Tondo Pitti*, along with works by Benvenuto Cellini and Giambologna. Upstairs, in the Gothic **Salone del Consiglio Generale**, are superb works by Donatello, including his stern *St George* (1416) and his bronze *David* (1430–40), the first freestanding nude created since Roman times. The room also contains reliefs submitted for the Baptistery doors by Ghiberti and Donatello and glazed terracotta Madonnas by Luca della Robbia. The second floor houses Renaissance bronzes, portrait busts and decorative arts.

Right: The Basilica di Santa Croce was once one of the largest churches in the Christian world

Palazzo Pitti

The vast Palazzo Pitti was the official residence of the Medici dukes of Tuscany. Today it houses the **Galleria Palatina** and is backed by a shady garden, the **Giardino di Boboli**. The Palatina's paintings are hung in the 17th-century style, in no chronological order. Aim to see the 11 Raphaels, among them the *Madonna della Seggiola*, the 14 Titians, the 17 works by Andrea del Sarto, and Caravaggio's *Sleeping Cupid*. You can visit the **Apartamenti Reali** (State Rooms) before moving on to the other collections, of which the **Museo degli Argenti**, a series of lavish rooms packed with luxury artefacts, is the most interesting.

Piazza della Signoria and the Palazzo Vecchio

At the heart of Florence is the Piazza della Signoria, a square ringed with fine buildings, chief of which is the **Palazzo Vecchio**, the town hall. The south side is dominated by the 1382 **Loggia dei Lanzi**, a former meeting place that now holds splendid late Renaissance sculpture – some original, some copies – including Cellini's *Perseus* (1545), Giambologna's *Rape of the Sabine Women*, and Donatello's *Judith and Holofernes*. Pass the replica of Michelangelo's *David* to visit the **Palazzo Vecchio**, headquarters of the Florentine council, which has a great tower containing the frescoed meeting hall, the **Salone del Cinquecento**, on the first floor, as well as the private quarters of Medici rulers.

Below: Cortona's celebrated ceiling fresco in the Sala di Marte, Palazzo Pitti

Northeast of the Arno

North of the river and east of the Piazza della Signoria, the church of **Santa Croce** is the main draw: a huge Franciscan building constructed between 1294 and 1450. Inside are the tombs of Michelangelo, Dante, Niccolò Machiavelli and Ghiberti; its side chapels include frescoes by Giotto. To its right stands Brunelleschi's **Cappella dei Pazzi** (1446), a tranquil chapel in severely classical style. North of here is Michelozzo's church of **Santissima Annunziata** (1444–81), with paintings by Perugino, Pontormo and Rosso Fiorentino; the **Museo di San Marco**, an ancient convent decorated with Fra Angelico's delicate frescoes; and the **Ospedale degli Innocenti**, a foundling hospital whose arched portico features lunettes by Andrea della Robbia. Near by, the **Museo Archeologico Nazionale** houses Egyptian and Etruscan collections.

Northwest of the Arno

West of the museum is the complex of **San Lorenzo**, the
Medici family church, designed in 1425 by Brunelleschi. Here
are buried many Medici family members, but their main
monuments are the adjoining **Cappelle Medicee**, the ostenta-
tious **Cappella dei Principi**, and the **Sagrestia Nuova**,
containing some of Michelangelo's most beautiful sculptures;
the tomb of Lorenzo dei Medici, decorated with the reclining
figures of *Dawn* and *Dusk*, and that of Giuliano, which
supports *Day* and *Night*. A few steps east is the main 15th-
and 16th-century Medici residence, the **Palazzo Medici-
Riccardi**, designed in 1444 by Michelozzo. Its exquisite first-
floor chapel is entirely frescoed with a *Procession of the Magi*
by Benozzo Gozzoli, the brightly dressed participants riding
through a Tuscan landscape. To the west, in the Gothic
church of **Santa Maria Novella**, you can admire Masaccio's
fresco, the *Trinità*, featuring the first successful use of
perspective in Western art.

South of the Arno

Besides the Palazzo Pitti, the area south of the river, the
Oltrarno, has two exquisite churches. The best approach is
across the Ponte Santa Trinità, a replica of the 1567 bridge
destroyed by bombing in 1941. This gives the best view of the
Ponte Vecchio, spanning the Arno upstream, which was built
in 1345 and is still lined with medieval shops. South of the
Trinità bridge is the huge, grey-and-white church of **Santo
Spirito**, designed by Brunelleschi between 1444 and 1481.
West of its pretty *piazza* is the church of **Santa Maria del
Carmine**, which contains some of Florence's greatest frescoes.
Most of the **Cappella Brancacci** was painted between 1425
and 1428 by two revolutionary artists of the early
Renaissance, Masolino (1383–1447) and Masaccio (1401–28).
While in Oltrarno, climb to the **Piazzale Michelangelo**, a
wonderful viewpoint overlooking the city.

The statue of
Neptune in the
Boboli Gardens

The elegant
façade of Santa
Maria Novella

The Ponte Vecchio (Old Bridge)

TAKING A BREAK
Try **Rivoire** in Piazza della Signoria or **Baldovino** (➤ 135) in Via San Giuseppe, near Santa Croce church.

FIRENZE (FLORENCE): INSIDE INFO

Top tips Book timed tickets in advance for the Uffizi, the Museo di San Marco and the Accademia (tel: 055 294 883).

• The Oltrarno district has wonderful **artisan, craft and antique shops**.

✚ 210 C4
Tourist Information Office
✉ Via Cavour 1r ☎ 055 290 832/3; www.firenzeturismo.it 🕔 Mon–Sat 8:30–6:30; Sun 8:30–1:30

Duomo, Museo dell'Opera del Duomo, Battistero, Campanile
✉ Piazza del Duomo ☎ 055 230 2885 🕔 Mon–Wed, Fri 10–5; Thu 10–3:30; Sat 10–4:45; Sun 1:30 4:45; museum: Mon–Sat 9–7:30, Sun 8:30–1:30; Battistero: Mon–Sat noon–6:30, Sun 8:30–1:30; Campanile: daily 9–7 💷 Duomo: free, Battistero: moderate; museum, Campanile: expensive

Galleria dell'Accademia
✉ Via Ricasoli 60 ☎ 055 238 8612; www.firenzemusei.it 🕔 Tue–Sun 8:15–6:50 (extended in summer) 💷 Expensive

Galleria degli Uffizi
✉ Piazzale degli Uffizi ☎ 055 238 8651; 055 294 883 to book in advance; www.firenzemusei.it 🕔 Tue–Sun 8:15–6:50 (extended in summer) 💷 Expensive

Museo Nazionale del Bargello
✉ Via del Proconsolo 4 ☎ 055 238 8606 🕔 Daily 8:15–1:50; closed 1st, 3rd, 5th Sun, 2nd, 4th Mon of month 🚌 14, 23, A 💷 Moderate

Palazzo Pitti
✉ Piazza Pitti ☎ 055 238 8614 🕐 Palatina, Appartamenti Reale Tue–Sun 8:15–6:50; Argenti daily 8:15–6:30, Apr–Sep; 8:15–4:30, rest of year; closed 1st, last Mon of month; gardens daily 8:15–7:30, Jun–Aug; 8:15–6:30, Apr, May; 8:15–5:30, Mar, Sep, Oct; 8:15–4:30, Nov–Feb
💷 Expensive; gardens: moderate

Palazzo Vecchio
✉ Piazza della Signoria ☎ 055 276 8465 🕐 Fri–Wed 9–7; Thu 9–2 💷 Expensive

Santa Croce
✉ Piazza Santa Croce ☎ 055 244 619 🕐 Mon–Sat 9:30–5:30; Sun 1–5:30 💷 Moderate

Santissima Annunziata
✉ Piazza SS Annunziata ☎ 055 239 8034 🕐 Daily 7–12:45, 4–6:30 💷 Free

Museo di San Marco
✉ Piazza San Marco 1 ☎ 055 238 8608 🕐 Mon–Fri 8:15–1:50, Sat–Sun 8:15–7; closed 1st, 3rd, 5th Sun, 2nd, 4th Mon of month 💷 Moderate

Ospedale degli Innocenti
✉ Piazza SS Annunziata ☎ 055 249 1708 🕐 Thu–Tue 8:30–2 💷 Inexpensive

Museo Archeologico Nazionale
✉ Via della Colonna 38 ☎ 055 23575 🕐 Mon 2–7; Tue, Thu 8:30–7; Wed, Fri–Sun 8:30–2
💷 Moderate

San Lorenzo
✉ Piazza San Lorenzo ☎ 055 216634 🕐 Church: Mon–Sat 10–5:30; cloister: Mon–Sat 10–6, Sun 9–1 💷 Inexpensive

Cappelle Medicee
✉ Piazza Madonna degli Aldobrandini 2 ☎ 055 238 8602 🕐 Daily 8:15–4:30; closed 2nd, 4th Sun, 1st, 3rd, 5th Mon of month 💷 Expensive

Palazzo Medici-Riccardi
✉ Via Cavour 3 ☎ 055 276 0340 🕐 Thu–Tue 9–7 (last entrance 6:30) 💷 Inexpensive

Santa Maria Novella
✉ Piazza Santa Maria Novella ☎ Church: 055 215 918; museum: 055 282 187 🕐 Church: Mon–Thu, Sat 9:30–4:30, Fri, Sun 1–4:30; museum: Mon–Sat 9–4:30, Sun 9–1:30
💷 Inexpensive

Santo Spirito
✉ Piazza Santo Spirito ☎ 055 210 030 🕐 Daily
💷 Free

Cappella Brancacci
✉ Piazza del Carmine ☎ 055 238 2195
🕐 Wed–Sat, Mon 10–5; Sun 1–5
💷 Moderate

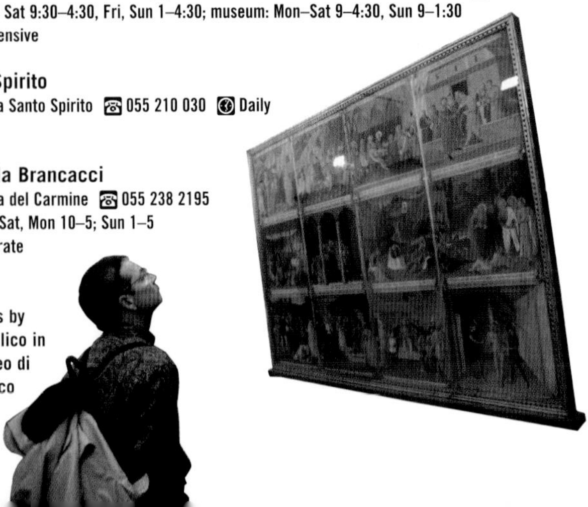

Paintings by
Fra Angelico in
the Museo di
San Marco

2 Assisi

Assisi is inextricably linked with St Francis (1182–1226), and a dramatic view of his burial place, the Basilica di San Francesco, opens up on the approach to this historic town clinging to the slopes of Monte Subiaso.

Above: Ceramic panel of St Francis

Basilica di San Francesco

In 1997 earthquakes inflicted severe damage on many of Assisi's historic buildings, including the 13th-century basilica and its glorious frescoes, but these have now been magnificently restored. In the Lower Church the vaults over the main altar are illustrated with allegories of the Franciscans' founding principles – chastity, poverty and obedience. Cimabue's portrait of Francis is in the right transept. The Upper Church contains a 28-fresco cycle showing the saint's life by Giotto, completed in 1300.

Basilica di Santa Chiara and beyond

St Clare (1194–1253), another native of Assisi, founded the Poor Clares, a new order of Franciscan nuns. Her remains lie in the basilica, which was built between 1257 and 1265 and contains frescoes and a crucifix that was said to have spoken to St Francis.

Assisi's main street, Via di San Francesco, leads to Piazza del Comune. From the cathedral you can walk up to the 14th-century Rocca Maggiore (castle) for stunning views.

Note: When visiting churches, dress modestly, avoiding shorts, miniskirts and sleeveless tops.

The Basilica di San Francesco is the town's greatest glory

TAKING A BREAK
Ristorante Medio Evo (Via Arco dei Priori 4) serves delicious Umbrian delicacies.

➕ 211 E2

Tourist Information Office
✉ Piazza del Comune 22 ☎ 075 812 534 🕐 Mon–Sat 8–6:30, Sun 10–1, Mar–Oct; Mon–Sat 8–2, 3–6, Sun 9–1, rest of year

Basilica di San Francesco
✉ Piazza San Francesco ☎ 075 819 001 🕐 Lower Church: daily 7:30–7; Upper Church: daily 8:30–7 🎟 Free

Basilica di Santa Chiara
✉ Piazza Santa Chiara ☎ 075 812 282 🕐 Daily 7:30–12, 2–6 🎟 Free

3 Siena

Hilltop Siena is built on three ridges, and near the point where they converge stands the Piazza del Campo, Europe's greatest medieval square, surrounded by palaces and forming the city's heart.

Piazza del Campo

Twice a year, on 2 July and 16 August, the Campo is the scene of the Palio, a bareback horse race held since the Middle Ages involving ten of Siena's 17 *contrade* (districts). Otherwise its chief sight is the vast **Palazzo Pubblico**, housing the **Museo Civico**. Its Sala della Pace features one of Europe's finest early medieval secular fresco cycles, Lorenzetti's *Allegories of Good and Bad Government* (1338). Climb the 102m (335-foot) **Torre del Mangia** (1338–48) on the Palazzo's eastern side for terrific views.

Top: The Palio – a spectacular bare-back horse race round the Campo

Piazza del Duomo

Three of the city's most interesting and beautiful buildings are found here. The Duomo has a magnificent façade and interior, with a floor consisting of 56 graffito (incised) marble panels, designed by 40 of Siena's finest artists between 1369 and 1547. Frescoes by Pinturicchio portray *Scenes from the Life of Pope Pius II* (1502–9) in the library entrance. The **Spedale di Santa Maria della Scala**, opposite the cathedral, was Siena's main hospital for almost 1,000 years, until the 1990s. Its medieval interior is now open to the public and includes a fresco cycle (1440) by Vecchietta, Domenico di Bartolo and

Above: Siena's Duomo is one of Italy's most beautiful churches

other Sienese artists, portraying aspects of the hospital's history. Masterpieces in the **Museo dell'Opera del Duomo** include an ethereal relief of the *Madonna and Child* (1456–9) by Donatello. On the first floor, La Sala di Duccio is dominated by Duccio's vast *Maestà* (1308–11), one of the greatest Italian medieval paintings.

The main art gallery, the **Pinacoteca Nazionale**, houses works by Guido da Siena, Duccio, Simone Martini, Sassetta, Vecchietta and Giovanni di Paolo, among many others.

TAKING A BREAK

Try the **Bar-Gelateria La Costerella** (no sign) at Via di Città 33 on the junction with Costa dei Barbieri and Via di Fontebranda.

Below: Palio pageantry

➕ 210 C3

Tourist Information
✉ Piazza del Campo 56 ☎ 0577 280 551; www.terresiena.it ⏰ Daily 9–7

Torre del Mangia
✉ Piazza del Campo ☎ 0577 292 232 ⏰ Daily 10–7 💷 Expensive; joint ticket only with museum

Museo Civico
✉ Piazza del Campo ☎ 0577 292 232 ⏰ Daily 10–7 💷 Expensive

Duomo
✉ Piazza del Duomo ☎ 0577 238 048 ⏰ Mon–Sat 10:30–7:30, Sun and pub hols 1:30–6:30, mid-Mar to Oct; Mon–Sat 10:30–6:30, Sun and pub hols 1:30–5:30, rest of year 💷 Moderate

Spedale di Santa Maria della Scala
✉ Piazza del Duomo 2 ☎ 0577 224 835 ⏰ Daily 10–6:30 💷 Expensive

Museo dell'Opera del Duomo
✉ Piazza del Duomo 8 ☎ 0577 283 048 ⏰ Daily 9–7 💷 Expensive

Pinacoteca Nazionale
✉ Palazzo Buonsignori, Via San Pietro 29 ☎ 0577 281 161 ⏰ Mon 8–2, Tue–Sat 8:15–7, Sun 8–1:15 💷 Moderate

SIENA: INSIDE INFO

Top tip Siena's centre is **easily explored on foot**, but if you come by train avoid the long uphill walk to the Campo and catch a bus from the station forecourt.

At Your Leisure

❹ Urbino

Urbino, the birthplace of Raphael (1483–1520), is one of Italy's best-preserved Renaissance cities. Duke Federico da Montefeltro's magnificent twin-towered home, the **Palazzo Ducale** houses the Galleria Nazionale delle Marche, whose collection includes two masterpieces by Piero della Francesca – *The Madonna of Senigallia* and *The Flagellation* – and Raphael's famous *La Muta* (*The Mute*), as well as works by Uccello and Titian. The **Duomo** (cathedral), restored after earthquake damage in 1997, contains a celebrated 16th-century painting of *The Last Supper* by Federico Barocci (1528–1612).

Casa di Raffaello, Raphael's birthplace, is now a small museum containing reproductions of his paintings and works by his father, Giovanni Santi, and his disciples Timoteo Viti and Giulio Romano.

The late 14th-century **Oratorio di San Giovanni Battista** has a stunning 1416 fresco cycle by the brothers Jacopo and Lorenzo Salimbeni.

Tourist information
🔢 211 E3 ✉ Piazza Rinascimento
☎ 0722 2613; www.comune.urbino.ps.it

Urbino is one of Italy's best-preserved Renaissance cities

🕐 Mon–Sat 9–1, 3–6, Sun 9–1, Jun–Sep

Palazzo Ducale
✉ Piazza Duca Federico ☎ 0722 325 655 🕐 Tue–Sun 8:30–7:45, Mon 8:30–2 💰 Expensive

Casa di Raffaello
✉ Via di Raffaello 57 ☎ 0722 320 105 🕐 Mon–Sat 9–1, 3–7, Sun 10–1, Mar–Oct; Mon–Sat 9–2, Sun 10–1, Nov–Feb
💰 Inexpensive

Exhibit in Gubbio's Palazzo dei Consoli

5 Gubbio

Gubbio's medieval streets and orange-tiled houses are set against the striking backdrop of Monte Ingino, which can be reached via cable car. The town is built on a series of terraces, with vertiginous views from Piazza della Signoria, the main square, dominated by the vast 14th-century **Palazzo dei Consoli**. The seven bronze *Tavole Iguvine* (Eugubine Tablets) are the pride of the palace's **Museo Civico**; they were ploughed up outside Gubbio in the 15th century and contain much of what we know of the ancient Umbrian language. The earliest dates from the 3rd century BC and together they contain the names of native gods, prayers, sacrificial instructions and curses.

The town's **Corsa dei Ceri** (Candle Race) has been celebrated every 15 May, St Ubaldo's Day, for centuries. The three *ceri* (wooden candles), weighing around 200kg (440 pounds) each, are surmounted by statues of St Ubaldo, the town's patron saint, St George and St Anthony, and teams of bearers race up Via Sant'Ubaldo to the Basilica di Sant'Ubaldo, near the summit of Monte Ingino. Inside the basilica is a glass casket containing the body of St Ubaldo.

Tourist information
🚩 211 E3 ✉ Piazza Oderisi 6 (off Corso Garibaldi) ☎ 075 922 0693; www.umbria2000.it 🕐 Mon–Sat 8–2, 3:30–6:30, Sun 8–2

Museo Civico
✉ Palazzo dei Consoli, Piazza Grande ☎ 075 927 4298 🕐 Daily 10–1, 3–6 💶 Moderate

6 Perugia

Umbria's capital is a lively, cosmo-politan city with a large student population. The main street, Corso Vanucci, leads from Piazza Italia to Piazza 4 Novembre, where the lovely 13th-century Fontana Maggiore once supplied water from the Monte Pacciano aqueduct. In the **Duomo** (cathedral) the Cappella del Sant'Annello holds the Holy Ring of the Virgin Mary, locked inside 15 boxes, each with a different key. The best fresco, a *Deposition* by Federico Barocci (1559), decorates the chapel of San Bernardino.

On the top floors of the 13th-century Gothic Palazzo dei Priori,

Perugia, Umbria's capital, retains its medieval heart

opposite, is the **Galleria Nazionale dell'Umbria**, exhibiting medieval and Renaissance works by Fra Angelica, Arnolfi di Cambio and Piero della Francesca, and paintings by Perugino.

The **Chiesa di San Pietro**, Perugia's first cathedral, was built as part of a Benedictine abbey in 966. Among the wealth of art and archi-tectural detail inside, look out for Perugino's *Pietà* in the left aisle, the *Adoration of the Magi* by Eusebio da San Giorgio and the magnificent choir stalls by Maestro Stefano (1526).

The delightful monastic garden behind San Pietro, the **Orto Botanico Medievale**, is laid out with medicinal plants and herbs.

Tourist information
🚩 211 E2 ✉ Palazzo dei Priori, Piazza IV Novembre 3 ☎ 075 573 6458 🕐 Mon–Sat 9–6:30, Sun 9–1, Mar–Sep; Mon–Sat 9–1:30, Sun 9–1, rest of year

Galleria Nazionale dell'Umbria
✉ Corso Vanucci ☎ 075 572 1009; www.galleentmaledellumbria.it 🕐 Daily 9–8 💶 Moderate

7 Spoleto

This ancient Umbrian city is best known for its international arts celebration, the Festival dei due Mondi, in June and July. Roman remains include the **Arco di Druso** (Arch of Drusus), built in AD 23, and the first-century AD **Casa Romana**, possibly the home of Vespasia Pollo, mother of Emperor Vespasian. The 14th-century **Ponte delle Torri** (Bridge of Towers), 80m (262 feet) high and 230m (755 feet) long, spans the Tessino gorge between Spoleto and Monteluco.

The graceful **Basilica di San Salvatore** has a splendid Renaissance porch, eight rose windows, and frescoes by Filippo Lippi (1406–69), who is buried here, and paintings by Pinturicchio (1454–1513).

An archaeological museum in the Monastery of Sant'Agata, in the upper town, displays Bronze Age finds from the imposing **Rocca** (Papal fortress), built in 1355 and once the home of Lucrezia and Cesare Borgia. It is now open as a museum.

Don't miss the **Pinacoteca** (picture gallery) in the Palazzo Comunale.

Tourist information
🔲 211 E2 ✉ Piazza della Libertà 7
☎ 0743 238920; www.conspoleto.com
🕐 Mon–Fri 9–1, 4–7, Sat–Sun 10–1, 4–7; closed Sun pm in winter

Rocca
✉ Piazza Campello ☎ 0743 43707
🕐 Daily 10–1, 3–7 💰 Expensive

Pinacoteca
✉ Piazza Municipio 1 ☎ 0743 45940
🕐 Wed–Mon 10:30–1, 3–6:30
💰 Moderate

8 Orvieto

Orvieto stands on a high volcanic plateau, surrounded by the vine-covered hills that produce its famous wines. Its Gothic-style **Duomo** (cathedral), with its dazzlingly ornate façade, was begun in the 13th century to celebrate the miracle of Bolsena, when blood dripped from the Communion Host on to the altar cloth in the nearby village of **Bolsena**. The sacred linen is housed in the Cappella del Corporale.

Opposite this is the Cappella di San Brizio, home to Luca Signorelli's masterpiece – the fresco cycle of *The Last Judgement*. Initially the painting was started in 1447 by Fra Angelico and Benozzo Gozzoli, but abandoned after only two panels had been

Spoleto's Ponte delle Torri crosses the Tessino chasm on ten pointed arches

completed. The work was finally finished by Signorelli in 1504, and influenced Michelangelo's work in the Sistine Chapel. Across the square the charming Palazzo Faina has been restored and houses a fine collection of Etruscan antiquities found in tombs surrounding the city.

Near the funicular station, in Piazza Cahen, is the Pozzo di San Patrizio, a 62m (203-foot) deep well

San Gimignano is celebrated for its medieval towers and beautiful skyline

Below: The highly decorative, twisting columns of Orvieto's magnificent Duomo

commissioned in 1527 by Pope Clement VII to supply water in the event of a siege.

Tourist information
✚ 211 D2 ✉ Piazza Duomo 24
☎ 0763 341772 🕐 Mon–Fri 8:15–1:50, 4–7, Sat 10–1, 3–6, Sun 10–12, 4–6

Duomo
☎ 0763 341167 🕐 Daily 7:30–12:45, 2:30–6:15, Mar–Oct; daily 7:30–12:45, 2:30–5:15, Nov–Feb 🖐 Free

Cappella di San Brizio
☎ 0763 342477 🕐 Mon–Sat 8–12:45, 2:30–7:15, Sun 2:30–7:15, Apr–Sep; one hour earlier rest of year 🖐 Moderate

❾ San Gimignano

San Gimignano's ancient towers form one of Tuscany's prettiest skylines. Its main focus is the Piazza del Duomo, site of the 12th- to 13th-century

Collegiata, whose interior is covered in frescoes, including a *Last Judgement* (1410) by Taddeo di Bartolo. Left of the Collegiata is the Palazzo del Popolo (1288), housing the **Museo Civico**, where the Sala del Consiglio (or Sala di Dante) is dominated by a painting of the *Madonna Enthroned* by Lippo Memmi (1317). The *palazzo*'s **Torre Grossa** (begun in 1300) is open to the public.

The **Church of Sant'Agostino** is best known for a 17-panel fresco cycle on the *Life of St Augustine* (1464–5), by Benozzo Gozzoli.

Tourist information
✚ 210 C3 ✉ Piazza Duomo 1
☎ 0577 940008 🕐 Daily 9–1, 3–7, Mar–Oct; 9–1, 2–6, Nov–Feb

Collegiata
✉ Piazza del Duomo ☎ 0577 940 008
🕐 Mon–Fri 9:30–7:30, Sat 9:30–5, Sun 1–5, Apr–Oct; Mon–Fri 9:30–5, Sun 1–5, Nov–Dec, Mar; services only Jan–Feb
🖐 Moderate

Pinacoteca and Torre Grossa
✉ Palazzo del Popolo, Piazza del Duomo ☎ 0577 940 340 🕐 Daily 9:30–7:30, Mar–Oct; daily 10–5:30, rest of year 🖐 Museum: moderate; Tower: moderate; combined ticket: moderate

Sant'Agostino
✉ Piazza Sant'Agostino 🕐 Daily 7–noon, 3–7, Apr–Oct; 7:30–noon, 3–6, Nov–Mar 🖐 Free

🔲 210 B3 ✉ Piazza Duomo 1
☎ 050 560464

Duomo, Baptistery, Museo dell'Opera, Camposanto
✉ Campo dei Miracoli ☎ 050 560 921
🕐 Mon–Sat 10–8, Sun 1–7, Apr–Oct;
Mon–Sat 10–dusk, Sun 3–dusk,
Nov–Mar 🎟 Moderate

🔟 Lucca

At Lucca's heart is Piazza San Michele, site of the old Roman forum, and the beautiful Romanesque church of **San Michele in Foro**. The main portal of Lucca's magnificent cathedral, the **Duomo di San Martino**, has carvings by Nicola Pisano; among the features inside is the Tempietto (1482–5), an octagonal chapel housing the *Volto Santo* (Holy Face), a cedar-wood Crucifix reputed to be a likeness of Christ carved by Nicodemus.

The **Museo Nazionale di Villa Guinigi** (Via della Quarquonia, tel: 0583 496033) has an eclectic collection of paintings, sculpture, textiles, Roman and Etruscan items, silverware, paintings by Fra Bartolommeo and sculpture by Matteo Civitali. Note the cathedral choir stalls (1529) decorated with inlaid wood images of Lucca.

🔟 Pisa

Pisa's Campo dei Miracoli (Field of Miracles) encompasses the celebrated leaning tower, the Duomo (cathedral), the Baptistery and a medieval cemetery, the Camposanto.

Begun in 1173, the **Leaning Tower** had started to keel by 1274. Intervention in the 1990s saved it from collapse and it reopened to the public in 2002. Construction of the **Duomo** started in 1064, and its ornate marble-striped exterior inspired similar churches across central Italy. Many of its treasures were destroyed by fire in 1595; survivors include the apse mosaic of *Christ in Majesty* (1302) by Cimabue and a carved pulpit (1302–11) by Giovanni Pisano.

Items from the Campo's buildings are displayed in the **Museo dell'Opera del Duomo**.

Tourist information
🔲 210 B4 ✉ Piazzale Verdi
☎ 0583 583150 🕐 Daily 9–7,
Apr–Oct, 9–5, rest of year

San Michele in Foro
✉ Piazza San Michele
🕐 Daily 7:30–12, 3–6; closed
during services 🎟 Free

Duomo di San Martino
✉ Piazza San Martino
☎ 0583 490 530 🕐 Daily
7–7, mid-Mar to end Oct; 7–5
rest of year 🎟 Cathedral:
free; sacristy: inexpensive

Top: Pisa's Leaning Tower
Left: Detail, San Michele, Lucca

Where to... Stay

Prices

Expect to pay per double room, per night
€ under €100   €€ €100–€180   €€€ over €180

FIRENZE (FLORENCE)

Brunelleschi €€€

The 4-star Brunelleschi has an excellent position in a quiet back-street between the Duomo and Piazza della Signoria. This conversion of an historic site was designed by architect Italo Gamberini and is built around a Byzantine chapel and the 5th-century Torre della Pagliazza, one of the city's oldest known structures. A small in-hotel museum is devoted to some of the items unearthed during construction. Rooms combine a modern feel with features retained or copied from the original buildings, notably the exposed brickwork.

 210 C4 ⊠ Via dei Calzaiuoli, Piazza Santa Elisabetta 3
☎ 055 290 311; fax: 055 219 653; www.hotelbrunelleschi.it

Casci €

The Casci is one of the best 2-star hotels in Florence, thanks to its position (just north of Piazza del Duomo), the warm welcome of its multilingual family owners, a good buffet breakfast, the fair prices, and the range of clean and pleasant rooms. All 25 have TVs; a handful face on to the Via Cavour (these have double glazing).

 210 C4 ⊠ Via Cavour 13 ☎ 055 211 686; fax: 055 239 6461; www.hotelcasci.com

Gallery Hotel Art €€€

This stylish 4-star hotel in a quiet square next to the Ponte Vecchio has a sleek, minimalist look – dark wood, neutral colours and modern art in the reception and the 65 rooms. There is a small, smart bar and a comfortable lounge area.

 210 C4 ⊠ Vicolo dell'Oro 5
☎ 055 27 263; fax: 055 268 557; www.lungarnohotels.com

Hermitage €€

Book early to secure one of the 28 rooms at this charming 3-star hotel. It owes its popularity to the amiable service, the good facilities and a superb position almost overlooking the Ponte Vecchio. Not all rooms have river or bridge views, and those that do can be noisy, despite double glazing; if this is a concern, request courtyard rooms. In summer, you can take breakfast on the roof terrace.

 210 C4 ⊠ Vicolo Marzio 1, Piazza del Pesce ☎ 055 287 216; fax: 055 212 208; www.hermitagehotel.com

ASSISI

Fontebella €€

Every room has its own, antique-furnished style in this intimate 16th-century *palazzo* between the Piazza del Pool and the Basilica di San Franceso. Paintings and tapestries hang on the walls and there are good views from the upper floors. The excellent Frantoio garden restaurant is attached.

 211 E2 ⊠ Via Fontebella 25
☎ 075 812 883; fax: 075 812 941; www.fontebella.com

SIENA

Antica Torre €€

The 3-star Antica Torre occupies a restored 16th-century tower. Book well in advance to secure one of the eight pretty but moderately sized rooms and try for rooms on the upper floor at the rear – they have the best views. The hotel lies about 600m (650 yards) east of the Campo on a side street off Via di

Pantaneto, near the church of Santa Maria dei Servi. There is no restaurant, but breakfast is served in the medieval cellar.

➕ 210 C3 ✉ Via Fieravecchia 7 ☎ 0577 222255; fax: 0577 222255

Hotel Santa Caterina €€

The Santa Caterina, just 5 minutes' walk outside the town wall and 15 minutes from the Piazza del Campo, is simply furnished in Tuscan style and has small but comfortable rooms with old dark wood and tiled floors. In summer, breakfast is served in the attractive secluded garden.

➕ 210 C3 ✉ Via E S Piccolomini 7 ☎ 0577 221 105; fax: 0577 271 087

SPOLETO

Palazzo Dragoni €€

This 14th-century building near the cathedral is run by the Diotallevi, local bakers, and not surprisingly provides unbeatable breakfast pastries. Rooms are individually decorated and equipped with modern facilities; there are great city views from the dining area.

➕ 211 E2 ✉ Via del Duomo 16 ☎ 0743 222 220; www.palazzodragoni.it

ORVIETO

Virgilio €

If you want to enjoy the authentic small-town experience, this hotel overlooking the main piazza is an ideal choice. Some rooms have good views of the Duomo; all are well equipped and comfortable, though on the small side, and an unpretentious breakfast is provided.

➕ 211 D2 ✉ Piazza del Duomo 5 ☎ 0763 341 882; www.hotelvirgilio.com

SAN GIMIGNANO

La Cisterna €€

This is one of San Gimignano's best 3-star hotels, tucked away in the eastern corner of Piazza della Cisterna in a medieval building which opened as a hotel in 1919. It has an excellent restaurant, Le Terrazze. Breakfast is included.

➕ 210 C3 ✉ Piazza della Cisterna 24 ☎ 0577 940 328; fax: 0577 942 080; www.sangimignano.com/lacisterna ⊘ Closed for a period between Epiphany and mid-Mar

PISA

Royal Victoria €€

Pisa has virtually no high-class hotels, so this one stands out. Its welcoming service and sedate if old-fashioned style are just what you would expect of an establishment that has been owned by five generations of the same family since 1839. Its position on the banks of the Arno, between the station and Campo dei Miracoli, is convenient for Pisa's main shopping street and piazza. The Leaning Tower and other sights are ten minutes' walk away. The 48 rooms may be a bit dated, but are clean and comfortable, with or without private bathroom, and there are also three- and four-bed rooms. Parking is available for a fee.

➕ 210 B3 ✉ Lungarno Pacinotti 12 ☎ 050 940 111; fax: 050 940 180

LUCCA

Palazzo Alexander €€

This charming and elegant residence in the heart of Lucca's historic centre makes it an ideal place for exploring the town, and is close to several good restaurants. The building dates back to the 12th century and has been restored in baroque style, with lavish use of yellow and gold. The rooms and apartments are spacious, with polished antique wood floors, large gilded mirrors and comfortable seats, and marble has been used in the bathrooms. Downstairs, part of the reception area is used for the buffet breakfast.

➕ 210 B4 ✉ Via Santa Giustina 48 ☎ 0583 583 571; fax: 0583 583 610

Where to...
Eat and Drink

Prices
Expect to pay for a three-course meal for one, excluding drinks and service
€ under €20   €€ €20–€40   €€€ over €40

FIRENZE (FLORENCE)

Baldovino €–€€

If you're in a dilemma over where to eat lunch or dinner close to the church of Santa Croce, look no further than Baldovino. An informal combination of modern and traditional, the restaurant has been one of Florence's great successes of recent years, if only because of its welcoming owner, Scotsman David Gardner. As a foreign restaurateur, Gardner has managed to satisfy a demanding Florentine clientele by mixing good food – Tuscan classics, plus innovative Neapolitan pizzas plus innovative salads and other non-Italian novelties – with a bright décor, young staff and a convivial, cosmopolitan atmosphere. Booking is strongly advised, especially on a Friday or Saturday. A sister *enoteca* (wine bar) just across the street serves snacks, coffee and wine.

➕ 210 C4 ⊠ Via San Giuseppe 22r ☎ 055 241 773 ❻ Tue–Sun noon–2.30, 7–midnight

Beccofino €–€€

A welcoming atmosphere, good, fairly priced modern Italian food, and a contemporary, if rather plain setting combines comfort with architectural and designer panache (the building was previously a mosque and art gallery). There's also an outside terrace.

➕ 210 C4 ⊠ Piazza degli Scarlatti 1, off Lungarno Guicciardini ☎ 055 290 076 ❻ Tue–Sat 7–11

Enoteca Pinchiorri €€€

An *enoteca* is usually an inexpensive wine bar: not here, although there is plenty of wine – some 80,000 bottles of Italian, French and other vintages, including some of the world's rarest (the cellar is one of the best in Europe). In fact, this is Florence's best and most expensive restaurant. Prices for the refined and elaborate Italian and international food are very high, while the service and surroundings are formal (men should wear a jacket and tie). *The* Florentine gastronomic treat.

➕ 210 C4 ⊠ Via Ghibellina 87 ☎ 055 242 777; www.pinchiorri.it ❻ Thu–Sat 12:30–2, 7:30–10, Tue 7:30–10 pm; closed Aug

Osteria del Caffè Italiano
€€–€€€

This combination of wine bar, restaurant and *trattoria* just west of Santa Croce offers a choice of dining experiences and prices. All three eating areas have the same distinctive medieval Florentine décor – terracotta floors, whitewashed walls and heavy beamed or vaulted ceilings – set in the restored 14th-century Palazzo Salviati. You can come here for a light lunch, a full meal, or a glass of wine and snack at any time of the day. Food is typically Tuscan.

➕ 210 C4 ⊠ Via Isole delle Stinche 11–13r ☎ 055 289 368 ❻ Tue–Sun 12:30–2, 7:30–11

Vivoli €

A Florentine institution that has been in the same hands for three generations. It once held the unofficial title for the best ice cream in Italy and you'll still have to go a long way to find *gelati*, sorbets or frozen yoghurts quite as good. It lies in a side street just west of Piazza Santa Croce off Via Ghibellina.

➕ 210 C4 ✉ Via Isole delle Stinche 7r ☎ 055 2302334 🕐 Closed Mon

SIENA

Le Logge €€

Few Tuscan restaurants are prettier than this former medieval pharmacy just off the Campo. The quality of the innovative food can be hit and miss: when it works, however, it's very good and a book of its recipes has been published.

➕ 210 C4 ✉ Via del Porrione 33 ☎ 0577 48 013 🕐 12:30–2:30, 7:30–10:30; closed Sun and periods in Jun and Nov

PERUGIA

Cantinone €–€€

Come here to enjoy a hearty meal of chicken in white wine or beef with Umbrian truffles. There's an extensive wine list and if you prefer more intimate surroundings there are private dining rooms off the hall. No credit cards.

➕ 211 E2 ✉ Via Ritorta 6 ☎ 075 573 4430 🕐 Wed–Mon 12:30–2:30, 7:30–10:30

ORVIETO

Grotte del Funaro €€

Over a thousand wines are on display in this huge, stone cellar, which has fine views across the Umbrian hills. Expect substantial and traditional meals along the lines of fire-roasted suckling pig or wild boar with truffles on toast.

➕ 211 D2 ✉ Via Ripa Serancia 41 ☎ 0763 343 276 🕐 Tue–Sun noon–3, 7–midnight

SAN GIMIGNANO

Dorandò €€–€€€

This restaurant re-creates recipes from Tuscany's Etruscan and medieval past, which may sound pretentious but the results are usually first rate. The restaurant is small and intimate and enjoys an elegant medieval setting. Prices, though, are high, even by San Gimignano's standards.

➕ 210 C3 ✉ Vicolo dell'Oro 2 ☎ 0577 941 862; www.tin.it/dorando 🕐 12:30–2:30, 7:30–10:30; closed mid-Jan to mid-Feb, Mon in winter

PISA

La Mescita €

A homely, central and inexpensive *trattoria*. Menus change daily to reflect what is available from the Vettovaglie market stalls near by, but always reflect local traditions – dishes might include *pappardelle con fiori di zucca* (pasta strips with courgette flowers), wild fennel and ricotta salad, or *baccalà bollito con i ceci* (boiled salt cod with pulses). The choice of cheese is excellent. The setting is attractive – the vaulted ceilings date from the 15th century – and the atmosphere warm and lively. The only drawbacks are the restaurant's popularity – best to book or arrive early.

➕ 210 B3 ✉ Via Cavalca 2, corner of Piazza delle Vettovaglie ☎ 050 544 294 🕐 12:30–2:30, 7:30–10:30; closed Mon and part of Aug

LUCCA

Buca di Sant'Antonio €€

The Buca lies in a half-hidden alley just off the southwest corner of Piazza San Michele and has long been the best of the city's central restaurants. The service is formal and the cooking is based on Lucchese traditions. Dishes might include *tordelli Lucchesi* (pasta filled with borage, beef, pork and nutmeg); *zuppa di farro* (vegetable soup made with a wheat-like grain); *capretto allo spiedo* (spit-roasted kid goat) and *semifreddo Buccellato*, a mixture of cream and wild berries.

➕ 210 B4 ✉ Via della Cervia 3 ☎ 0583 312 199 🕐 12:30–2:30, 7:30–10:30; closed Sun pm, Mon and a period in Jul

Where to... Shop

When it comes to shopping you'll be spoilt for choice in central Italy, where incomes are high and the sense of style is all-pervading. In this major tourist region shops cater for discerning souvenir-hunters, and there's a strong tradition of artisan and traditional products. You'll find the usual specialities such as fashion, jewellery, leather and lingerie, along with wines and oils, ceramics and pottery.

Florence, capital of Tuscany, is the main centre, but Perugia in Umbria also offers great retail opportunities,

as do Spoleto and Orvieto, albeit on a lesser scale.

Florence's main shopping area lies north of the Arno, with the high-class designer stores lining the Via Tornabuoni, and department stores, such as **Coin** and **La Rinascente**, and mid-range shops in and around the Piazza della Repubblica and along the Via dei Calzauoli.

The city has two permanent street markets: the rambling stalls of **San Lorenzo**, selling everything from leather goods to football shirts, around the church of the same name, and the souvenir-packed **Mercato Nuovo**, west of Piazza della Signoria. Florence's huge **Mercato Centrale**, the daily food market, is also near San Lorenzo.

Florence is renowned for its jeweller's shops, based since 1593 on the **Ponte Vecchio**; gold here is still sold by weight and there are affordable trinkets and coral pieces on sale along with serious rocks.

Across the river are dozens of tiny artisan shops and workshops in the **Oltrarno** district, where you'll find everything from furniture and top-quality antiques to quirky fashion, accessories, marbled-paper stores and print shops.

Siena's shops have less to offer, but there's a good selection of leather and shoe shops and branches of the major fashion chain stores. Good buys here are colourful ceramics, books, paper products, sticky *panforte* – Siena's trademark confection – and *contrade* flags and T-shirts, all found on and near the main shopping street, the **Via di Citta**.

There's more of the same in **San Gimignano**, where the main street is lined with gift shops crammed with pottery, olive-wood bowls and platters and table and bed linen.

If you're in northern Tuscany, well-heeled **Lucca** has excellent shops; it's particularly strong on jewellery and exclusive, low-key fashion.

Moving on to Umbria, **Perugia** attracts the crowds from all over the region. Its main street, the **Corso Vanucci**, is worth a browse for souvenirs, but the serious shopping is down the hill in the modern part of town, around the railway station.

It's the same story in **Spoleto**, where the modern, lower part of town has more on offer, but the historic centre has a lively daily market in the **Piazza di Mercato** and some fashion boutiques and antique stores.

In **Assisi** the accent is on religious souvenirs and ceramics; you'll find a wide range of the latter in **Orvieto** as well. To shop at source for Umbrian pottery head for **Deruta**, where it's made.

Food shopping is excellent all over central Italy; in both Tuscany and Umbria look out for fine wines – which you can often buy straight from the vineyards – olive oil, cheese, honey, cured meats, hams, sausages and cured meats of every description.

Where to...
Be Entertained

For many visitors central Italy's main attraction is its traditional festivals – historic celebrations in towns all over the region.

Topping the list is **Siena**'s famous **Palio**, the most exciting and authentic of all Italy's *festas*. This twice-yearly (2 July and 16 August) bareback horse race takes place around the main *piazza*, the Campo, in honour of the Virgin Mary, and is preceded by weeks of preparation and pageantry; advance planning is essential (www.wilpaliodisiena.com).

Florence celebrates Easter with the **Scoppio del Carro**, when a ceremonial cart stuffed with fireworks is ignited outside the

Duomo, and **Gubbio** welcomes the **Festa dei Ceri** (5 May; www.gubbio.com/ceri), a parade of 6m (20-foot) wooden 'candles' through the streets to the mountain.

Virtually every town and village in the region has its own festival, often dedicated to the local saint. Most feature processions, music and plenty of food and wine. *Sagre* (food festivals), celebrating the local speciality, are common and great fun; you'll see banners announcing them, or ask at the APT.

Music festivals feature throughout the region, with Florence topping the bill. Its major event is the **Maggio Musicale Fiorentino** (May and June), Italy's longest-running music festival, with a good mix of opera, ballet and classical

music. From June to August the **Estate Fiesolana**, a summer music and dance festival, takes place at **Fiesole**, with performances in the Roman amphitheatre (www.estate-fiesolana.it). Umbria stages two major music festivals: **Spoleto**'s **Festival dei Due Mondi** (June to August) and **Perugia**'s jazz fest, **Umbria Jazz** in July and August, while in **Arezzo** Italy rocks to **Arezzo Wave**, a huge July rock festival with up to 150 events.

Florence also has a year-round succession of music, opera and ballet: the **Teatro Comunale** is the main venue. Many smaller centres stage summer music events; ask at the local tourist office and look out for leaflets and posters.

Nightlife throughout central Italy flourishes in the university cities, so head for Florence, Siena and Perugia for funky clubs and live music. In summer the action tends to move to the coast; **Viareggio** in Tuscany is noted for its summer party scene.

Central Italy is a walker's paradise, particularly in early summer before the heat builds and when the country is at its floral best. Strike off along the *strade bianche* (white roads) that thread through the Tuscan countryside or head for the hills of Umbria for superb upland hiking. Autumn is another good time. Some local tourist offices will recommend routes; **San Gimignano** is good in this respect.

Many *agriturismo* establishments offer riding, a great way to see the country; some also have their own tennis courts and swimming pools. You can swim in public pools in most towns of any size, or find a river for a lazy day's relaxation.

For something more strenuous, you could rent a bicycle – ask at local tourist offices about availability. For the more adventurous, hang-gliding is an option; Umbria is a good venue, particularly in the Sibillini mountains, southeast of Perugia.

Southern Italy

Getting Your Bearings

South of Rome is a harsher, more impoverished Italy, where the climate is hotter and drier, the landscape mountainous and arid in places, astonishingly fertile in others, and the sea coast is supremely beautiful. The ancient Greek and Roman civilisations left their mark here as nowhere else, in the ruins of their great cities and shrines.

The south's main city is vibrant Naples, packed with treasures and set on one of the Mediterranean's most beautiful bays. This Bay of Angels is dominated to the south by Vesuvio (Vesuvius), an active volcano that destroyed Pompei and Ercolano, leaving these Roman towns preserved in the midst of their everyday life. South of Vesuvius the Sorrento Peninsula juts west, its sinuous coast scattered with mesmerising villages like Ravello, its offshore island of Capri an idyllic holiday spot for thousands of years. South again is the great Greek temple of Paestum, and there are more reminders of the past at Matera, famous for its cave dwellings, and in the extraordinary conical *trulli* houses round Alberobello. Further south, Lecce is home to some of Italy's most extravagant baroque architecture, and north are the coastal delights and outdoor pleasures of the Gargano, a limestone peninsula where pine trees cling to white rocks above an the sea. There's more stupendous scenery to the north in the Abruzzo, where the wilderness area of the Parco Nazionale d'Abruzzo provides a habitat for chamois, raptors, deer and brown bears.

Above: Pompei's amphitheatre

Previous page: Sorrento

Right: The campanile of Amalfi's Duomo

Dining out in Ravello

Italy's south is a vast, sprawling region that spans virtually a third of the country. Five days should be enough to take in some of the region's great cities, the stunning coast and a little of the spectacular country that's representative of the whole area. Naples and the coast to its south are a must, but you'll have to choose whether to visit one of the national parks or head far into the deep south for fascinating Alberobello and Lecce.

Southern Italy in Five Days

Day One

Morning
Head up Spaccanapoli in **2** **Napoli (Naples)** (➤ 146–147), taking in Santa Chiara and the Duomo (left), before visiting the Museo Archeologico Nazionale.

Afternoon
After lunch go to the Museo e Parco di Capodimonte for superb art and cool, green suroundings, before heading for the Certosa and its great city views.

Evening
Evening is the time for shopping and experiencing the lively downtown *passeggiata* before a typically Neapolitan dinner.

Day Two

Morning and Afternoon
Travel round the Bay to visit the ruins of **3** **Pompei** (fresco, right) and drive up **3** **Vesuvio** (➤ 148–149); en route is **5** **Ercolano** (➤ 152), another intriguing ruin of a Roman city destroyed by a volcanic eruption.

Evening
Settle in for the night at the pretty resort of **Sorrento** (➤ 150).

Day Three

Morning

Set out to drive round the lovely **4 Sorrento Peninsula** (Positano, left, ➤ 150) to **Amalfi** (➤ 151), following a tortuous road that's one of the Mediterranean's most scenic. If you want to visit **12 Capri** (➤ 156), there are regular sailings from Sorrento.

Afternoon and Evening

Spend the afternoon exploring some of the coast's attractive villages, before heading into the hills to spend the night in **6 Ravello** (below, ➤ 152).

Day Four

Morning

An early start will give time to explore the great Greek temple at **7 Paestum** (➤ 153), before cutting east via Potenza to **8 Matera** and its *sassi* (➤ 153).

Afternoon and Evening

Aim to leave Matera by late afternoon, picking up the A14 north to the fringes of the **11 Parco Nazionale del Gargano** (➤ 155), where you can decide whether to explore this beautiful peninsula or head further north to the **1 Parco Nazionale d'Abruzzo** (➤ 144–145). Alternatively, if you're making for **9 Lecce** (➤ 154), head south from Matera via **10 Alberobello** (➤ 154). From Lecce, you can head up to the Gargano if there's time.

Day Five

If you're concentrating on the Gargano spend time exploring some of the interior before heading for the stunning coastline and its fishing villages. If you've chosen to visit the Abruzzo, head for the visitor's centre at Pescasseroli.

Parco Nazionale d'Abruzzo

Having started life as a royal hunting reserve, the Parco Nazionale d'Abruzzo was created in 1923 to protect and preserve the native flora and fauna. It now covers around 44,000ha (108,720 acres) of wilderness in the southern Abruzzo region, and is one of Italy's natural jewels.

The landscape is one of ancient forests of beech and maple, interspersed with ash, hawthorn and hornbeam. The park provides a safe habitat for a variety of wild animals threatened with extinction, including chamois deer, mountain goats, Appenine lynxes, Appenine wolves and the rare brown *marsicano* bear (*Ursus arctos marsicanus*).

In spring and summer the alpine meadows are a riot of colour and you are likely to see golden eagles, goshawks and peregrine falcons circling overhead. This is a great place for birdwatchers – more than 300 species of birds have been spotted in the area. There are also around 1,200 species of plants and trees, including more than 250 types of fungi alone.

Pescasseroli

A good starting point for exploring the park is the visitor centre in the attractive old village of Pescasseroli, west of the park's central point, where a small natural history museum gives an excellent overview of the Abruzzo's habitats and there are facilities for rehabilitating injured animals. You can pick up a map here with details of the 150 walks and trails in the park, as well as information about *rifugi* (refuge huts), where you can spend the night. Horse-riding and mountain-biking are further options.

The village of Scanno in the heart of the Abruzzo region

Around the Park

While you are here take time to visit some of the little towns and villages in and around the park. **Scanno**, to the east, is a perfectly preserved medieval hill town. **Opi**, southwest of Pescasseroli, has a chamois museum. **Sulmona**, northeast of Scanno, is known for its

Chamois

The chamois is a small wild antelope with short, vertical horns, native to the mountains of southern Europe. A herd of around 500 lives in the park. In the past its skin was used for soft, pliable leather, but modern 'shammy' leather is more usually made from specially treated goatskin or sheepskin.

PARCO NAZIONALE D'ABRUZZO: INSIDE INFO

Top tips The village of **Civitella Alfedena**, southeast of Pescasseroli, has a wolf museum, the **Centro Lupo**, where you can find out more about the Appenine wolves that inhabit the national park.
• The philosopher, writer and politician **Benedetto Croce** was born in Pescasseroli (1866–1952); **you can visit his birthplace**, Palazzo Sipari, in the *piazza* that now bears his name.

---

confetti – sugared almonds – and as the birthplace of Roman poet Ovid (43 BC–AD 17).

The scrub-covered lower slopes of the national park

TAKING A BREAK
Try **Hotel Ristorante Il Bucaneve**, Viale Cabinovia in Pescasseroli or **Lo Sgabello**, Via Pescatori 45 in Scanno for local and national dishes.

✚ 214 B4
Tourist information
✉ Via Santa Lucia 6, Pescasseroli ☎ 0863 910461; www.abruzzoturismo.it ⏱ Daily 9–1, 4–7, Easter–Sep
🚉 Avezzano, then bus to Pescasseroli

Natural History Museum
✚ 214 B4 ✉ Park Visitor Centre, Viale Cabinovia, Pescasseroli ☎ 0863 91 13221 ⏱ Tue–Sun 10–1, 3–7
💶 Expensive

Centro Lupo
✚ 214 C4 ✉ Via Santa Lucia, Civitella Alfedena ☎ 0864 890141 ⏱ Daily 10–1, 3–7, Apr–Sep; 10–1, 2–5 rest of year 💶 Moderate

The park is the haunt of the golden eagle

② Napoli (Naples)

For decades visitors avoided Naples, aware of its high crime rate. Since the 1990s, however, much has been done to reopen this vibrant city to the world, and now it is firmly back on the tourist map as the home of the pizza and of one of the best Roman archaeological collections in the world.

The untidy sprawl at the heart of this city is one of its authentic charms. The tourist office is on Piazza Gesù Nuovo, at one end of the main thoroughfare, Spaccanapoli. Lying roughly parallel to the harbour, and largely pedestrianised, this long street slices through the old centre and is lined with shops, churches, squares, bars and restaurants. The archaeological museum and the Duomo lie north of here, and the hilltop complex of Certosa di San Martino, surrounded by terraced gardens, to the southwest.

Just east of the tourist office is **Santa Chiara**, a restored 14th-century Gothic church with tranquil cloister gardens remodelled by Domenico Vaccaro in 1742.

Majolica-tiled columns in the church of Santa Chiara

Museo Archeologico Nazionale

Though chaotic, old fashioned and poorly labelled, the archaeological museum contains some of the world's best preserved Roman artefacts. There are vivid wall paintings, the famous *Cave Canem* ('beware of the dog') mosaic, glass and silverware, bizarre erotica and statues, all excavated from the immediate area and the cities of Pompei and Ercolano (► 148–149 and 152). Treasures from the Farnese collection, brought from Rome, include superb sculptures of a bull and the hero Hercules.

Museo e Parco di Capodimonte

For a complete contrast to the Roman remains, visit this 18th-century palace, built by Charles III to house his mother Elizabeth Farnese's fabulous collection of fine art and porcelain – including many pieces made by the local Capodimonte factory. The paintings include major works by Renaissance artists, with portraits by Titian and Raphael, Pieter Brueghel's *Parable of the Blind* (1568) and Caravaggio's *Flagellation of Christ* (1609).

Below: Shopping in Via Tribunali's marketplace

TAKING A BREAK

You are spoiled for choice in Naples, where pizza was invented – the **Pizzeria di Matteo** at Via Tribunali 94 is a good place to start.

Above: Boats at rest in Santa Lucia harbour

🚹 214 C2
Tourist information
✉ Piazza Gesù Nuovo ☎ 081 5523328; www.inaples.it
🕐 Mon–Sat 9–7:30, Sun 9–2
🚉 Napoli Centrale

Museo Archeologico Nazionale
✉ Piazza Museu 19, 80135 ☎ 081 440166 🕐 Wed–Mon 9–7
💰 Expensive

Museo e Parco di Capodimonte
✉ Via Miano 1, 80132 ☎ 081 749 9111 🕐 Tue–Sun 8:30–7:30
💰 Expensive

NAPOLI (NAPLES): INSIDE INFO

Top tips Petty theft can still be a problem, **so be careful with your belongings**, don't carry more cash than you need and avoid backstreets.
• **Naples' traffic is chaotic** and moves at a very slow pace; if you are driving get a detailed map and don't take short cuts. Better still, use public transport.
• If you're bewildered by the choice in a *pizzeria*, **opt for the classic Pizza Marguerita**, flavoured with tomato and cheese, and eaten *a libretto*, or folded in half.

Hidden gem Naples has a second stunning museum dedicated to porcelain – the **Museo Nazionale della Ceramica**, next to the beautiful setting of the Villa La Floridiana, at Via Cimarosa 77 (open Tue–Sun 9:30–12:30, moderate).

③ Pompei and Vesuvio

Together, the live volcano and the extensive remains of the Roman city, which it destroyed at a stroke on 24 August AD 79, form one of the greatest sights of southern Italy.

Vesuvio

The unmistakable bulk of Vesuvio, or Mount Vesuvius, looms inland to the east of Naples. It has erupted several times over the years, overwhelming the settlements on its lower slopes – most recently in 1944. While scientists monitor the mountain and try to predict the next blowout, you can walk up the steep, broad, cinder-strewn track to the crater's rim and look in, but the best views are behind you: on a clear day you can see for miles.

Detail of a fresco in Pompei

Pompei

Pompei is remarkable for the story of its destruction and preservation, and for the details of everyday life which it has revealed over the course of 250 years of excavation. You can walk along the streets and peer into the houses and shops, exploring the details of murals, bath-houses and shop signs. Smaller finds have been removed to the Museo Archeologico Nazionale in Naples (▶ 146), but here you can see the squares and temples, private villas and public buildings, markets and

A section of the excavated ruins

Eyewitness Report
Thanks to a letter written by Pliny the Younger (*c*62–113), we have a first-hand account of the eruption. Pliny's uncle, the great scholar Pliny the Elder, was less fortunate – in his curiosity he ventured too near the city and was killed by poisonous fumes at Castellamare.

The Bay of Naples, with Vesuvio in the background

theatres. Highlights include the frescoed House of the Vettii, the Villa dei Misteri, the colonnades of the Foro and the extensive House of the Faun, with its restored gardens.

Life ended here in AD 79, when Vesuvio spewed out a cloud of poisonous volcanic gas, followed by a blanket of ash. Many citizens died where they stood; plaster casts of the spaces left in the ash layer by their long-since decomposed bodies can be seen, some raising their arms against the onslaught.

TAKING A BREAK

There is a **bar/restaurant** with self-service at the site, and numerous restaurants just outside.

🚋 214 C2
✉ Scavi di Pompei, Villa dei Misteri 2 ☎ 081 857 5111; www.pompeiisites.org 🕓 Daily 8:30–7:30 (last entrance 6), Apr–Oct; 8:30–3 (last entrance 1:30), Nov–Mar 🚆 Circumvesuviana to Pompei Scavi Villa dei Misteri 💶 Expensive

Tourist Information
✉ Via Sacra 1, Pompei ☎ 081 850 7255 🕓 Mon–Fri 9–7, Sat 9–2, Apr–Oct; Mon–Fri 9–9:30, Sat 9–2, rest of year

---

POMPEI AND VESUVIO: INSIDE INFO

Top tips The site at Pompei is huge, so **get a detailed map or guide** and be prepared for a lot of walking. The Via dell'Abbondanza is the main thoroughfare, running west from the Porta Marina (harbour entrance to the city), via the Foro (main public square) and past the Terme (public baths) to the Porta di Sarno and the Anfiteatro (amphitheatre). The entrance to the site is near the eastern end.

• When exploring either of these sites in the heat of the day, **take a bottle of drinking water** with you.

Hidden gem You'll see the *Cave Canem* ('beware of the dog') image reproduced on souvenirs all around this area. The original was a mosaic at the threshold of the House of the Tragic Poet, off Via di Nola.

4 Sorrento Peninsula and Amalfi Coast

Sorrento

Boats busily ply to and from Sorrento's harbours – fishing craft from the old harbour (Marina Grande) to the south, and ferries to Ischia, Capri and Naples from the more central Marina Piccola. This is a well-established and laid-back tourist stopover, with a great choice of grand hotels and interesting restaurants. Relax with a cappuccino in one of the cafés on Piazza Tasso, the main square, or stroll through the narrow streets full of shops selling ceramics, marquetry (pictures created with inlaid wood) and other local souvenirs. Just about every outlet sells the vivid yellow lemon liqueur, *limoncello*.

Amalfi Coast

This thrilling 80km (50-mile) stretch of coast between Positano and Salerno is a

Above: Looking down over the town and coastline of Sorrento

Left: Detail of a fountain in the heart of Amalfi

SORRENTO PENINSULA AND AMALFI COAST: INSIDE INFO

Top tips Driving on the narrow and winding Amalfi coast road requires constant vigilance, with little chance to admire the views. For a more relaxing experience **consider a coach tour or the public SITA bus**, which has the added advantage of a viewpoint above the traffic.

• Escape the summer crowds in Amalfi by taking the **popular walk through the Valle dei Mulini**, a narrow ravine studded with old watermills, once part of the town's famous paper-making industry. For details, ask at the tourist office.

• **Two of the best beaches** along the Amalfi coast are found at the village of Cetara, east of Amalfi.

Hidden gem The **Chiostro del Paradiso** (Paradise Cloister), beside the Duomo, was designed as the last resting place of Amalfitan aristocracy, and you can find peace and quiet amid its palm trees and pointed arches.

highlight of any visit to southern Italy. A zig-zag road along jagged cliffs links vertiginous villages that seem to tumble into the azure sea – a sleepy confusion of pastel-painted houses with red-tiled roofs and steeply terraced fields, overflowing with a bounty of vines, olives and citrus fruits. Highlights include picturesque **Positano**, a favourite haunt of artists; **Amalfi**, with the extraordinary Moorish black-and-white frontage to its Duomo dating from the 12th century; and lovely **Ravello** (➤ 152).

TAKING A BREAK

For dining with a difference in Sorrento, try **La Favorita-O' Parrucchiano**, a restaurant among the tropical foliage of a 19th-century greenhouse. *Sorrentine peproni ripieni* (stuffed peppers) is a local speciality (Corso Italia 71, tel: 081 8781321).

Positano's houses cling precariously to the hillside

A Doll's House

In an unlikely juxtaposition of northern temperament and southern climes, Norwegian playwright Henrik Ibsen (1828–1906) wrote one of his most famous plays, *A Doll's House* (1879), while staying at the Luna Convento hotel, a converted 13th-century Franciscan monastery in Amalfi.

➕ 214 C2
Tourist information
✉ Corso Roma 19, Amalfi ☎ 089 871107; www.sorrentoweb.it 🕐 Mon–Sat 8:30–1:30, 3:30–7:30, Jul–Oct; Mon–Sat 3:30–5, Nov–Jun 🚃 Sorrento: Circumvesuviana light railway from Naples to Sorrento

At Your Leisure

5 Ercolano (Herculaneum)

When Vesuvio erupted in AD 79, smothering Pompei to the south in burning ash, it swamped this coastal town to the west in a river of mud. All Pompei's wooden structures were burned but Ercolano survived rather better, and houses up to two storeys high remain on the site, notably along Cardus IV street. In the Villa dei Papiri 1,700 Greek and Roman papyrus documents were preserved; they can now be seen in the Museo Archeologico Nazionale in Naples (► 146). Ercolano's attractive location above the bay and the wealth apparent in the wall paintings and mosaics of its houses suggests it was an up-market small town. A highlight is the wine merchant's **Casa di Nettuno**, with its shelves of wine jars and superb mosaic of Neptune and Amphitrite. Excellent rail connections to Sorrento and Naples make this the better site to explore if you have limited time – allow half a day.

🚲 214 C2 ✉ Ercolano Scavi, Ercolano
☎ 081 777 7008 🕐 Daily 8:30–7:30, summer; 8:30–5, rest of year
🚇 Circumvesuviana railway connects Ercolano to Sorrento and Naples
💰 Expensive

The garden terrace of Villa Rufolo, Ravello

6 Ravello

The peaceful village of Ravello, high above the sea, has cafés around a wide medieval main square and two notable villas to explore. The 13th-century **Villa Rufolo** is the more famous, with ornate Moorish-influenced architecture and a beautiful terraced garden overlooking the roofs of Ravello to the sea. Giovanni Boccaccio, author of the *Decameron*, was inspired here in the 14th century, and Richard Wagner composed part of his opera *Parsifal* while staying here in 1877, an event celebrated with an annual open-air Wagner festival. **Villa Cimbrone** dates from the 18th century but incorporates much older carved stone fragments. Its lush gardens, with their spectacular belvedere, were designed by Edmund Denison (1816–1905), an English lawyer whose other claim to fame was the rebuilding of Big Ben, the clock on London's Houses of Parliament.

Tourist Office
🚲 215 D2 ✉ Piazza del Duomo 10
☎ 089 857096 🕐 Daily 9–7

Villa Rufolo
✉ Piazza del Vescovado ☎ 089 857657 🕐 Daily 9–8, May–Sep; 9–sunset, rest of year 💰 Moderate

Villa Cimbrone
✉ Via Santa Chiara ⏱ Daily 9–8,
May–Sep; 9–sunset, rest of year
💶 Moderate

7 Paestum

Set on the coast 35km (22 miles) south of Salerno, Paestum was a Greek city taken by the Romans in the 3rd century BC. In flower-filled meadows are the substantial remains of three temples, effectively forgotten until their rediscovery in the 18th century. The biggest was dedicated to the sea-god Poseidon (Neptune to the Romans); the whole settlement was named Poseidonia in his honour. You can learn more about this, and admire the exquisite 480 BC wall painting from the Tomba del Tuffatore (Diver's Tomb), at the **Museo Nazionale Archeologico**.

The superb Doric Temple of Neptune at
Paestum (formerly Poseidonia)

Tourist Office
➕ 215 D1 ✉ Via Magna Grecia 887
☎ 0828 811016

Ancient site
⏱ Daily 9–1 hour before sunset
🚉 Paestum (1km/0.6 mile from site)
💶 Expensive

Museo Nazionale Archeologico
☎ 0828 811023 ⏱ Daily 9–7; closed
1st, 3rd Mon of month 💶 Expensive

Above: Matera's extraordinary *sassi*
(cave dwellings)

8 Matera

People have been living in houses (*sassi*) scraped out of the limestone ravines at Matera for around 7,000 years. The best way to approach this UNESCO World Heritage Site is via the specially built **strada panoramica** (scenic route), which gives views over the two old town areas of Sassa Caveoso to the southeast and Barisano to the northwest. As well as houses there are some 120 churches (*chiesi rupestri*) built into the rock, including San Pietro Caveoso and Santa Maria de Idris, both adorned with 14th-century rock paintings. As residents have moved to the comforts of the new town, some houses have become chic apartments, but until the latter half of the 20th century Matera was a very dark place to live, notorious for the severe poverty of its peasant dwellers and rife with disease.

Tourist Office
➕ 216 C4 ✉ Via de Viti de Marco 9
☎ 0835 331983 🚉 Matera

9 Lecce

There's an appealing light-hearted-
ness about the baroque decoration
of the buildings in this historic town.
Churches and *palazzi* built in the
local pale golden stone are encrusted
with carvings – exuberant swags of
flowers and foliage, cherubs and
mythical creatures, and stylised
columns and curlicues. All this dates
from the 16th and 17th centuries, a
period of prosperity when the town
was under Spanish rule. Bankers and
merchants built splendid mansions
along the Via Palmieri and Via
Libertini, along with churches galore.
The architect chiefly associated with
this boom is Giuseppe Zimbalo, and
his masterpiece is generally considered to be the façade of the **Basilica
di Santa Croce** (1646), on Via
Umberto I, with its ornate pediment
and deeply set rose window. The
Chiesa del Rosario (Rosary
Church), on Via Giuseppe Libertini,
was his final and most elaborate
contribution (1691). Zimbalo was
also responsible for the rebuilt
cathedral on the central square,
Piazza del Duomo (1659–70).

Elsewhere around the town you'll
find relics of its earlier inhabitants,
notably the Roman amphitheatre,
which dates back to the first
century AD.

Lecce is also known for its local
cuisine, so look out for lamb and
baby goat (*capretto*) dishes on the
menu, accompanied by wines such as
Leverano, Alezio and Copertino.

Tourist Office
🗺 217 F3 ✉ Corso Vittorio

Lecce's Roman amphitheatre

Emanuele 24 ☎ 08324 8092;
www.pugliaturismo.it ⏰ Mon–Fri
9–1, 4–7, Sat 9–1

**One of Alberobello's mysterious *trulli*, with
its distinctive conical-shaped roof**

10 Alberobello

One of the strangest and most
delightful sights of southern Italy is
Alberobello, a village of *trulli* –
hundreds of little round houses with
conical roofs, made of neatly laid
slabs of limestone (*chiancarelle*),
apparently without the use of mortar.
There's a fairytale quality to the
place, which dates back mainly to
the 18th century. The reason for the
distinctive design of its houses is
unknown, but similar dwellings are
found in parts of Syria. Most of
Alberobello's buildings are white-
washed, and some have mysterious

hieroglyphic symbols painted on their roofs. Several now contain exclusive hotels and restaurants, art galleries, craft shops and souvenir outlets, and there's a *trullo* church, Sant'Antonio, which dates to 1926. An unusual 19th-century two-storey house, the Trullo Sovrano (Sovereign Trullo), on Piazza Sacramento, is preserved as a museum. Other *trulli* in a more rustic setting can be seen along the road to Martina Franca.

Tourist Office

🗺 217 D4 ✉ Piazza Sacramento 19
☎ 080 432 6030; www.alberobellon-line.it 🚇 Alberobello

Trullo Sovrano

✉ Piazza Sacramento 🕐 Daily 10–8 summer; 10–5 winter 💰 Inexpensive; www.trullosovrano.org

🄫 Parco Nazionale del Gargano

Designated in 1995, this national park covers most of the densely wooded area known as the spur of Italy's boot (*sperone d'Italia*). The peninsula juts 65km (40 miles) into the Adriatic Sea, and is approximately 45km (28 miles) at its widest point, so it is not difficult to explore in a day. Rocky cliffs, sandy beaches and whitewashed resort villages are the main appeal of the coastal fringe, while the ancient and varied woodland of the interior offers an escape from the heat. Find out about opportunities for walking and other activities at the Corpo Forestale visitor centre at **Vico**.

The old walled fishing village of **Péschici**, on the northern tip, has narrow, winding streets, sandy bays that are good for swimming, and access to the offshore **Isole de Tremiti** island group and inland to the **Foresta Umbra**, a superb area of beech, maple, hornbeam, lime and birch woodland. To the west of Péschici, the lagoons of **Varano** and **Lesina** are good places for bird-watching.

There are two notable pilgrimage sites on the peninsula. **San Giovanni Rotondo** was home to the 20th-century miracle worker Padre Pio da Petralcino, and the 13th-century church in **Monte Sant'Angelo**, Santuario di San Michele, celebrates visions of St Michael witnessed in a cave here at the end of the 5th century and repeated in the 8th century.

Tourist Office

🗺 215 F4 ✉ Via San Antonio Abate 121, Monte Sant'Angelo ☎ 084 568911;
www.parks.it/parco.nazionale.gargano/
🕐 Tue and Thu 9:30–12:30, 3–6
🚇 Péschici

Aerial view over the heavily farmed tableland of the Gargano Peninsula

Further Afield

🔢 Capri

The first visitors to leave their mark on this beautiful rock at the mouth of the Gulf of Naples were the Romans. Caesar Augustus liked it so much that he swapped it for wealthier Ischia in around 29 BC, and Tiberius moved his whole court here, charmed by its lush, mountainous landscape and fabulous views back to the mainland. Today you can get here by ferry or hydrofoil on a day trip from Naples or Sorrento, or stay in one of the hotels or rented villas – but remember that jet-set locations command jet-set prices.

From Marina Grande a funicular takes you up from the harbour to the main centre, Capri town. Designer shops and restaurants surround the Piazzetta square, overlooked by the Moorish Santo Stefano church. A switchback road leads halfway up Monte Solaro to the quieter, white-washed village of **Anacapri**, where the main attraction – apart from the views – is the **Villa San Michele**, former home of Swedish physician Axel Munthe (1857–1949), who wrote a best-selling book about the place. From the nearby Piazza della Vittoria a chairlift takes you up the mountain (580m/1,900 feet). A hike back down through the Anginola woods brings you past the ruins of a villa which belonged to Compton Mackenzie, author of *Whisky Galore*.

Other writers who fell in love with the island include D H Lawrence, Graham Greene and Maxim Gorky.

Boat trips to the **Grotta Azzurra** (Blue Grotto), a low sea cave which glows turquoise in the sunlight, leave regularly from the Marina Grande.

Tourist Office

🔲 214 C1 ✉ Piazza Umberto 1, Capri

☎ 081 837 0686; www.capri.it

🕐 Daily 8:30–8:30, Easter–Oct; 9–1, 3:30–6:30, Nov–Easter

✉ Via G Orlando 59, Anacapri ☎ 081 837 1524 🕐 Mon–Sat 9–3 🚢 Regular ferry or hydrofoil services from Sorrento and Naples on the mainland

Looking over Capri towards the jagged rocks called the Faraglioni

Villa San Michele

✉ Off Piazza della Vittoria, Anacapri

☎ 081 837 1401; www.sanmichele.org

🕐 Daily 9–6, Apr–Oct; 10:30–3:30, Nov–Mar 💷 Moderate

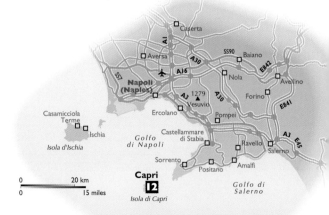

Where to... Stay

Prices
Expect to pay per double room, per night
€ under €100 **€€** €100–€180 **€€€** over €180

PARCO NAZIONALE D'ABRUZZO

Pagnani €€
This charming, modern hotel is based in the mountains near Pescasseroli. It has 24 sunny and spacious rooms, many with balconies. Facilities include televisions, parking and a restaurant.

214 B4 ✉ Viale Cabinovia, Pescasseroli ☎ 0863 912 866; www.hotelpagnani.it

NAPOLI (NAPLES)

Europa €–€€
There's a cheeriness about this 19th-century building near the old centre of Naples, enhanced by paintings in the bedrooms and the pot plants and frescoes that adorn the common areas – which include a library. Among the facilities are televisions, phones, safe deposit boxes and minibars. You can eat in the attached restaurant, La Grande Abbuffata.

214 C2 ✉ Corso Meridionale 14 ☎ 081 267 511; www.grandhoteleuropa.com

Grand Hotel Vesuvio €€€
Since the Grand opened its doors in 1882 many a star has taken advantage of its luxury service, including Humphrey Bogart, Errol Flynn and Grace Kelly. The bedrooms are furnished with antiques and the star treatment includes a limousine service and a boat for guests. There are fine views from Caruso, the rooftop restaurant, and the Echia Club's health and beauty facilities are available to guests.

214 C2 ✉ Via Partenope 45 ☎ 081 764 0044; www.vesuvio.it

Hotel il Convento €–€€
Refurbishment has added to the discreet charms of this 17th-century palace adjacent to the Santa Maria Francesca convent, and period furniture rounds off the classy image. All modern conveniences are provided in the guest rooms (TV, minibar and other facilities) and breakfast is served in a small roof garden.

214 C2 ✉ Via Speranzella 137/A ☎ 081 403 977; fax: 081 400 332; www.hotelilconvento.com

Miramare €€–€€€
Before its conversion into a modern and comfortable hotel this was the US consulate and, in the 19th century, an aristocratic villa. It's now idiosyncratically decorated with paintings and art nouveau furnishings, and guests can enjoy satellite TV, free video rental, tea and coffee and a minibar in their rooms, as well as the wonderful views from the terrace.

214 C2 ✉ Via Nazario Sauro 24 ☎ 081 764 7589; fax: 081 764 0775; www.hotelmiramare.com

POMPEI

Amleto €
From the roof garden and solarium of this bright and peaceful hotel you can gaze out over the ruins of Pompei and Ercolano, and the volcano that destroyed them both. Art and mosaics decorate the guest rooms and the whole building is given an air of serenity with its marble floors and low-key lighting. There is free parking.

214 C2 ✉ Via Bartolo Longo10 ☎ 081 863 1004; www.hotelamleto.it Circumvesuviana train to Pompei

AMALFI

Lidomare €-€€

The Camera family run this hotel near the main square. The 14th-century building has an airy atmosphere, with tiled floors, modern and period furnishings. Rooms have TVs, safe deposits and phones, and you can have your breakfast on a terrace with great views.

🛏 215 D2 ⬛ Largo Piccolomini 9
🕿 089 871 332; www.lidomare.it

POSITANO

Villa Franca €€€

Relaxed elegance is the pervading impression of this well-equipped hotel, where the common areas are given a touch of style with ferns, urns and plinths. The guest rooms are similarly tasteful, and you can enjoy Neapolitan dishes on the terrace or a swim in the pool, both of which overlook the beach. There's a health club and gym plus a solarium available to guests.

🛏 214 C2 ⬛ Viale Pasitea 318
🕿 089 875 655; fax: 089 875 735;
www.villafrancahotel.it

SORRENTO

Imperial Tramontano €€€

Antiques, period furnishings and the greenery of the winter garden all contribute to the air of class in this 16th-century *palazzo*, which was turned into a hotel in 1812. Royals and literati (Lord Byron, Shelley and Goethe to name a few) have stayed here and present-day guests can enjoy terrific views (from some rooms) and access to a private beach and pool.

🛏 214 C2 ⬛ Via Vittorio Veneto 1
🕿 081 878 1940; fax: 081 807 2344;
www.tramontana.com ⊗ Closed
Jan–Feb

ALBEROBELLO

Dei Trulli €€

For a truly unique experience book a room in this luxury hotel occupy-ing a cluster of *trulli*, Alberobello's ancient conical dwellings. Beyond the exterior the hotel is tranquil and comfortable, with gardens, and simply decorated rooms that are available only on a half-board basis.

🛏 217 D4 ⬛ Via Cadore 32 🕿 080
432 3555; fax 080 432 3560;
www.hoteldeitrulli.it

GARGANO PENINSULA

Hotel dei Mandorli €

There's a slightly dated feel to the furnishings in this comfortable hotel, but it makes the perfect place to stay if you plan to explore the Gargano National Park, San Giovanni Rotondo or Sant'Angelo. A *pizzeria* serves dishes cooked in a wood-burning oven and you can organise several outdoor activities from the hotel.

🛏 215 F4 ⬛ Località Montagna,
Ruggiano 🕿 and fax: 0884 530
400/1; www.hoteldeimandorli.it
🚍 Manfredonia then local bus to
Ruggiano

CAPRI

Belsito €-€€

You can soak up the wonderful island views from the Belsito's terrace restaurant while tucking in to a Neapolitan meal. There are balcony views from some rooms too, and all are cheerfully decorated. The hotel is just a brief walk away from the Piazzetta di Capri and Arco Naturale.

🛏 214 C1 ⬛ Via Matermania 11
🕿 081 837 0969; fax: 081 837 6622;
www.hotelbelsito.com

Grand Hotel Quisisana €€€

You don't get much grander than this. The emphasis on luxury and efficient service. Rooms are decorated in a mix of modern and period style, and have extensive views. Facilities include a spa and the island's best restaurant, Quisi. Standards are high; so are the prices.

🛏 214 C1 ⬛ Via Camerelle 2
🕿 081 837 0788; www.quisi.com
⊗ Closed Nov to mid-Mar

Where to...
Eat and Drink

Prices

Expect to pay for a three-course meal for one, excluding drinks and service

€ under €20 €€ €20–€40 €€€ over €40

NAPOLI (NAPLES)

Dora €€€

Seafood and showbiz are the unusual mix here; after finishing your meal you may well be entertained by the staff. The restaurant's signature dish is *pasta alla Dora* (pasta with a tomato sauce and shellfish), and there's a wide range of grilled and baked fish recipes as well as a good quality selection of wines.

➕ 214 C2 ☒ Via Ferdinando Palasciano 30 ☎ 081 680 519 ⏰ Mon–Sat noon–3, 8–midnight; closed 3 weeks in Aug

Gran Caffè la Caffetteria €

Sit indoors in the elegant tea room or outside where you can watch the comings and goings of the Piazza dei Martiri. Neapolitan pastries are served here, including the delicious *baba* cakes and crispy *sfogliatelle* pastry.

➕ 214 C2 ☒ Piazza dei Martiri 26 ☎ 081 764 4243 ⏰ Sat–Sun 7.30 am –midnight, Mon–Fri 7.30 am–10 pm

Trattoria San Ferdinando €–€€

Local wines are on offer at this friendly *trattoria* near the San Carlo theatre, as well as a wide choice of desserts. But first sample the tasty

savouries – good choices are the peppers and buffalo cheese and penne pasta with courgettes.

➕ 214 C2 ☒ Via Nardones 117 ☎ 081 421 964 ⏰ Mon and Sat 12–3, Wed–Fri 12–3, 8–11:30

POMPEI

Ristorante-Pizzeria Carlo Alberto €–€€

Pasta, pizzas and seafood are the staples at this little restaurant near the site of the ruined Roman town. There's a choice of delicious desserts and you can finish off the proceedings with a *grappa del vesuvio*, produced from the Lacrima Christi grape grown on Vesuvio.

➕ 214 C2 ☒ Via Carlo Alberto 15 ☎ 081 863 3231 ⏰ Daily 12–3, 7–11:30

President €–€€

The daily catch is traditionally cooked at this excellent seafood eatery, and served up as wonderful first and second courses – try the

calamari served in a subtle sauce. There's a very good choice of wines.

➕ 214 C2 ☒ Piazza Schettino 12 ☎ 081 850 7245; www.ristorante president.it ⏰ Tue–Sun 12:30–3, 7–midnight; closed 10–25 Aug

SORRENTO

Buco €€

Traditional fish and meat dishes are given a modern twist at this superb restaurant housed in a former monastery in the heart of Sorrento. Enjoy one of the good wines on offer with a *fusilli al ragù Genovese* (pasta in lamb sauce) or mullet on a bed of orange slices and *pecorino* cheese, and round it off with one of the mouth-watering desserts.

➕ 214 C2 ☒ Rampa Seconda Marina Piccola 5 ☎ 081 878 2354; www.ilbucoristorante.it ⏰ Thu–Tue 12:30–2:45, 7–11; closed Jan

Caruso €€–€€€

Enrico Caruso, the world-famous tenor, is the star of the show here –

not only in the restaurant's name but also in its collection of photographs and memorabilia, not to mention the records of the great man's voice. An extensive choice of vegetable and seafood dishes includes a delicious seafood platter and the daily catch, and there are some inventive and tasty desserts.

⊞ 214 C2 ⊠ Via Sant'Antonino 12 ☎ 081 807 3156; www.restorante-museocaruso.com ⊙ Daily 12–3.30, 7:30–11:30; closed Mon in Jan

AMALFI

Tari €–€€

Fresh ingredients and traditional techniques combine to provide superb seafood, pasta and pizza dishes at this informal, family-run restaurant. There's a wide-ranging wine list, which naturally includes a selection of locally produced tipples.

⊞ 215 D2 ⊠ Via Capuano ☎ 089 871 832 ⊙ Wed–Mon 11:30–3, 7–11:30; closed Nov

there are also plenty of meat options. The local wines are delicious and leave some room for the sublime desserts.

⊞ 217 F3 ⊠ Via Idomeneo 14 ☎ 0832 332 383 ⊙ Tue–Sun 12:30–3:30, 8–11

GARGANO PENINSULA

Medievo €–€€

Local recipes are the inspiration for the terrific food served in this Monte Sant'Angelo establishment, using *salumi* and cured meats and accompanied by a good wine from the select list. The regional speciality, *orecchiette pasta*, is served in a lamb sauce, and desserts include an unforgettable concoction of dried figs with rum-soaked almonds.

⊞ 215 F4 ⊠ Via Castello 21, 71013 Monte Sant'Angelo ☎ 0884 565 356; www.ristorantemedievo.it ⊙ Daily 12:30–3:30, 8–10, Aug–Sep; Tue–Sun 12:30–3:30, 8–10, Oct–Jul; closed 2 weeks in Nov

MATERA

Da Mario €–€€

Locals crowd into this brick vault, which was once part of a *palazzo* and which now houses an unpretentious bar and restaurant. For prices at the lower end of the scale you can enjoy regional dishes such as *strascinate con rape* (turnip tops with home-made pasta) and *orecchiete con funghi* (pasta 'ears' with wild mushrooms).

⊞ 216 C4 ⊠ Via XX Settembre 14 ☎ 0835 336 491; www.ristorantedamario.net ⊙ Mon–Sat 2–3, 8–midnight; closed 10–17 Aug

LECCE

Picton €–€€

Traditional regional food is spiced up with new inventions at this fine restaurant in Lecce's baroque centre. Seafood is a predominant feature – try the potato gnocchi with swordfish for starters – but

CAPRI

Da Gemma €€–€€€

This eatery is part of Capri's glamorous history, having attracted a glittering society crowd since the 1930s. It still serves up unbeatable *pizza napoletana*, fisherman's risotto, *ravioli alla caprese* and *maccheroncelli* with potatoes and mussels. The desserts and the wine are superb.

⊞ 214 C1 ⊠ Via Madre Serafina 6 ☎ 081 837 0461; www.dagemma.com ⊙ Daily noon–3.30, 7–midnight; closed 3 weeks in Jan

Da Tonino €–€€

Wine buffs should head to this restaurant near the Arco Naturale to examine the vast list of regional and international labels. The food is traditional southern, with highlights including the *millefoglie d'alici* (pastry with anchovies) and quail with chestnuts.

⊞ 214 C1 ⊠ Via Dentecalla 12 ☎ 081 837 6718 ⊙ Daily 12:30–2.30, 7–10.30; closed 6 Jan–15 Mar

Where to...
Shop

South of Naples, you're in Italy's Mezzogiorno region, traditionally – and currently – the poorest part of the country, where the consumer boom has yet to hit. Naples itself is the place to shop if you're in the spending mood, and the villages and resorts of the Sorrento Peninsula are also good trawling grounds. Other towns worth a visit include Bari and Lecce.

Naples' chic, high-fashion stores lie in the Santa Lucia area, particularly on Via Chiaia and, just north, along the Via Toledo, where you'll find the department stores and fashion chains. Jewellery, antiques and artwork are good buys for serious shoppers, and even budget-conscious purchasers can pick up a cameo brooch or a piece of coral jewellery at prices that won't break the bank.

Look out also for the miniature figurines – shepherds, angels, Three Kings and the Holy Family – which are made for presepi (Christmas cribs), a tradition that goes back 600 years.

It's worth taking in the tiny specialist shops in the Spaccanapoli area, where there are bright ceramics and pottery and outlets for the traditional Christmas crib figures, many of which make lovely ornaments. Naples' markets are a joy, with each neighbourhood having its own street market. To sample the best head for Pignasecca, the Mercato di Sant'Antonio, both food markets, or the dazzling and sweet-scented flower market, the Mercato dei Fiori, at Castel Nuovo. You might want to check out the museum shops in Naples and at Pompei, where good reproductions of Roman artefacts and excellent art books are on sale.

Heading south from Naples, the best of the region's shopping is found in the tiny villages of the Sorrento Peninsula and the Amalfi coast, where chic boutiques sell eye-catching beachwear and cool and elegant resort and evening wear.

There's a wealth of bright ceramics on sale all down this coast – look for the huge serving platters and decorative stands of pottery lemons and oranges.

Amalfi, Sorrento and the island of Capri are noted for limoncello, a lemon-based liqueur that makes a good souvenir. It's great mixed with champagne or prosecco, or as an after-dinner digestivo. Local wines, grown on the rich volcanic soil of Vesuvius, are excellent, and many of the villages have a good enoteca, where you can sample before you buy.

In much of the rest of southern Italy, shopping lacks the range and style of the north. To dismiss it out of hand would be unfair, however; enterprising locals are increasingly experimenting with out-of-the-ordinary shops, and the situation is improving all the time. For clothing, high-class leather and general shopping it's best to stick to the Naples area, but in places like the Gargano Peninsula, Alberobello and Lecce quirky little design and art galleries are opening up, along with ceramic and pottery studios and jewellers who'll make inexpensive, pretty pieces to order.

Food is also worth hunting out. Puglia is a major olive oil producer, and the standard of its wines is rising – you can buy both straight from the producers. Look out for local pasticcerie and salumerie – goats' cheeses are excellent, and you could take home some orecchiette, the local ear-shaped pasta.

Where to...
Be Entertained

For entertainment in the south Naples reigns supreme. The main venue for classical music is the Teatro San Carlo, Italy's oldest opera house, whose opera season runs from December to May; the rest of the year is devoted to classical concerts and ballet. You can also see dance at the Teatro Politeama, which stages lavish productions featuring international companies.

To find out what's on pick up a copy of *Qui Napoli*, or the more youth-orientated *Pagine dell'Ozio*, from the tourist office.

If you're a music fan and heading south, you could aim to take in the **Festival Musicale di Ravello** (June to August; www.ravellofestival.it); some performances are held in the stunning surroundings of the **Villa Rufolo** and its gardens. **Lecce** has the beautiful 19th-century **Teatro Paisello**, which stages a year-round mix of classical, jazz and pop music concerts, with occasional ballet productions.

Naples' main traditional celebration is the **Festa di San Gennaro** (first Sun in May, 19 Sep, 16 Dec), dedicated to the city's patron saint, when, amid huge rejoicing, a vial of his desiccated blood is exhibited to the crowds. The blood liquefies and the time it takes to do so portends the city's fortunes for the year ahead.

For summer clubbing you can't do better than to head for the **Sorrento Peninsula and Amalfi coast**, home to some of Italy's most chic seasonal clubs, some sited in caves above the sea; **L'Africana** at Praiano and **Music on the Rocks** at Positano are the pick of the bunch. Further south and off the beaten track, evening entertainment will probably be limited to a stroll and a nightcap at an outside table in some glorious *piazza*.

Outdoor Fun

For the sports-minded, the stretch of coast around **Sorrento** provides some of Italy's best watersports experiences. Sailing, windsurfing and scuba diving are all on offer, and this area is one of the few where you'll find excellent tuition from English-speaking instructors, and a full range of equipment for hire. Snorkelling is popular too, and there are masks and flippers for sale in all the coastal villages. Floodlit tennis courts are a feature of many of the smarter hotels, and golfers can get a game at **Arco Felice** just outside Naples. As you head into the deep south, there's less on offer, though the **Gargano Peninsula** is the honourable exception, with watersports and diving at Vieste and the surrounding villages. The east coast resorts, with their wide, sandy beaches, also hire out pedalos, perfect gentle exercise on the water.

Boat trips are a good way to enjoy the fresh air and sun; boats run from Naples to **Capri** and **Ischia** and from Sorrento to **Capri**, and from the Gargano you can reach the stunning **Isole Tremiti**.

Inland

Walking is a good spring and early summer option, and by far the best way to get a taste of the **Parco Nazionale d'Abruzzo**. Head for Pescasseroli, where the park office can help with information; you can also go riding and mountainbiking on the park trails.

Sicily and Sardinia

Getting Your Bearings

Sicily and Sardinia, two scenically beautiful and culturally unique islands, are destinations in their own right. Sicily, lying off the toe of Italy's boot, has lively, historic cities, classical sites, mountains and international resorts. Sardinia's attractions range from its interior uplands, with their hidden, tranquil villages, to the glitz of its jet-set resort coast.

Above: Shepherd with his flock in Sardinia
Previous page: Interior of Palermo's cathedral

Trapani

Marsala

Mazara del Vello

Monreale 6   **Palermo** 5

Alcamo

Castelvetrano

Sciacca   SS115

Agrigento 3

SICILY

Licata   Gela

SS115

Capo d'Orlando   Milazzo

Messina

Cefalù 4

A20

Randazzo   A18

Prizzi   Alia   Nicosia   Adrano

Enna   A19

2 **Taormina and Mount Etna**

Catania

Golfo di Catania

7 **Piazza Armerina**

Caltagirone

Palazzolo Acreide

Ragusa

Modica   Noto

Capo Passero

Siracusa 1

0   60 km
0   40 miles

★ Don't Miss

At Your Leisure

Don't Miss

In Sicily's eastern corner, a clutch of sights includes the Greek temples at Agrigento and the ancient city of Siracusa, where buildings and monuments span over 3,000 years. North from here Mount Etna, Europe's largest active volcano, is the backdrop for Taormina, the island's best-known holiday centre. Inland to the east are the remarkable mosaics at the Roman palace of Piazza Armerina, and north, through the mountains, the road leads to Sicily's capital, Palermo. On its outskirts is the great Norman cathedral of Monreale; west along the coast is amiable Cefalù, a seaside town with wonderful beaches, good restaurants and a splendid cathedral.

Detail of a column in Agrigento's Valle dei Templi

Sardinia's exquisite coastline is its main draw. The Costa Smeralda attracts the well-heeled from all over the world, and the west coast Coral Riviera round Alghero contrasts with the rocky drama of Cala Gonone on the east. Inland is the wilderness of the Parco Nazionale del Gennargentu, where rare birds, animals and flora flourish, as do the area's traditional crafts. South lie the capital, Cagliari, an ancient walled town surrounded by a modern city, and Nora, a Roman archaeological site set beside the sea.

Exploring Sicily in five days is a challenge. Concentrate on the major draws, leaving time for a few days on the coast. This itinerary could be altered to allow two nights in Taormina rather than Cefalù, though the best way to tackle Palermo is by train, only feasible along the north coast.

Sicily in Five Days

Day One

Start your exploration of **1 Siracusa** (➤ 168–169) in Ortygia, before heading out to the Parco Archeologico Neapolis. Leave Siracusa in the afternoon and drive to **2 Taormina** (➤ 170–171). Spend the evening relaxing in Taormina.

Day Two

Explore Taormina (Greek Theatre, right) before heading out for an optional drive up **2 Mount Etna** (➤ 170–171), or south to **7 Piazza Armerina** (➤ 174). Aim to reach **3 Agrigento** (➤ 172) that night.

Day Three

Start early to visit the Greek temples at Agrigento. After lunch drive through the hills to **6 Monreale** (➤ 174), where you can spend the night.

Day Four

Visit Monreale; bypass Palermo and head for **4 Cefalù** (left, ➤ 173) for two nights.

Day Five

If you want to visit **5 Palermo** (below, ➤ 173), take the train in from Cefalù, or spend the day on the beach.

If you want to explore all Sardinia's diversity, it's best to choose two areas for overnighting. From the Costa Smeralda, Alghero becomes an option, while staying in the south would allow you to explore the Parco Nazionale del Gennargentu, the west coast and Cagliari. Another option would be to head for the beach and stay there for the duration of your visit!

Sardinia in Three Days

Day One

Spend the day in **Cagliari** (right, ► 175), concentrating on the medieval quarters and Castello. In the late afternoon, drive west on the S125 towards the west coast. Book in for the night on the fringes of the **Parco Nazionale del Gennargentu** (► 176).

Day Two

Drive through the unspoilt beauty of the Gennargentu, aiming to reach Olbia and the Costa Smeralda in the late afternoon. Take an evening swim, do some trendy shopping, or watch the rich on holiday before finding somewhere for dinner.

Day Three

Morning
Spend a relaxed morning on the beach or pottering around the idyllic northeast corner of the island.

Afternoon
Drive west to Alghero, arriving in time to take in the pleasures of this busy port.

Evening
A drink in a *piazza* café and a fish dinner will round the day off perfectly.

⓵ Siracusa

Modern Siracusa, rebuilt after severe bomb damage in World War II, is a workaday place, but the old heart, around the tiny island of Ortygia, is another matter, with appealing squares, narrow streets, well-worn baroque buildings and a scattering of good shops, cafés and restaurants.

Piazza del Duomo is at the heart of the city

Below: Fishing boat tied up on the quayside

This old quarter, linked to the mainland by a causeway bridge, suffered its own cataclysm in 1693, when it was hit by a major earthquake. It was rebuilt with a flourish of baroque façades, centred around Piazza Pancale. Here you'll find an ancient temple to Apollo (6th century BC), and an even older temple to Athena, which has been absorbed into the fabric of the Christian cathedral.

Greek influences

Both temples date from a period when the city, founded in 733 BC, was under Greek control, an outpost of Magna Graecia (Greater Greece). So successful was this power base that it threatened the might of Athens itself, and an Athenian armada sent here to pull the colony into line was defeated

Eureka!

This was the famous cry of Archimedes as he jumped from his bath, suddenly realising that a body in water displaces a volume of liquid equal to its own volume. The great mathematician, born in Syracusa in c287 BC, also invented formuli to calculate the relative volume of spheres and cyclinders. He died during the Roman invasion in 213 BC, apparently too deep in calculation to notice his attacker.

SIRACUSA: INSIDE INFO

Top tips If it's too hot above ground, head for the comparative **cool of the 4th-century catacombs** west of the Museo Archeologico Regionale, on Viale San Giovanni.

• If you don't want to stay in modern Syracuse, **consider the town of Noto** instead. Lying to the southwest, it also has outstanding baroque architecture.

Hidden gem The **Grotta dei Cordari**, or Cave of the Ropemakers, lies near the Teatro Greco. Its unusually humid interior created the ideal conditions for early ropemakers, who could twist their hemp without fear of it becoming brittle and splitting.

Above: Roman amphitheatre

Below: Statue on the Duomo

in 415 BC. The Romans succeeded where the Athenians had failed, with a conquest in 213 BC, and subsequent occupiers included Byzantines, Saracens, Normans and Spanish.

The best of the ancient Greek remains are preserved in the **Parco Archeologico Neapolis**, an open site to the northwest of the city. The **Teatro Greco**, a 15,000-seat amphitheatre carved out of the white rock of the hillside, predates the **Roman amphitheatre** by about 500 years. The ancient quarry of Latomia del Paradiso is the gruesome spot where thousands of Athenian prisoners were shut up and left to die in 413 BC. For more gore, look out for the huge sacrificial altar, the **Ara di Ierone II**, near the visitor centre, where up to 450 bulls at a time were slaughtered to appease the gods.

TAKING A BREAK

Don Camillo, at Via Maestranza 96, serves fine seafood and locally made cheeses.

🕂 219 F4
Tourist information office
✉ Via Sebastiano 45 ☎ 0931 67710; www.apt/siracusa.it
🕐 Mon–Sat 8:30–1:30, 3–6, Sun 9–1, Easter–Oct; closed Sat pm and Sun rest of year 🚉 Siracusa

Parco Archeologico Neapolis
✉ Largo Paradiso ☎ 0931 66206 🕐 Daily 9 am–2 hours before sunset 💰 Moderate

2 Taormina and Mount Etna

The town of Taormina, on Sicily's northeast coast and backing up the flank of Monte Tauro, is widely considered to be the most attractive on the island. Its stylish shops reflect a chic holiday clientele, and in the height of summer it bulges at its elegant seams with visitors eager to enjoy the views down to the sparkling sea and behind it to Europe's most famous volcano, Etna. Little alleyways and flower-filled balconies set the scene around the central Piazza IX Aprile and the main street, Corso Umberto I.

If you can tear yourself away from the cafés and bars, the folk art museum, the **Museo Siciliano d'Arte e Tradizione Popolari**, is well worth a look, with a bit of everything from religious paintings to domestic items. Taormina's biggest attraction is its **Teatro Greco** (Greek theatre), dating from the 3rd century, a perfect arc of tiered seats above the Ionian Sea, with the stunning natural backdrop of Mount Etna.

To experience Etna fully you should visit the summit

Etna Facts

Formed around 60,000 BC
Known to the Greeks as Aipho, 'I Burn'
Known to the Arabs as Jebel, 'Mountain of Mountains'
At 3,323m (10,900 feet), Europe's highest volcano
Subsidiary volcanic cones: more than 200
First recorded eruption: c700 BC
Major eruptions to date: around 90
Minor eruptions to date: around 135
Last major eruption: 1992
Worst ever eruption: 1669, lasted 122 days

Mount Etna

This sleeping giant of a volcano with its snow-capped peak often appears to float in the air. It is still active, and unlike Vesuvio (► 148) generally bursts in long fissures rather than blowing from the top. Small eruptions are frequent, so check locally for areas of current volcanic activity before you explore on your own. The fertile and

Etna smoulders under a blanket of snow

wooded lower slopes are generally more interesting than the bleak tops, and can be seen from the encircling private Circumetnea railway route from Catania, or by road along a similar route.

TAKING A BREAK

The **Porta Messina** is an inexpensive restaurant tucked under the walls of Taormina, overlooking a little *piazza*, and serving local delicacies as well as pasta and pizza (Largo Giove Serapide, tel: 0942 23205).

🗺 219 F5
Tourist information office
✉ Palazzo Corvaja, Corso Umberto 1, Taormina ☎ 0942 23243 🕐 Mon–Sat 8:30–2, 4–7
🚆 Taormina-Giardini, then steep climb up to town or bus
✉ Via Garibaldi 63, Nicolosi ☎ 095 911505; www.aast-nicolosi.it 🚆 Nicolosi

Museo Siciliano d'Arte e Tradizione Popolari
✉ Palazzo Corvaja, Palazzo Corvaja, Corso Umberto 1 ☎ 0942 610 274 🕐 Tue–Sun 9–1, 4–8
💵 Inexpensive

Teatro Greco
✉ Via Teatro Greco ☎ 0942 23220 🕐 Daily 9–7, Apr–Oct; 9–5:30, rest of year 💵 Moderate

---

TAORMINA AND MOUNT ETNA: INSIDE INFO

Top tips Avoid attempting to drive into Taormina in July and August, when the town is packed out with holidaymakers and **parking is almost impossible**.
• **Guided tours** to view the crater of Mount Etna are available from Catania, Taormina and Nicolosi, when conditions allow. Contact local tourist offices for details.
• To **explore the summit of Etna yourself**, take the cable-car from the mountain refuge at Rifugio Sapienza, then follow the rough road to the top. Allow a full day for this expedition, and wear suitable footwear and warm, waterproof clothing.

❸ Agrigento

Apart from shops and restaurants, there's little to hold your attention in the modern city of Agrigento: its main interest is its role as the gateway to the Valle dei Templi (Valley of the Temples) to the south, the best classical site outside Greece.

There are the remains of nine temples on the site, which are an indication of the scale and importance of the original Greek settlement of Acragas, founded in 582 BC. Earthquakes and later settlers took their toll, but the weathered columns of the temples still stand. The best preserved is the **Tempio della Concordia**, east of the main entrance, which dates from 450 BC, its majestic Doric pillars almost all complete. Stroll along the **Via Sacra** for temples dedicated to Juno and Herakles. To the west the **Tempio di Giove**, planned as the biggest ever, was interrupted by a battle and never completed. The Museo Archeologico contains interesting finds from the site.

The amazingly intact Doric Tempio della Concordia

TAKING A BREAK
The **Black Horse** is a busy, inexpensive restaurant just off the main street of Agrigento, where the home-cooked food is some of the best in Sicily (Via Celauro 8, tel: 0922 23223).

➕ 219 E4
Tourist information office
✉ Viale della Vittoria 522 ☎ 0922 401352 🕐 Tue–Thu 9–1, Wed 9–1, 3–6 🚉 Agrigento

Valle dei Templi
☎ 0922 26191 🕐 Daily 8:30–1, 3–7 🖐 Moderate

Museo Archeologico
✉ Viale Panoramica ☎ 0922 401565 🕐 Wed–Sat 9–7, Sun and Mon 8:30–1 🖐 Moderate

---

AGRIGENTO: INSIDE INFO

Top tips Sightseeing in the Valle dei Templi is blisteringly hot in summer so be prepared and **take a hat, sunscreen and plenty of drinking water** with you. All these can be bought at the kiosks near the car parks at the main entrance.
• To avoid the crowds and the worst of the heat, come here **first thing in the morning** – the site is open daily from 8:30 am.

At Your Leisure

Boat at rest in Cefalù

◿ Cefalù

Cefalù is a charming medieval town, wedged between a high cliff and the sea, which has managed to remain relatively unspoiled despite the attractions of its cafés, restaurants and sandy beaches. Dominating all is the vast, solid, golden-brown cathedral, founded in 1131 by Sicily's first king, Ruggiero II. Inside, its chief treasure is a mosaic in the apse of the Christ Pantocrator, dating from 1148 – Sicily's earliest example of this familiar image. The cathedral overlooks the main square, Piazza del Duomo, where you can relax with a cool drink among the palm trees. If you're feeling energetic, you can climb the 278m (912-foot) crag, La Rocca. There are excellent views over the town from here, and the remains of a 2nd-century BC temple dedicated to Diana.

Tourist information office
➕ 219 E5 ✉ Corso Ruggiero 77
☎ 0921 421050; www.cefalu-tour.pa.it
🚇 Cefalù

◻ Palermo

Sicily's capital is a decaying beauty riven with slums and chaos, petty crime and poverty, but look past this to the vibrant markets, the baroque architecture and the varied museums, and you're unlikely to be disappointed. Elegant shops line the Viale della Libertà and Via Maqueda, a contrast to the teeming, jostling street markets of the Vucciria around Piazza San Domenico. Other highlights include fabulous Byzantine mosaics in the 12th-century Cappella Palatina, and the carved masonry of Il Capo, the cathedral, on Corso Vittorio Emanuele, where royal tombs include that of Roggeiro II. For a grisly but unforgettable sight visit the catacombs of the **Convento dei Cappuccini**, west of the centre. The Capuchins preserved dead bodies by drying them in the sun and treating them with lime and arsenic; they lie here in rows, dressed in their funeral finery.

Tourist information office
➕ 219 E5 ✉ Piazza Castelnuovo 35
☎ 091 583847;
www.palermotourism.com 🕐 Mon–Fri 8:30–2, 3–7, Sat–Sun 9–1 🚇 Palermo Centrale

Convento dei Cappuccini
✉ Via G Mosca-Via Piedmonte ☎ 091 212117 🕐 Daily 9–noon, 3–5
🎟 Inexpensive

The Cappella Palatina, Palermo

⑥ Monreale

Set in the foothills southwest of Palermo, with great views over that city to the sea, Monreale has one claim to fame – and what a claim it is. Its 12th-century Duomo, designed to outshine its rival in the capital below, is one of Europe's great cathedrals, a Norman beauty with sublime Arab and Byzantine decoration. Inside, once your eyes have adjusted to the light, you gradually become aware of the shimmering golden mosaics that seem to cover every surface from floor to ceiling, enhanced by marble inlay and paintings. Reflecting the work of Greek, Byzantine and local craftsmen, the mosaics were completed around 1182, and depict everything from elaborate and intricate patterns, saints and angels to the Christ Pantocrator. Attached to the cathedral is the 12th-century cloister of a former Benedictine abbey, with more than 200 carved and inlaid pillars supporting Arab-style arches.

Tourist information office
🏠 219 D5 ✉ Salita Belmonte 43, Villa Igea, Palermo ☎ 0916 398011
🕐 Mon–Fri 8–2:30, Thu also 3–6:30

⑦ Piazza Armerina

This small town lies in the central, mountainous heartland of Sicily, and is the access point for a stunning display of Roman pictorial mosaics. They decorate the floors of what was once the Villa del Casale, reached down a narrow lane 5km (3 miles) southwest of the town, and were preserved by a 12th-century landslide which destroyed the building's

View over the formal gardens of Monreale's cathedral

walls but covered the mosaics until their excavation in 1929. Their quality and quantity suggest that the palatial villa may have belonged to the wealthy co-emperor (with Diocletian), Maximianus Herculius, who ruled at the end of the 3rd century AD. Many depict hunting scenes; the best of these, 59m (193 feet) long, lines the corridor in the courtyard and shows a range of exotic creatures from elephants and tigers to ostriches and rhinos being captured for gladiatorial combat and circus appearances. Athletic Roman maidens in bikinis pose and play ball in another mosaic, and a humorous scene shows children being chased by their prey – peacocks and hares.

Tourist information office
🏠 219 E4 ✉ Via Cavour 15 ☎ 0935 680201 🕐 Mon–Fri 8–2, Thu 3–6:30

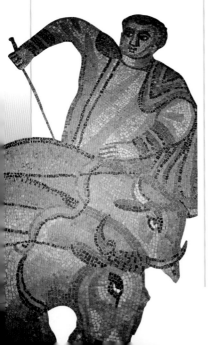

Detail of a mosaic in Villa Imperiale, Piazza Armerina

8 Sardinia

Sandy beaches and sparkling waters make Sardinia a hedonist's delight. The 272km (170-mile) long, 144km (90-mile) wide island – the Mediterranean's second largest – offers beautiful coastline, crystal-clear seas, windsurfing, snorkelling, boating and wildlife.

Above: Fresco in Cagliari's Duomo

Below: The Sunday market, Cagliari

The rich and famous head straight for the Costa Smeralda, a 55km (34-mile) stretch of sandy bays and luxurious resorts in the northeast, which became a fixture on the celebrity map in the early 1960s. For mere mortals there are many other lovely areas of Sardinian coast to explore, such as the resorts south of Olbia, where accommodation comes at a fraction of the price.

Cagliari

The island's sprawling modern capital is on the southern coast, overlooking the Bay of Angels. Established in Phoenician days, it changed hands many times over the centuries, and you can enjoy the historical layers around the medieval quarter, the Castello. Concerts and poetry readings are still given in the **Roman amphitheatre**, which was built to seat 10,000. Several terraces give great views over the city, including the Bastione San Remy, where an antiques and flea market is held on Sunday mornings.

Alghero

This busy fishing port in northwest Sardinia came under Spanish rule from the 14th century, and the Catalan influence is still evident in street names and the local dialect.

At its heart was a walled medieval town, and seven towers survive from this period, including the Porte Torre. At the **Mare Nostrum Aquarium** you can get nose-to-nose through the glass with fragile sea horses and toothy piranhas. This part of the coastline is famous for the production of coral jewellery in fabulous shades of pink and red.

Parco Nazionale del Gennargentu

Away from the beach resorts, Sardinia has a dry, rocky interior, where wild boar and moufflon roam in the cork oak forests, and where isolated farming communities preserve an ancient way of life. Hazelnuts, honey and aniseed are some of the local products; look out also for bamboo flutes called *launeddas*, and fine embroidery on the traditional costumes still worn by some of the older women. **Punta la Marmora**, at 1,834m (6,017 feet), is the highest peak in the Gennargentu mountain range and gives its name to the park.

Rooftop view of the Costa Smeralda from Porto Cervo

TAKING A BREAK

At the **Al Tuguri** restaurant in Alghero fish of the season tops the bill – try a little of everything on the appetising *menu degustazione* (Via Maiorca 113, tel: 0799 76772).

➕ 219 E2
Tourist information
✉ Piazza Matteotti 9, Cagliari ☎ 070 669255; www.regione.sardegna.it 🕐 Mon–Sat 8:30–1:30, 2:30–7:30, Sun 9–12, 4–8, Apr–end Sep; Mon–Sat 9–1, 3–6, rest of year

Mare Nostrum Aquarium
✉ Via XX Settembre 1, Alghero ☎ 079 978333; www.aquariumalghero.com 🕐 Daily 10–1, 4–8, Apr–Oct; Sat 3–8, Sun 10–1, 3–8, rest of year 💰 Expensive

---

SARDINIA: INSIDE INFO

Top tips The **humidity and heat** drive even locals out of Cagliari in August, so save your visit for another time.
• To explore the Gennargentu, take a ride on the **Trenino Verde**, a five-hour train trip (with stops) between Mandas and Arbatax on the coast. The **SS125** is a scenic road between Arbatax and Dorgali, and there's good access to the interior from Nuoro and Mandas.

Don't miss Intricate embroidery is a feature of traditional Sardinian costumes. The **Museo della Vita e Tradizioni Popolari** at Nuoro has an excellent display (open daily, moderate).

Where to... Stay

Prices

Expect to pay per double room, per night

€ under €100   €€ €100–€180   €€€ over €180

SICILY

SIRACUSA

Domus Mariae €€

Orsoline nuns run this small and well-located seafront hotel on the Ortigia promontory. From the terrace you can see the smoke plumes emerging from Mount Etna. The guest rooms have balconies and plenty of room, and the bathrooms are rather small but well designed. Sicilian food is served in the restaurant and there is a bar and a solarium.

🔢 219 F4 ⊠ Via Vittorio Veneto 76
☎ 0931 24854; fax: 0931 24858;
www.sistemia.it/domusmariae

Gutkowski €

Expect no extras or gimmicks at this straightforward hotel within easy reach of local sights, including the Tempio di Apollo. Breakfast is served on the terrace, with fine views of the Mediterranean.

🔢 219 F4 ⊠ Lungomare Vittorini 26
☎ 0931 465861; www.guthotel.it

TAORMINA

Villa Belvedere €€–€€€

Set among the palm trees near the public gardens, this is a comfortable hotel with a lovely, flowery garden and balconied rooms, some of which have great views towards Mount Etna.

🔢 219 F5 ⊠ Via Bagnoli Croce 79
☎ 0942 23791 ⏰ Closed Nov–Mar

AGRIGENTO

Kaos €€

A winning combination of activities and tranquillity mark out this hotel in an 18th-century villa among the olive groves. There's a private beach and extensive grounds; rooms are spacious and airy.

🔢 219 E4 ⊠ Villagio Pirandello
☎ 0922 598622; fax: 0922 598770

PALERMO

Principe di Villafranca €€–€€€

Local crafts and produce provide the focus for this roomy guesthouse near the Teatro Politeama. Fabrics and furniture are made by Sicilian craftspeople and traditional dishes using local ingredients are served in the restaurant.

🔢 219 E5 ⊠ Via Giuseppina Turrisi
Colonna 4 ☎ 091 6118523;
www.principedivillafranca.it

SARDINIA

CAGLIARI

Forte Village €€–€€€

This 5-star resort has a wide choice of accommodation, eateries and activities – including ice-skating and go-karting – available to guests.

🔢 219 E1 ⊠ Santa Margherita di
Pula ☎ 070 92171; www.fortevil-
lageresort.com ⏰ Mar–Oct

ALGHERO

Continental €–€€

Though not central – it's a bus ride from the city centre – this quiet, family-run hotel has spacious rooms, some of which have balconies, and guests can use the swimming pool and private beach of the neighbouring Hotel Calabona.

🔢 219 D2 ⊠ Via F.lli Kennedy 66,
Alghero ☎ 0799 75250; fax: 0799
81046; www.hotelcalabona.it
⏰ May–Sep

Where to...
Eat and Drink

Prices
Expect to pay for a three-course meal for one, excluding drinks and service

€ under €20   €€ €20–€40   €€€ over €40

SICILY

SIRACUSA

Don Camillo €–€€

Chef Giovanni brings a touch of creativity to this seafood restaurant, reached via a complimentary city-centre bus service. Highlights are the gourmet cheeses, raw shrimp, octopus, squid and *piselli e vongole* (mussels with peas).

➕ 219 F4 ☒ Via Maestranza 96
☎ 0931 67133; www.ristorante-doncamillosiracusa.it ◷ Mon–Sat noon–3, 7–10; closed 2 weeks in Nov, and 23–27 Dec

Jonico 'a Rutta 'e Ciauli €–€€

Friendly staff make you welcome at this art nouveau restaurant which has fine views from the terrace. Interesting choices might include pasta and marinated octopus, or roasted aubergines (eggplants) with sardines. Desserts are equally tasty.

➕ 219 F4 ☒ Riviera Dionisio il Grande 194 ☎ 0931 65540
◷ Wed–Mon noon–3, 8–10.30

Ristorante Gioia €–€€

Join the mixed crowd of locals and tourists at this inexpensive eatery very near the cathedral. Fresh vegetables and seafood are used in pasta dishes and there are intriguing options such as *gambieri al menta* (minted prawns).

➕ 219 F4 ☒ Via dei Tolomei 5
☎ 0931 66386 ◷ Tue–Sun 12.30–3, 7.30–midnight

TAORMINA

Casa Grugno €€–€€€

Rich recipes and a huge wine list are part of the appeal of this popular restaurant near the Duomo in the city's historic heart. Enjoy shellfish in Cognac or fresh made ravioli stuffed with goat's cheese.

➕ 219 F5 ☒ Via Santa Maria de' Greci ☎ 0942 21208;
www.casagrugno.it ◷ Mon–Sat noon–2.30, 7–10.30. Dec–Jan, Mar–Apr, Oct; Mon–Fri 7–10.30 pm, May–Sep; closed Feb and Nov

Porta Messina €€–€€€

Choose from seafood, pasta or pizza at this welcoming restaurant on a small square near the city walls. The daily catch of fish is simply grilled and served with a spicy salad, and the dessert list includes traditional Sicilian dishes.

➕ 219 F5 ☒ Largo Giove Serapide 4
☎ 0942 23205 ◷ Daily noon–2.30, 7–midnight, Jul–Aug; Thu–Tue noon–2.30, 7–midnight, Sep–Dec, Feb–May; closed Jan

Ristorante la Griglia €–€€

Local recipes are used at this quiet place, where dishes ranging from roasted pig to raw scampi can be served outside on the shady terrace. Leave room for one of the tasty desserts – the crêpes are great.

➕ 219 F5 ☒ Corso Umberto 54
☎ 0942 23980 ◷ Wed–Mon noon–2.30, 7.30–10.30

AGRIGENTO

Black Horse €

It's a stiff climb from the centre of modern Agrigento to this popular little restaurant, but it's worth it to enjoy the exquisite home-made Sicilian food, served by very welcoming staff. Highlights include *spaghetti con le sarde* (spaghetti with sardines), pasta with *melanzane* (aubergines/eggplants, tomato and melted mozzarella), ricotta salata (aubergines and salted ricotta) and grilled fish.

➕ 219 E4 ✉ Via Celauro 8 ☎ 0922 23223 ⏰ Mon–Sat 12:30–2:30, 7:30–10; closed 1 Jan

CEFALÙ

Ostaria del Duomo €–€€

It's especially busy at lunchtimes, but it's worth it for the excellent local dishes, which include the sweet-and-sour specialities, grilled fish and *caponata* (sweet and sour vegetables). There are good local and national wines on the list too. The restaurant sits right next to the Duomo and you can eat outside and make the most of its location.

➕ 219 E5 ✉ Via Seminario 5 ☎ 0921 421838 ⏰ Daily 12:30–3, 7–midnight, May–Sep; Tue–Sun 12:30–3, 7–midnight, Oct–Apr

Frutti di Mare €–€€

The daily catch is cooked to perfection at this famous restaurant overlooking the Mediterranean. Regulars on the menu are the *vongole e fasolari zuppetta* (mussel and clam soup) and spicy seafood spaghetti. No credit cards.

➕ 219 E5 ✉ Via Messina Marine 204 ☎ 091 471699 ⏰ Daily noon–3, 7–midnight

Osteria dei Vespri €–€€

Book in advance to get a table at this cosy and atmospheric restaurant, one of the best in Sicily. If you do manage to secure a place, try the *caponata* or penne pasta with tuna sauce. Tables are available on the square outside in summer.

➕ 219 E5 ✉ Piazza Croce Dei Vespri 6 ☎ 091 6171631 ⏰ Mon–Sat noon–3, 8–midnight, Sep–Jul; Mon–Sat 8–midnight, Aug; closed 1 week in Aug

Antica Hostaria €–€€

Formality and grandness are the watchwords here, as staff tend to the social stars of Sardinia, serving such delicacies as mussels and lobster in local white wine and *burrida* (fish marinated in walnut and garlic sauce).

➕ 219 E1 ✉ Via Camillo Benso Cavour 60 ☎ 070 665870 ⏰ Mon–Sat 1:30–3, 7:30–11; closed Aug and 23 Dec–6 Jan

Corsaro €€–€€€

Prices are high and the dishes are inventive, including antipasti such as hot *carasau* (thin, crispy bread) drizzled with olive oil and main meals such as *saccaia* (lamb with broth) and pasta stuffed with ricotta and vegetables. Reservations.

➕ 219 E1 ✉ Viale Regina Margherita 28 ☎ 070 664318 ⏰ Mon–Fri 12:30–3, 7:30–11, Sat

7:30–11; closed 2 weeks in Aug and 23–27 Dec

Flora €€

Creative dishes on offer at this pleasant little *trattoria* include tagliatelle with sea anemone, pasta with *bottarga* (sun-dried fish roe) and *fregola* (Sardinian couscous).

➕ 219 E1 ✉ Via Sassari 45 ☎ 070 664735 ⏰ Mon–Sat 1–4, 8–midnight; closed 2 weeks in Aug and 25 Dec

Al Tuguri €€

Sardinian and Catalan influences are combined in the dishes which major on fish and seafood. The menu changes according to the season, but is likely to include home-made pasta with *cozze, piselli* and *gamberi* (mussels, peas and lobster) and *acciughe marinate* (white marinated anchovies).

➕ 219 D2 ✉ Via Maiorca 113 ☎ 0799 76772 ⏰ Mon–Sat 12:30–2, 8–10:30; closed 20 Dec–20 Jan

Where to...
Shop

SICILY

Shopping on Sicily is centred on **Palermo**, the capital, home to possibly Italy's most vibrant markets, where you'll be spoilt for choice if you want to pick up a picnic or track down food specialities to take home.

Palermo is also the place for mainstream shopping, but you might prefer to head for the distinctly more up-market **Taormina**, where trendy boutiques sell holiday clothing, beautiful linens and lingerie, jewellery and local specialities. The best of these is pottery, found all over the island, and particularly at **Caltagirone**, a town on the north coast that makes and sells nothing else. Siracusa and Cefalù have great little artisan shops tucked down their narrow streets, and evening is the time to hit Agrigento's lively main street, packed with little shops.

SARDINIA

Sardinia's main shopping centre is **Cagliari**, the island's capital. Shops cater for every need, with department stores, chain store fashion, home accessory and linen shops, book stores, galleries, art and antique shops. You'll find souvenir shops in the old walled quarter, but for serious shopping head for the more modern area along the water's edge and off Largo San Felice. There's an antiques and handicrafts market in Piazza Carlo Alberto on the second Sunday of the month.

There's more shopping to be had in **Alghero** and **Olbia**, but the pick of Sardinia's trendiest and most elegant stores can be found in the chic developments of the Costa Smeralda.

The island is also famous for its traditional handwoven carpets and tapestries.

Where to...
Be Entertained

SICILY

Palermo's **Teatro Massimo** is the venue for opera and classical music throughout the year, but it's better perhaps to take in one of the summertime outdoor theatrical performances in the unrivalled settings of the **Greek theatres** at Taormina and Siracusa, where performances include the original Greek tragedies. For other nightlife head for Taormina's clubs and bars, or try Cefalù for a lower-key scene; Palermo's clubs and bars are mainly in the northern section of the city.

Outdoor pursuits include swimming, sailing and diving; hotels often have their own pool or private beach. Tennis features, too, and tourist offices can provide details for walking and riding. You can ski in winter in the inland mountains.

SARDINIA

For a musical evening in Cagliari head for the **Teatro Comunale**, which hosts first-rate musical, theatrical and dance events. The city is good for late-night bars; you'll find similar possibilities in Alghero, and more trendy options along the Costa Smeralda.

Traditional festivals are strong on Sardinia – the best include **La Sartiglia**, a horseback pre-Lent tournament in Oristano, the **Sagra di Sant'Efisio** in Cagliari (1 May), celebrating the island's patron saint, and the **Cavalcata**, a horseback event with richly-costumed processions in Sassari (Ascension Day).

Outdoor activities include boat trips, sailing, diving and windsurfing, and there's also hiking in the interior of the Gennargentu.

Walks & Tours

1 AROUND PIAZZA NAVONA

Walk

DISTANCE 3km (2 miles) **TIME** 3 hours
START/END POINT Piazza Navona ⊞ 210 D3

This walk around the heart of Rome takes in some of the city's best-known sights as it meanders between Piazza Navona and Piazza di Spagna before returning to its starting point.

1–2
Leave from the northern end of Piazza Navona. From Via Agonale, turn right on to Piazza Sant'Agostino. On the left you will see the **church of Sant'Agostino**, known for three superb works of art: Caravaggio's 1605 painting of the Madonna (first chapel in the left aisle), Raphael's fresco of St Isaiah (third pillar on the left), and Jacopo Sansovino's statue of the Madonna del Parto (1521).

2–3
Cross the piazza, turn left on Via della Scrofa (it becomes Via di Ripetta), right on to Via Tomacelli, then left on to Piazza Augusto Imperatore. Cross the piazza and turn right on to Via dei Pontefici. The **Accademia Nazionale**

People-watching in Piazza Navona

di Santa Cecilia is at the end of the street. Rome's national school of music has an orchestra of 90 musicians and has staged more than 14,000 concerts.

3–4
Turn right on to Via del Corso, then left on to Via della Croce, which is lined with food shops and cafés. Continue until the road comes to **Piazza di Spagna** (➤ 53). Turn right to reach the bottom of the Spanish Steps.

Cooling off in the *piazza*

With the steps behind you, walk across the *piazza* to Via dei Condotti, Rome's smartest shopping street. Bear left on to Via Belsiana, just before you reach Via del Corso again, and follow it to Piazza San Silvestro. Cross Via Frattina and Via della Vite, then cross the square diagonally and walk into a little street called Via del Pozzetto. Turn right on to Via Poli, crossing over Via del Tritone, and on to Piazza di Trevi and the **Fontana di Trevi** (► 54).

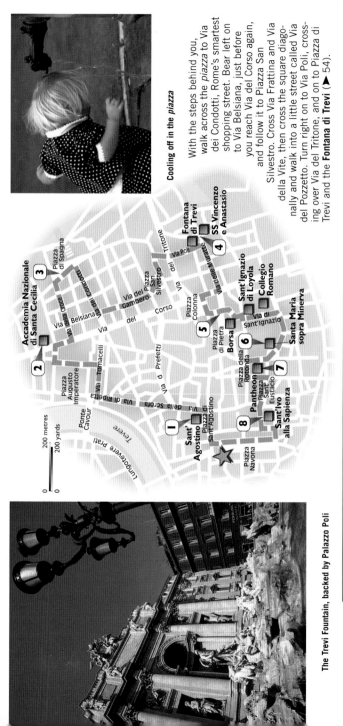

The Trevi Fountain, backed by Palazzo Poli

The Pantheon – one of Europe's best-preserved ancient buildings

6–7

Continue down Via di Sant'Ignazio until you come to Piazza del Collegio Romano. Turn right on to Via Piè di Marmo. This leads to Piazza della Minerva and the Gothic **church of Santa Maria sopra Minerva**, founded in the 8th century and built over a Roman temple to Minerva. Look out for Bernini's elephant statue, which supports an ancient Egyptian obelisk. Inside, be sure to see the frescoes of the *Annunciation* and *Assumption* by Filippino Lippi.

7–8

With the church to your right, follow Via della Minerva to Piazza della Rotonda and the **Pantheon** (▶ 50–51). With the Pantheon in front of you, take Via della Rotonda, then the first right, Via della Palombella, to Piazza Sant'Eustachio. Leave the square on the opposite side, following Via dei Staderari, which passes along the side of the church of **Sant'Ivo alla Sapienza**, one of Borromini's most eccentric churches, dominated by its strange spiral lantern. Take Via dei Sediari back to Piazza Navona.

This church is celebrated for its magnificent *trompe-l'oeil* painting by Andrea Pozzo, which creates the striking illusion of a dome.

Taking a Break

Try the popular **Antica Enoteca**, a traditional wine bar with a restaurant at the rear (Via della Croce 76b, tel: 06 679 0896, daily 12:30 pm–1 am; restaurant daily 12:30–midnight).

4–5

The **church of Santi Vincenzo e Anastasio** stands opposite the fountain. It is particularly renowned for the grisly tradition of keeping the hearts and lungs of past popes, 22 in all, in urns in the crypt. With the Trevi before you, take Via delle Muratte to the left, and follow it to Via del Corso. Turn right on to the Corso, towards Piazza Colonna. With the Corso behind you, take Via dei Bergamaschi, in the far left-hand corner of the *piazza*, to Piazza di Pietra.

5–6

On the right-hand side of the *piazza* is the 17th-century **Borsa** (stock exchange), which incorporates the last remaining columns of Hadrian's temple. Carry on along Via de' Burro to Piazza di Sant'Ignazio, and the beautiful church of **Sant'Ignazio di Loyola**.

2 Southern Tuscany

Tour

This tour takes you south through the historic small towns south of Siena and some of the richest and most archetypal landscapes in Tuscany.

1–2

Take the SS2 from Siena. In 3km (2 miles) you will see signs saying 'Buonconvento 25'. Turn left after 8km (5 miles), still on the SS2, for Buonconvento. At a crossroads, continue on the SS2 to **Buonconvento**, which is unusual in that it's not built on a hill like most towns in Tuscany. Turn right after the bridge to enter the town. The tiny, brick-built old centre and the Museo d'Arte Sacra are worth a brief exploration.

2–3

Leave Buonconvento on the SS2, turning right to join the SP45 for Montalcino, passing through beautiful, unspoiled countryside. In about 9km (6 miles), bear right at the top of the hill and join the SP14, following signs for

DISTANCE 261km (162 miles) **TIME** 11 hours (best spread over two days)
START/END POINT Siena ✚ 210 C3

The crypt of the 9th-century Abbazia di Sant'Antimo

Montalcino. Follow the city wall anti-clockwise (counterclockwise) to the roundabout (traffic circle) at the top of the hill. There's free parking left of the roundabout, or pay parking on the right-hand side, next to the Rocca (La Fortezza). **Montalcino** is one of Tuscany's most ancient settlements and is famous for its red wines.

3–4

After exploring Montalcino, follow signs from the roundabout at the top of the hill for **Abbazia di Sant'Antimo**, about 10km (6 miles) south of town, joining the SP55. Take the right turning to reach the abbey. Its beautiful situation, among olive groves and wooded hills, and its fascinating history and superb architecture make it well worth a stop.

4–5

Return to the main road and drive on up to Castelnuovo dell'Abate. At the top of the hill turn right, following the sign saying 'Stazione Monte Amiata' on the SP22. The road now begins to wind downhill. Go over a level

View of Pienza's cathedral from the city walls

5–6

Drive through the village, then head downhill. After 5km (3 miles) turn left at the intersection to join the SS2. Continue until you reach **Bagno Vignoni**. Park at the top of the hill just outside town. This ancient spa has been used since Etruscan times and has at its centre not a *piazza* but an enormous outdoor pool of warm, sulphurous water from a natural hot spring.

6–7

Go back downhill and turn left at the end of the road. Take the next right to join the SP53 for Pienza, then turn left on to the SP18 and drive uphill. **Pienza**, a UNESCO World Heritage Site, is a tiny medieval and Renaissance jewel of considerable charm. Its focal point is its grand central square, Piazza Pio II, bordered by a handful of palaces and the cathedral.

7–8

Leave Pienza, continue uphill and when you come to an intersection, turn right for the SR146 and Montepulciano. Follow the road until you reach Montepulciano; park outside the city walls. **Montepulciano** is one of Tuscany's most perfect hill towns, with

The rolling hills around Castiglione d'Orcia

crossing by Monte Amiata station, cross the River Orcia and continue to Monte Amiata. The road then begins to climb uphill again. At the intersection, go to the left towards Castiglione d'Orcia. The road becomes even more steep, with superb views. When you come to a junction, turn left and join the SR323, continuing towards **Castiglione d'Orcia**. This little village huddles around its imposing fortress, the Rocca d'Orcia.

sweeping views, and turn right for Pienza on the SS146. One of Italy's foremost Renaissance churches – San Biagio – and a wealth of fabulous art and architecture.

8–9

Drive downhill and turn right for Pienza on the SS146. Some 7km (4 miles) further, turn right to join the SP15, which goes towards Torrita di Siena. Turn left just in front of a bar on the corner to join the SP57. Follow the road to an intersection, turn sharp left past Petroio and continue for another 4km (2.5 miles), then turn right for Montisi.

At an intersection, turn left and follow the SP14 through the small medieval town of Montisi, to the outskirts of San Giovanni d'Asso. At the next intersection, turn right towards Abbazia di Monte Oliveto Maggiore. Follow this road to Montefresco, then turn left at the intersection and drive for another 3km (2 miles). Go left at the next intersection, shortly turning off to **Abbazia di Monte Oliveto Maggiore**. This late 13th-century Benedictine abbey sits in splendid isolation on a pretty hillside amid woods of oak, pine, cypress and olive. The beauty of its setting is matched by the charm of its buildings, and there is a famous fresco cycle on the *Life of St Benedict* in the main cloister.

Leave the abbey, continuing along the SR451 to Buonconvento. Take the SS2 that leads back to Siena.

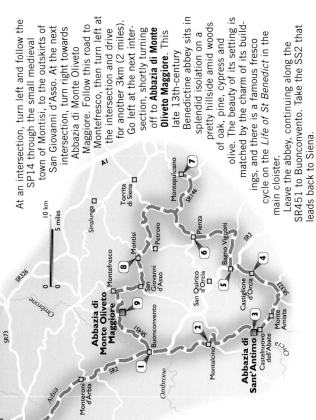

SR326 · Ombrone · SR73 · Arbia · SR223 · Siena · Monteroni d'Arbia · SR2 · Ombrone · Buonconvento · **Abbazia di Monte Oliveto Maggiore** · Montefresco · Montisi · Petroio · San Giovanni d'Asso · Torrita di Siena · Sinalunga · A1 · Montepulciano · SR146 · Pienza · Bagno Vignoni · SR2 · San Quirico d'Orcia · Montalcino · **Abbazia di Sant'Antimo** · Castelnuovo dell'Abate · Castiglione d'Orcia · Monte Amiata · Orcia · SR223

10 km
5 miles

Taking a Break

The **Fiaschetteria Italiana** in Montalcino is recommended for lunch; it serves coffees, cakes, light meals and wine (Piazza del Popolo 6, open daily 7:30 am–midnight, Apr–Oct; closed Thu rest of year). Or try **Silene** in Monte Amiata, whose cooking makes good use of local ingredients – mushrooms, asparagus, boar, truffles (signed from Pescina, 4km/2.5 miles east of Seggiano).

3 The Gargano Peninsula

Tour

Explore the spur of Italy's 'boot', a hilly, forested limestone peninsula that juts into the Adriatic. Sensational views unfold as you wind along the rugged coast, occasionally dipping inland.

DISTANCE 208km (130 miles) **TIME** 2–3 hours
START POINT Southwest of Manfredonia ⊞ 215 E3
END POINT San Severo/A14 *autostrada* ⊞ 215 E4

Limestone arches are a feature along the coastline of the Gargano Peninsula

1–2

Take the Foggia exit from the A14 autostrada and follow signs for Manfredonia on the SS89. Just before Manfredonia, fork right on to the SS159, past the **church of Santa Maria di Siponto**, a fine 11th-century Romanesque church set among Roman ruins.

2–3

Drive for 3km (2 miles) to the old imperial city of **Manfredonia**. The castle was built by King Manfred (1232–1266), and is now a museum on the history of the Gargano Peninsula.

Castle ruins in the mountain town of Monte Sant'Angelo

3–4

Continue northeast on the SS89 and follow the road as it goes left towards the popular pilgrimage town of **Monte Sant'Angelo**, site of one of Italy's most revered Christian shrines, where visions of the Archangel Michael appeared in the 5th century to the Bishop of

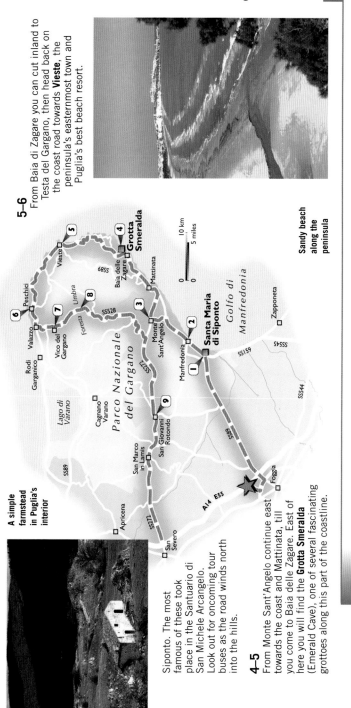

5–6

From Baia di Zagare you can cut inland to Testa del Gargano, then head back on the coast road towards **Vieste**, the peninsula's easternmost town and Puglia's best beach resort.

Sandy beach along the peninsula

A simple farmstead in Puglia's interior

Siponto. The most famous of these took place in the Santuario di San Michele Arcangelo. Look out for oncoming tour buses as the road winds north into the hills.

4–5

From Monte Sant'Angelo continue east towards the coast and Mattinata, till you come to Baia delle Zagare. East of here you will find the **Grotta Smeralda** (Emerald Cave), one of several fascinating grottoes along this part of the coastline.

Boats pulled up on the beach below the town of **Peschici**

6–7

Follow the coast road from Vieste northwest to **Peschici**, a pretty, walled medieval fishing village, which makes an ideal base for exploring the **Parco Nazionale del Gargano** (Gargano National Park). Past Peschici, turn south off the coast road at the village of Valazzo and drive inland to **Vico del Gargano**, which has long been associated with the production of olive oil.

7–8

Take the narrow, winding road into the heart of the **Foresta Umbra**, a vast forest of beech, maple, hornbeam and birch. If you are lucky you may catch sight of rare orchids, deer or moufflon on the limestone plateaux.

Taking a Break

The **Locanda Dragone** in Vieste (Via Duomo 8, tel: 0884 701212) is a good place to stop for lunch, or you could wait until you reach Peschici and eat later at **La Collinetta** (Madonna di Loreto, tel: 0884 964151).

8–9

The SS528 continues south through the forest till it meets the SS272 (west of Mont Sant'Angelo). Drive through the little pilgrimage town of **San Giovanni Rotondo**, and San Marco in Lamis to the end of the tour at the San Severo entrance to the A14 *autostrada*.

Practicalities

Websites
- Italian State Tourist Board: www.enit.it
- Italian Tourist Office for US: www.italiantourism.com
- Rome Tourist Office: www.romaturismo.it

In Italy
Ente Provinciale per Il Turismo (ENIT)
Via Parigi 5, Roma
☎ 06 3600 4399/
06 488 991

BEFORE YOU GO

WHAT YOU NEED

		UK	Germany	USA	Canada	Australia	Ireland	Netherlands	Spain
● Required ○ Suggested ▲ Not required △ Not applicable	Some countries require a passport to remain valid for a minimum period (usually at least six months) beyond the date of entry – contact their consulate or embassy or your travel agent for details.								
Passport/National Identity Card		●	●	●	●	●	●	●	●
Visa (regulations can change – check before booking your trip)		▲	▲	▲	▲	▲	▲	▲	▲
Onward or Return Ticket		○	○	●	●	●	○	○	○
Health Inoculations (tetanus and polio)		▲	▲	▲	▲	▲	▲	▲	▲
Health Documentation		●	●	▲	▲	▲	●	●	●
Travel Insurance		○	○	○	○	○	○	○	○
Driver's Licence (national)		●	●	●	●	●	●	●	●
Car Insurance Certificate		●	●	●	●	●	●	●	●
Car Registration Document		●	●	●	●	●	●	●	●

WHEN TO GO

Rome

High season   Low season

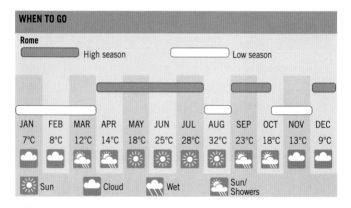

JAN	FEB	MAR	APR	MAY	JUN	JUL	AUG	SEP	OCT	NOV	DEC
7°C	8°C	12°C	14°C	18°C	25°C	28°C	32°C	23°C	18°C	13°C	9°C

☀ Sun   ☁ Cloud   🌧 Wet   🌦 Sun/Showers

Italy's climate is **predominantly Mediterraean**, with Alpine trends in the mountainous far north and arid heat in the far south. In between, there's likely to be a bit of everything, but in summer temperatures soar and the sun shines all day. In the hottest months, July to September, temperatures can reach over 30°C (86°F), with humidity boosted by the Sirocco, a hot wind from Africa. Inland, temperatures can stay high at night, too, and many Romans desert their city in the stickiest months of July and August.

Winter brings rain and fog, even to the south, and localised flooding can become a problem, most notably in Venice. In the far north the snowfields of the mountains become a sparkling winter sports ground.

In the UK
ENIT
1 Princes Street
London W1R 8AY
☎ 020 7408-1254

In the US
ENIT
630 Fifth Avenue
Suite 1565
New York NY 10111
☎ 212/245-5618

In Australia
ENIT
Level 45
1 Macquarie Street
Sydney NSW 2000
☎ (02) 9392 7900

GETTING THERE

By Air Italy has major international airports at Rome, Milan, Venice, Pisa and Naples, plus smaller connecting airports across the country and on Sardinia and Sicily. International flights from within Europe also land at smaller airports such as Palermo and Rimini.

From the UK, airports are served by Italy's international carrier, Alitalia (tel: 0870 544 8259; www.alitalia.co.uk), British Airways (tel: 0870 850 9850 in UK; 199 712266 in Italy; www.ba.com), BMI Baby (tel: 0870 264 2229; www. bmibaby.com), easyJet (tel: 0871 750 0100; www.easyjet.com), and Ryanair (tel: 0870 156 9569; www.ryanair.com). Flying time varies from about 2 to 3.5 hours.

From the US, numerous carriers operate direct flights, including Alitalia (tel: 800 223 5730; www.alitliausa.com), American Airlines (tel: 800 433 7300; www. aa.com), Continental (tel: 800 231 0856; www.continental.com), Delta (tel: 800 241 4141; www.delta.com), Northwest Airlines (tel: 800 447 4747; www.nwa.com) and United (tel: 800 538 2929; www.ual.com). Flying time varies from around 11 hours (US west coast) to 8 hours (eastern US).

Ticket prices tend to be highest at Christmas, Easter and throughout the summer. Airport taxes are generally included in ticket prices.

By Rail Numerous fast and overnight services operate to Rome from most European capitals, with connections from major towns. Florence, Milan, Turin and Venice are other popular direct destinations. A weekly Motorail service on Friday enables you to take your car on the train from Denderleeuw in Belgium to Bologna, between April and September.

TIME

Italy is one hour ahead of GMT in winter, one hour ahead of BST in summer, six hours ahead of New York and nine hours ahead of Los Angeles. Clocks are advanced one hour in March and turned back in October.

CURRENCY AND FOREIGN EXCHANGE

Currency Italy is one of the 12 European countries to use a single currency, the euro (€). Euro coins are issued in denominations of 1, 2, 5, 10, 20 and 50 cents and €1 and €2. Notes are issued in denominations of €5, €10, €20, €50, €100, €200 and €500.

Exchange Most major **travellers' cheques** – the best way to carry money – can be changed at exchange kiosks (*cambio*) at the airports, at Termini railway station and in exchange offices near major tourist sights. Many banks also have exchange desks, but queues can be long.

Credit cards Most credit cards (*carta di credito*) are widely accepted in larger hotels, restaurants and shops, but cash is often preferred in smaller establishments. Credit cards can also be used to obtain cash from ATM cash dispensers. Contact your card issuer before you leave home to find out which machines accept your card.

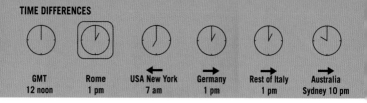

TIME DIFFERENCES

GMT	Rome	USA New York	Germany	Rest of Italy	Australia
12 noon	1 pm	← 7 am	→ 1 pm	→ 1 pm	→ Sydney 10 pm

WHEN YOU ARE THERE

CLOTHING SIZES

UK	Rest of Europe	USA	
36	46	36	
38	48	38	
40	50	40	
42	52	42	Suits
44	54	44	
46	56	46	
7	41	8	
7.5	42	8.5	
8.5	43	9.5	
9.5	44	10.5	Shoes
10.5	45	11.5	
11	46	12	
14.5	37	14.5	
15	38	15	
15.5	39/40	15.5	
16	41	16	Shirts
16.5	42	16.5	
17	43	17	
8	34	6	
10	36	8	
12	38	10	
14	40	12	Dresses
16	42	14	
18	44	16	
4.5	38	6	
5	38	6.5	
5.5	39	7	
6	39	7.5	Shoes
6.5	40	8	
7	41	8.5	

NATIONAL HOLIDAYS

1 Jan	New Year's Day
6 Jan	Epiphany
Mar/Apr	Easter Monday
25 Apr	Liberation Day
1 May	Labour Day
2 Jun	Republic Day
15 Aug	Assumption of the Virgin
1 Nov	All Saints' Day
8 Dec	Feast of the Immaculate Conception
25 Dec	Christmas Day
26 Dec	St Stephen's Day

OPENING HOURS

- ○ Shops
- ● Offices
- ◑ Banks
- ● Post Offices
- ○ Museums/Monuments
- ○ Pharmacies

8 am 9 am 10 am noon 1 pm 2 pm 4 pm 5 pm 7 pm

☐ Day ▨ Midday ☐ Evening

Shops Hours vary, but they are usually open Tue–Sat 8–1, 4–8; Mon 4–8 pm. Shops in larger cities may open all day (*orario continuato*).
Restaurants Usually 12:30–3, 7:30–10:30 pm; many close Sun evening and Mon lunchtime, with a statutory closing day (*riposo settimanale*). Many restaurants close for the whole of August.
Museums Hours vary greatly, according to location. Most close one day a week – often Monday.
Banks Major branches may also open Sat and have longer weekday hours.
Post offices Usually Mon–Fri 8:15–2, Sat 8:15–noon or 2.

EMERGENCY 113

POLICE 112

FIRE 115

AMBULANCE 118

PERSONAL SAFETY

Petty crime, particularly theft of wallets and handbags, is fairly common in the major cities. Be aware of scruffy, innocent-looking children: they may be working in gangs, fleecing unwary tourists. If approached, hang on to your possessions, raise your voice and – if necessary – use force to push them away. To be safe:

- Carry money in a belt or pouch.
- Wear your camera – never put it down.
- Leave valuables in the hotel safe.
- Stick to main, well-lit streets at night.

Police assistance:
 113 from any phone

TELEPHONES

from post offices, shops or bars. Tear the corner off the card before use.

When calling within Italy, simply dial the full number. Rome numbers all begin with 06. Cheap rate is Mon–Sat 10–8. Hotels usually add a surcharge to calls from rooms. Dial 12 for operator or directory enquiries.

Telecom Italia (TI) payphones are on streets and in bars, tobacconists and restaurants. Most take coins or a phone card (*carta telefonica*), bought

International Dialling Codes
Dial 00 followed by

UK:	44
USA / Canada:	1
Irish Republic:	353
Australia:	61
Germany:	49

POST

Post boxes are red for normal post and blue for priority post (*posta prioritaria*). Most offices (*posta*) open Mon–Fri 8:15–2, Sat 8:15–noon/2. Stamps (*francobolli*) can be bought from post offices, tobacconists showing a 'T' sign and bars.

ELECTRICITY

Current is 220 volts AC, 50 cycles. Plugs are two-round-pin continental types; UK and North American visitors will require an adaptor. North American visitors should check whether 110/120-volt AC appliances require a voltage transformer.

TIPS/GRATUITIES

Tipping rates in Italy are low. Restaurant, café and hotel bills include a service charge so a tip is not expected, although many people leave a few coins in restaurants, and up to 10 per cent in smart ones.

Taxis	Round up to nearest €0.50
Tour guides	Discretion
Porters	€0.50–€1 per bag
Chambermaids	€0.50–€1 per day
Bar service	Up to €0.25
Lavatory attendants	Small change

CONSULATES and EMBASSIES

UK
☎ 06 4220 0001

USA
☎ 06 46 741

Ireland
☎ 06 697 9121

Australia
☎ 06 852 721

New Zealand
☎ 06 441 7171

HEALTH

 Insurance Nationals of EU countries can get medical treatment at reduced cost in Italy with the relevant documentation (on presentation of form E111 for Britons; contact the post office for new regulations), although medical insurance is still advised, and is essential for all other visitors. Ask at your hotel for details of English-speaking doctors.

 Dental Services As for general medical treatment (see Insurance above), nationals of EU countries can obtain dental treatment at reduced cost, but private medical insurance is still advised for all.

 Weather Minor health worries include too much sun, dehydration or mosquito bites, so drink plenty of fluids, and wear sunscreen and a hat in summer. Insect repellent may be useful if you sleep with the windows open in summer.

 Drugs Prescription and other medicines are available from a pharmacy (*una farmacia*), indicated by a green cross. Pharmacies usually open at the same as shops (Tue–Sat 8–1, 4–8, Mon 4–8 pm), and take it in turns to stay open through the afternoon and into late evening.

 Safe Water Tap water is safe. So, too, is water from public drinking fountains unless marked '*Acqua Non Potabile*'.

CONCESSIONS

Young People/Senior Citizens Young visitors and children under 18 from EU countries are entitled to free entrance or reduced rates to most galleries. Similar concessions are available to senior citizens over 65. A passport is required as proof of age.

Combined Entry Tickets If you are planning a lot of sightseeing in one area, enquire at the tourist office or at participating sites about combined tickets, which can offer much better value than buying individual tickets. For example, in Venice, a combined ticket for 15 of the most important churches costs just €8.

TRAVELLING WITH A DISABILITY

Wheelchair access is improving in larger cities, but is almost non-existent in the rest of the country. In old towns, you'll find few pavements or dropped kerbs; streets can be narrow, cobbled and congested with parked vehicles. **In the UK**, Holiday Care (tel: 0845 124 9971; www.holidaycare.org.uk) publishes information on accessibility.
In the US, SATH (Society for Accessible Travel and Hospitality; www.sath.org) has lots of tips for travellers with visual impairment or reduced mobility.

CHILDREN

Most bars and restaurants welcome children, but few have baby-changing facilities.

TOILETS

There are public lavatories at railway stations and in larger museums, but otherwise they are rare. Ask for *il bagno* or *il gabinetto*.

CUSTOMS

The import of wildlife souvenirs from rare and endangered species may be illegal or require a special permit. Before buying, check your home country's customs regulations.

SURVIVAL PHRASES

Yes/no **Sì/non**
Please **Per favore**
Thank you **Grazie**
You're welcome **Di niente/prego**
I'm sorry **Mi dispiace**
Goodbye **Arrivederci**
Good morning **Buongiorno**
Goodnight **Buona sera**
How are you? **Come sta?**
How much? **Quanto costa?**
I would like... **Vorrei...**
Open **Aperto**
Closed **Chiuso**
Today **Oggi**
Tomorrow **Domani**
Monday **lunedì**
Tuesday **martedì**
Wednesday **mercoledì**
Thursday **giovedì**
Friday **venerdì**
Saturday **sabato**
Sunday **Domenica**

DIRECTIONS

I'm lost **Mi sono perso/a**
Where is...? **Dove si trova...?**
  the station **la stazione**
  the telephone **il telefono**
  the bank **la banca**/
  the toilet **il bagno**
Turn left **Volti a sinistra**
Turn right **Volti a destra**
Go straight on **Vada dritto**
At the corner **All'angolo**
the street **la strada**
the building **il palazzo**
the traffic light **il semaforo**
the crossroads **l'incrocio**
the signs for...
  le indicazione per...

IF YOU NEED HELP

Help! **Aiuto!**
Could you help me, please?
  Mi potrebbe aiutare?
Do you speak English? **Parla inglese?**
I don't understand **Non capisco**
Please could you call a doctor
  quickly? **Mi chiami presto un
  medico, per favore**

RESTAURANT

I'd like to book a table
  Vorrei prenotare un tavolo
A table for two please
  Un tavolo per due, per favore
Could we see the menu, please?
  Ci porta la lista, per favore?
What's this? **Cosa è questo?**
A bottle of/a glass of...
  Un bottiglia di/un bicchiere di...
Could I have the bill?
  Ci porta il conto

ACCOMMODATION

Do you have a single/double room?
  Ha una camera singola/doppia?
with/without bath/toilet/shower
  **con/senza vasca/gabinetto/
  doccia**
Does that include breakfast?
  E'inclusa la prima colazione?
Does that include dinner?
  E'inclusa la cena?
Do you have room service?
  C'è il servizio in camera?
Could I see the room?
  E' possibile vedere la camera?
I'll take this room **Prendo questa**
Thanks for your hospitality
  Grazie per l'ospitalità

NUMBERS

0	zero	12	dodici	30	trenta	200	duecento
1	uno	13	tredici	40	quaranta	300	trecento
2	due	14	quattordici	50	cinquanta	400	quattrocento
3	tre	15	quindici	60	sessanta	500	cinquecento
4	quattro	16	sedici	70	settanta	600	seicento
5	cinque	17	diciassette	80	ottanta	700	settecento
6	sei	18	diciotto	90	novanta	800	ottocento
7	sette	19	dicianove	100	cento	900	novecento
8	otto	20	venti			1000	mille
9	nove			101	cento uno	2000	duemila
10	dieci	21	ventuno	110	centodieci		
11	undici	22	ventidue	120	centoventi	10,000	diecimila

acciuga anchovy
acqua water
affettati sliced
cured meats
affumicato
smoked
aglio garlic
agnello lamb
anatra duck
antipasti
hors d'oeuvres
arista roast pork
arrosto roast
asparagi
asparagus
birra beer
bistecca steak
bollito
boiled meat
braciola
minute steak
brasato braised
brodo broth
bruschetta
toasted bread
with garlic or
tomato
topping
budino pudding
burro butter
cacciagione
game
cacciatore, alla
rich tomato
sauce with
mushrooms
**caffè corretto/
macchiato**
coffee with
liqueur/spirit,
or with a drop
of milk
caffè freddo
iced coffee
caffè latte
milky coffee
caffè lungo
weak coffee
caffè ristretto
strong coffee
calamaro squid
cappero caper
carciofo
artichoke
carota carrot
carne meat
carpa carp

casalingo
home-made
cassata
Sicilian fruit
ice-cream
cavolfiore
cauliflower
cavolo cabbage
ceci chickpeas
cervello brains
cervo venison
cetriolino
gherkin
cetriolo
cucumber
cicoria chicory
cinghiale boar
cioccolata
chocolate
cipolla onion
coda di bue
oxtail
coniglio rabbit
contorni
vegetables
coperto
cover charge
coscia
leg of meat
cotolette cutlets
cozze mussels
crema custard
crostini canapé
with savoury
toppings or
croutons
crudo raw
digestivo after-
dinner liqueur
dolci cakes/
desserts
erbe aromatiche
herbs
fagioli beans
fagiolini
green beans
fegato liver
faraona
guinea fowl
facito stuffed
fegato liver
finocchio fennel
formaggio
cheese
forno, al baked
frittata omelette
fritto fried
frizzante fizzy
frulato whisked

frutti di mare
seafood
frutta fruit
funghi
mushrooms
gamberetto
shrimp
gelato ice-cream
ghiaccio ice
gnocci potato
dumplings
granchio crab
gran(o)turco
corn
griglia, alla
grilled
imbottito
stuffed
insalata salad
IVA VAT
latte milk
lepre hare
lumache snails
manzo beef
merluzzo cod
miele honey
minestra soup
molluschi
shellfish
olio oil
oliva olive
ostrica oyster
pancetta bacon
pane bread
panna cream
parmigiano
Parmesan
passata sieved
or creamed
pastasciutta
dried pasta
with sauce
pasta sfoglia
puff pastry
patate fritte
chips
pecora mutton
pecorino
sheep's milk
cheese
peperoncino
chilli
peperone red/
green pepper
pesce fish
petto breast
piccione
pigeon
piselli peas

pollame fowl
pollo chicken
polpetta
meatball
porto port wine
prezzemolo
parsley
primo piatto
first course
prosciutto
cured ham
ragù meat sauce
ripieno stuffed
riso rice
salsa sauce
salsiccia
sausage
saltimbocca
veal with
prosciutto and
sage
secco dry
secondo piatto
main course
senape mustard
servizio compreso
service charge
included
sogliola sole
spuntini snacks
succa di frutta
fruit juice
sugo sauce
tonno tuna
uova strapazzate
scambled egg
**uovo affrogato/
in carnica**
poached egg
**uovo al tegamo/
fritto**
fried egg
uovo alla coque
soft boiled egg
uovo alla sodo
hard boiled egg
vino bianco
white wine
vino rosso
red wine
vino rosato
rosé wine
verdure
vegetables
vitello veal
zucchero sugar
zucchini
courgette
zuppa soup

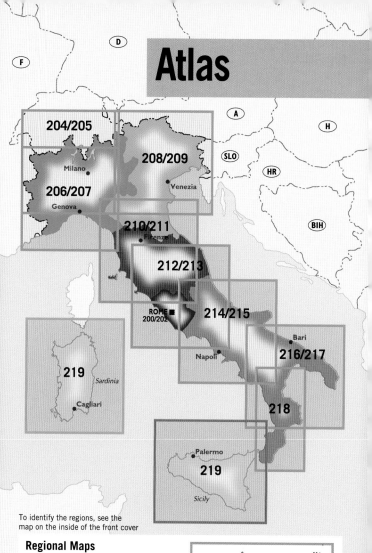

Atlas

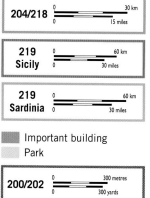

Regional Maps

▬▬▬	Major route
▬▬▬	Motorway/main road
▬▬▬	International boundary
▬▬▬	Regional boundary
▫	City/town
▣	Featured place of interest
■	Place of interest

City Plans

	Main road/minor road
▬▬▬	Railway
▣	Place of interest
●	Metro

To identify the regions, see the
map on the inside of the front cover

| **204/218** | 0 ▬▬▬ 30 km |
| | 0 ▬▬▬ 15 miles |

| **219** **Sicily** | 0 ▬▬▬ 60 km |
| | 0 ▬▬▬ 30 miles |

| **219** **Sardinia** | 0 ▬▬▬ 60 km |
| | 0 ▬▬▬ 30 miles |

| ▨ | Important building |
| ▨ | Park |

| **200/202** | 0 ▬▬▬ 300 metres |
| | 0 ▬▬▬ 300 yards |

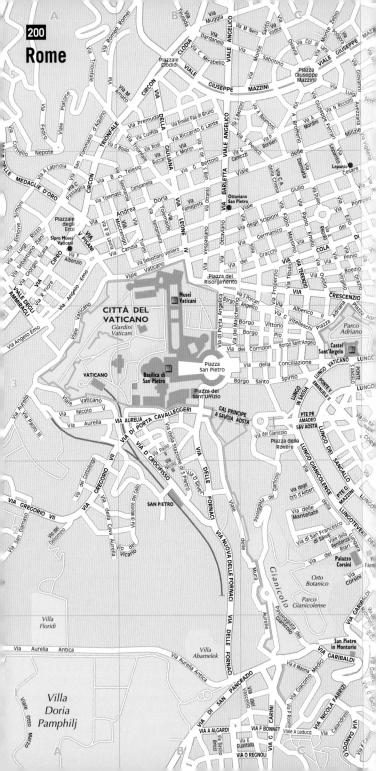

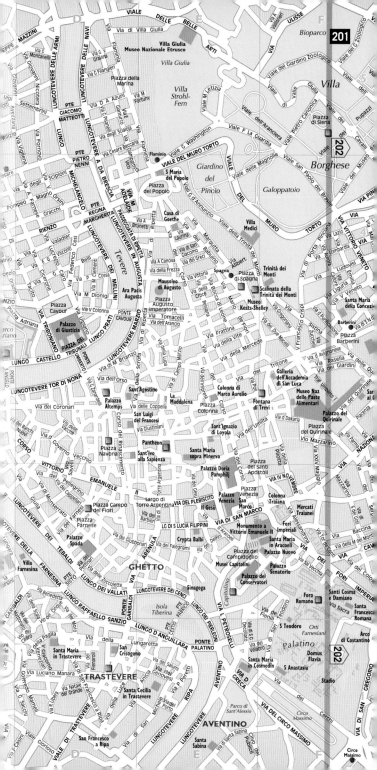

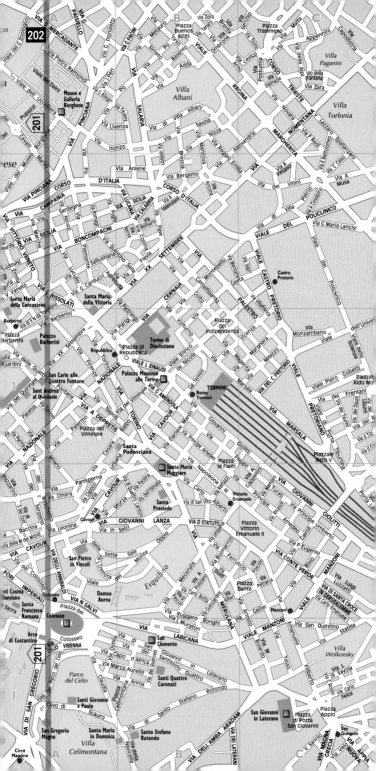

Rome Index

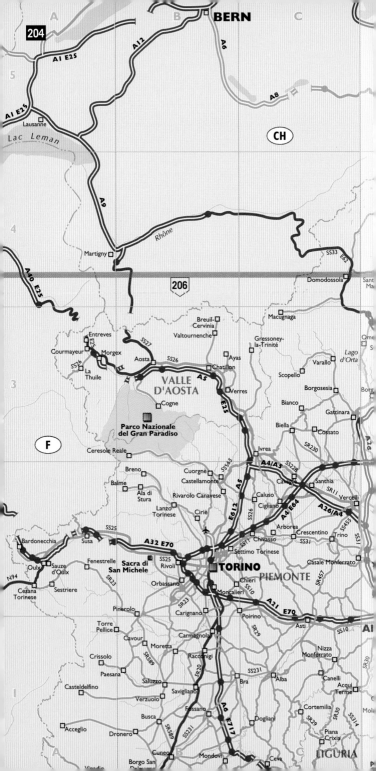

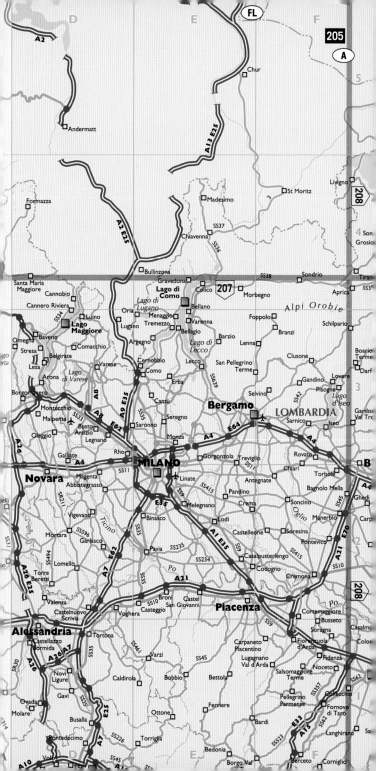

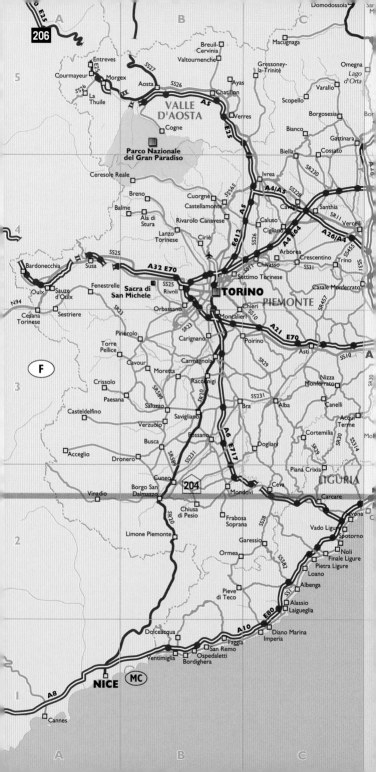

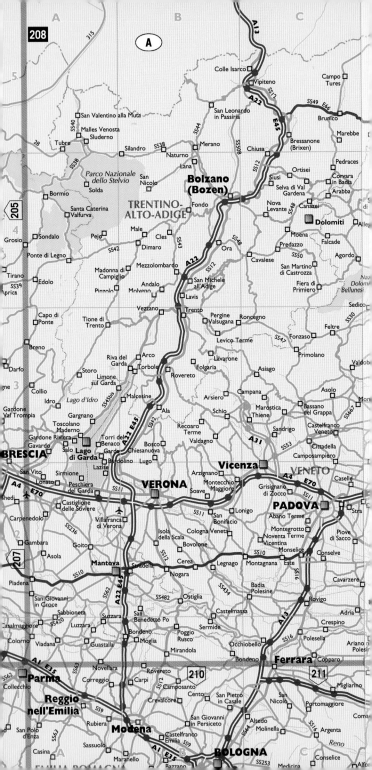

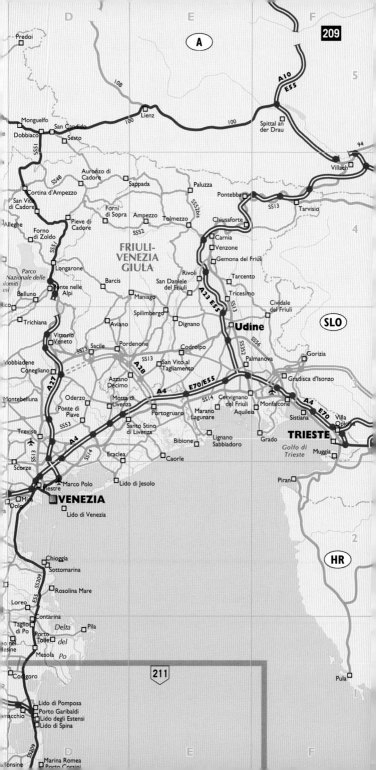

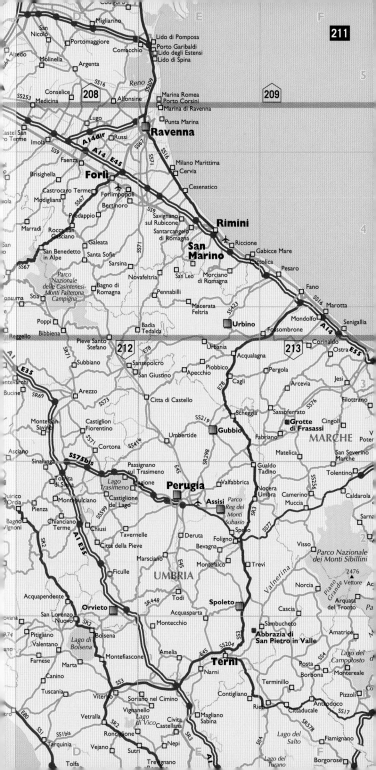

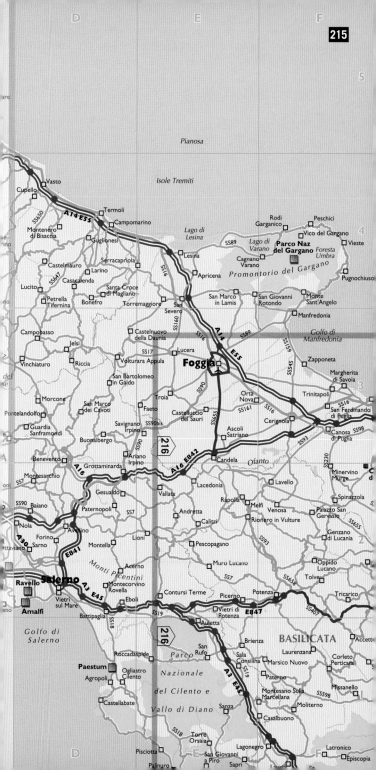

BARI
SS16
Mola di Bari
Capurso
Rutigliano
Polignano a Mare
massima
Conversano
Monopoli
Turi
Savelletri
Castellana
Grotte
Torre Canne
Putignano
Fasano
Gioia
del Colle
Noci
Alberobello
Locorotondo
SS379
Ostuni
Martina Franca
San Vito
dei Normanni
Celle
Messapica
SS16
Brindisi
PUGLIA
Grottaglie
Francavilla
Fontana
Latiano
Mesagne
Massafra
E90
SS7
San Pietro
Vernotico
alagiano
SS7
Oria
San Donaci
Squinzano
San Cataldo
TARANTO
SS7ter
Manduria
San Pancrazio
Salentino
Campi
Salentina
Lecce
Marina di Ginosa
Campomarino
Porto
Cesareo
Copertino
SS16
Martano
Nardo
Galatina
Otranto
Galatone
Maglie
SS16
Golfo di
Taranto
Gallipoli
Parabita
Santa Cesarea
Terme
Casarano
Ugento
SS274
Gagliano del Capo
Marina
di Leuca

Cariati
SS106
Ciro Marina
E90
Strongoli
SS107
E846
Crotone
Cutro
E90
Isola di
Capo Rizzuto
SS106

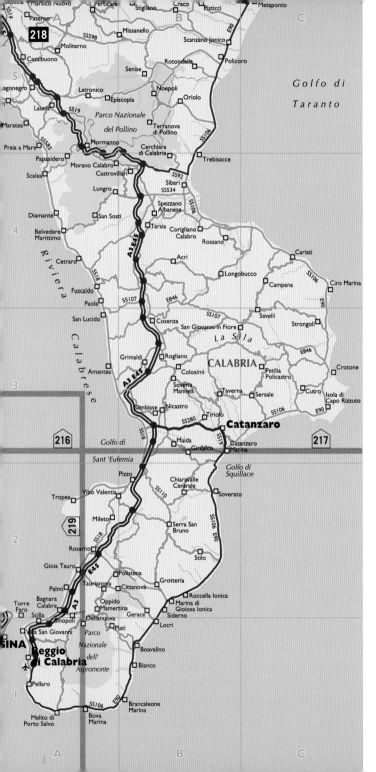

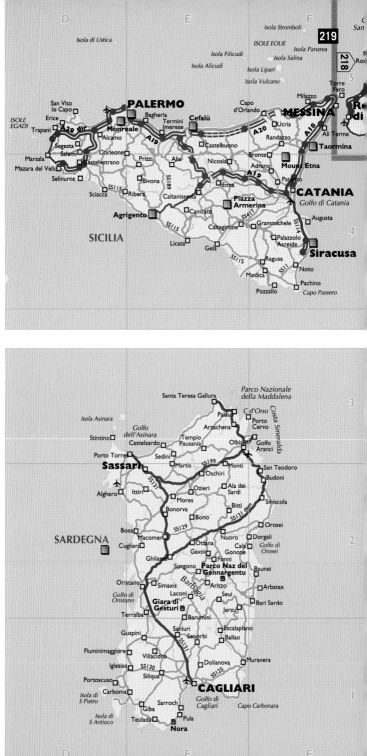

Atlas Index

Picture credits

The Automobile Association would like to thank the following libraries and the Italian State Tourist Board for their assistance with the preparation of this book.

Front and back cover: (t) AA World Travel Library/Max Jourdan; (ct) AA World Travel Library/ Clive Sawyer; (cb) AA World Travel Library/Max Jourdan; (b) AA World Travel Library/Simon McBride

THE BRIDGEMAN ART LIBRARY, LONDON (www.bridgeman.co.uk) 14c Portrait of Lord Byron (1788–1824) (oil on canvas), Phillips, Thomas (1770–1845)/Private Collection; 16t The Molo, Venice, Canaletto (Giovanni Antonio Canal) (1697–1768) Private Collection/Christie's images; 21b The Birth of Venus, c1485 (tempera on canvas) Botticelli, Sandro/Galleria degli Uffizi, Florence, Italy, Giraudon.
ITALIAN STATE TOURIST BOARD, by courtesy of 72b, 73c.
MARY EVANS PICTURE LIBRARY 7r.
RONALD GRANT ARCHIVE 10b.
WORLD PICTURES 71b, 78t, 83, 84t, 84b, 91, 92c, 94c, 95t, 96, 97, 105b, 117b, 126t, 127t, 128t, 144, 149, 152, 153t, 156.

The remaining photographs are held in the Automobile Association's own photo library (AA World Travel Library) and were taken by the following photographers:

PETE BENNETT 7b, 71t, 76; JERRY EDMANSON 6t, 9, 13t, 114c, 115br; TERRY HARRIS 115t, 125c, 128b, 128bg; JIM HOMES 15t, 36c, 39t, 47t, 50l, 54/55, 56/57, 183r; ALEX KOUPRIANOFF 39c, 40/41, 47b, 48cl, 49, 51, 59t; MAX JOURDAN 10b, 12b, 13b, 12/13bg, 16b, 20cl, 68, 69tl, 69tr, 70, 74b, 75t, 74/75, 80b, 81, 141c, 142c, 142b, 143c, 146b, 146b, 147t, 147c, 148t, 150t, 150b, 151; SIMON MCBRIDE 8/9, 11b, 13c, 17b, 18, 18/19bg, 22, 36b, 42b, 43c, 45, 48cr, 50r, 52, 53t, 54, 55, 56, 57, 59c, 60, 100t, 101c, 103, 102/3, 113, 117t, 118c, 118b, 119b, 120, 120/121, 120/121bg, 122b, 182, 184, 185, 186r, 191; DARIO MITIDIERI 14t, 19t, 19c, 21t, 42t, 53b, 92b, 101t, 102t, 102b; RICH NEWTON 95c; KEN PATERSON 20t, 114b, 116c, 121, 125t, 128c, 131, 132b, 186l; CLIVE SAWYER 6c, 8, 10t, 17c, 21c, 38cr, 38bl, 58, 67, 7lc, 74c, 74/75bg, 76/77bg, 78c, 79, 80t, 80c, 82, 93b, 94b, 98t, 98c, 99, 101b, 105t, 106b, 115bl, 116b, 119t, 122c, 123, 124, 126c, 132t, 139, 140c, 140b, 143t, 145c, 148b, l54c, 155br, 155bl, 163, 164c, 164b, 165b, 166t, 166c, 166b, 167, 168t, 168c, 169c, 169b, 170c, 170b, 171, 172, 173t, 173b, 174t, 174b, 175t, 175b, 176b, 183l, 181l, 189l, 189r, 190; RICK STRANGE 19b; TONY SOUTER 11t, 12t, 20cr, 40b, 69b, 93c, 106t, 130, 130/1, 153c, 154t, 181, 188r; PETER TIMMERMANS 145b, 149; PETER WILSON 5, 38cl, 39b, 41, 43b, 46, 71t.

Abbreviations for terms appearing above: (t) top; (b) bottom; (l) left; (r) right; (c) centre (bg) background.

SPIRAL GUIDES

Questionnaire

Dear Traveler

Your comments, opinions and recommendations are very important to us. So please help us to improve our travel guides by taking a few minutes to complete this simple questionnaire.

Send to: Spiral Guides, MailStop 66, 1000 AAA Drive, Heathrow, FL 32746–5063

Your recommendations...

We always encourage readers' recommendations for restaurants, nightlife or shopping – if your recommendation is added to the next edition of the guide, we will send you a FREE AAA Spiral Guide of your choice. Please state below the establishment name, location and your reasons for recommending it.

_____

_____

_____

_____

_____

Please send me AAA Spiral _____

(see list of titles inside the back cover)

About this guide...

Which title did you buy?

_____ **AAA Spiral**

Where did you buy it? _____

When? m m / y y

Why did you choose a AAA Spiral Guide? _____

_____

_____

_____

Did this guide meet your expectations?

Exceeded ☐   Met all ☐   Met most ☐   Fell below ☐

Please give your reasons _____

_____

_____

_____

continued on next page...

Were there any aspects of this guide that you particularly liked?

Is there anything we could have done better?

About you...

Name (Mr/Mrs/Ms)

Address

Zip

Daytime tel nos.

Which age group are you in?

Under 25 ☐ 25–34 ☐ 35–44 ☐ 45–54 ☐ 55–64 ☐ 65+ ☐

How many trips do you make a year?

Less than one ☐ One ☐ Two ☐ Three or more ☐

Are you a AAA member? Yes ☐ No ☐

Name of AAA club

About your trip...

When did you book? m m / y y   When did you travel? m m / y y

How long did you stay?

Was it for business or leisure?

Did you buy any other travel guides for your trip? ☐ Yes ☐ No

If yes, which ones?

Thank you for taking the time to complete this questionnaire.